The Editor

JARED GARDNER is Joseph V. Denney Designated Professor of English at The Ohio State University. He is the author of three monographs, including *Projections: Comics and the History of 21st-Century Storytelling* and *The Rise and Fall of Early American Magazine Culture*, and he is the editor or coeditor of several volumes, including *The Comics of Charles Schulz: The Good Grief of Modern Life*. He has worked closely for many years with the Billy Ireland Cartoon Library and Museum at Ohio State, including serving as curator on several exhibits.

NORTON CRITICAL EDITIONS
Modernist & Contemporary Eras

ANDERSON, Winesburg, Ohio
AZUELA, The Underdogs
BURGESS, A Clockwork Orange
CATHER, My Ántonia
CATHER, O Pioneers!
CONRAD, Heart of Darkness
CONRAD, Lord Jim
CONRAD, The Secret Agent
CONRAD, The Secret Sharer and Other Stories
CUMMINGS, E. E. Cummings: Selected Works
Eight Modern Plays
EISNER, A Contract with God and Other Stories of Dropsie Avenue
ELIOT, The Waste Land and Other Poems
FAULKNER, As I Lay Dying
FAULKNER, The Sound and the Fury
FITZGERALD, The Great Gatsby
FORD, The Good Soldier
FORSTER, Howards End
FORSTER, A Passage to India
FREUD, Civilization and Its Discontents
FRIEDAN, The Feminine Mystique
HEMINGWAY, In Our Time
HEMINGWAY, The Sun Also Rises
JOHNSON, The Autobiography of an Ex-Colored Man
JOYCE, Dubliners
JOYCE, A Portrait of the Artist as a Young Man
KAFKA, Kafka's Selected Stories
KAFKA, The Metamorphosis
LARSEN, Passing
LARSEN, Quicksand
MANN, Death in Venice
MANSFIELD, Katherine Mansfield's Selected Stories
Modern African Drama
Modern and Contemporary Irish Drama
PROUST, Swann's Way
RHYS, Wide Sargasso Sea
RICH, Adrienne Rich: Poetry and Prose
SHAW, George Bernard Shaw's Plays
SOYINKA, Death and the King's Horseman
STEIN, Three Lives and Q.E.D.
TOOMER, Cane
WATSON, The Double Helix
WHARTON, The Age of Innocence
WHARTON, Ethan Frome
WHARTON, The House of Mirth
WOOLF, Jacob's Room
WOOLF, Mrs. Dalloway
YEATS, Yeats's Poetry, Drama, and Prose

A NORTON CRITICAL EDITION

Will Eisner

A CONTRACT WITH GOD AND OTHER STORIES OF DROPSIE AVENUE

PRIMARY TEXTS

EISNER ON THE GRAPHIC NOVEL AND COMICS

REVIEWS AND ASSESSMENTS

CRITICISM

Edited by

JARED GARDNER
THE OHIO STATE UNIVERSITY

W. W. NORTON & COMPANY
Celebrating a Century of Independent Publishing

W. W. Norton & Company has been independent since its founding in 1923, when William Warder Norton and Mary D. Herter Norton first published lectures delivered at the People's Institute, the adult education division of New York City's Cooper Union. The firm soon expanded its program beyond the Institute, publishing books by celebrated academics from America and abroad. By mid-century, the two major pillars of Norton's publishing program—trade books and college texts—were firmly established. In the 1950s, the Norton family transferred control of the company to its employees, and today—with a staff of five hundred and hundreds of trade, college, and professional titles published each year—W. W. Norton & Company stands as the largest and oldest publishing house owned wholly by its employees.

Printed in the United States of America

Manufacturing by Lakeside Book Company
Book design by Antonina Krass
Production manager: Brenda Manzanedo

Library of Congress Cataloging-in-Publication Data

Names: Eisner, Will, author, artist. | Gardner, Jared, editor.
Title: A contract with god and other stories of Dropsie Avenue : primary texts, Eisner on the graphic novel and comics, reviews and assessments, criticism / Will Eisner ; edited by Jared Gardner.
Description: First edition. | New York : W. W. Norton, [2023] | Series: Norton critical editions | Includes bibliographical references and index.
Identifiers: LCCN 2022009824 | **ISBN 9780393284836 (paperback)**
Subjects: LCSH: Tenement houses—New York (State)—New York—Comic books, strips, etc. | Jews—New York (State)—New York—20th century—Comic books, strips, etc. | Bronx (New York, N.Y.)—Comic books, strips, etc. | Eisner, Will—Criticism and interpretation. | Graphic novels—History and criticism. |
LCGFT: Graphic novels. | Literary criticism.
Classification: LCC PN6727.E4 C63 2023 | DDC 741.5/973—dc23/eng/20220629
LC record available at https://lccn.loc.gov/2022009824

W. W. Norton & Company, Inc., 500 Fifth Avenue, New York, N.Y. 10110
www.wwnorton.com
W. W. Norton & Company Ltd., 15 Carlisle Street, London W1D 3BS

1 2 3 4 5 6 7 8 9 0

Contents

Introduction: A Life in Pictures

I

In the history of comics in the United States, one individual plays a key role in almost every major development in the form. From the establishment of the first comic book studio in 1938, to his pioneering work in educational comics in the 1950s and '60s, to his work in popularizing the concept of the graphic novel in the late 1970s, to his foundational work in comics theory and instruction in the 1980s and '90s, Will Eisner's impact on the history of American comics remains unparalleled.

Today this impact is recorded in various institutions, including the Eisner Awards (the equivalent of the Oscars for comics) and Will Eisner Week, an annual celebration of graphic novels, literary comics, and free speech. Much of the research that went into this introduction was conducted in the Will Eisner Seminar Room at the Billy Ireland Cartoon Library & Museum at The Ohio State University, an institution to which Eisner contributed as a founding donor.

Despite these and other memorials to Eisner's importance to comics, he is today less familiar to younger students of the form than many of those whose careers he influenced, such as Art Spiegelman, Frank Miller, and Scott McCloud. Part of the reason for this, as noted by Don McGregor—an early practitioner of the graphic novel form—is that paradoxically Eisner's influence was so pervasive that it was often not recognized even by those who were profoundly shaped by his work: "Will Eisner influenced me when I wasn't even aware of it. . . . [E]ven if you hadn't had a lot of exposure to Will's work, the chances are you were affected by it, in some form, through another artist who had been influenced with Will's work."[1]

Another reason Eisner's contributions are not as visible today is that Eisner tended to be the first one through the door at each major development in the comics form, making his pioneering contributions at times appear "old fashioned" to those who showed up a generation or two later, after conventions and marketplaces had been regularized. This is the case, for example, with Eisner's work in the graphic novel form. Eisner's interest in outsized emotions has not always been in tune with the alternative comics generation that emerged in the '90s. While Eisner's characters are often theatrical and highly emotional, the most celebrated graphic novels at the turn of the twenty-first century often featured characters defined by emotional detachment and alienation. The art critic Peter Schjeldahl articulates this disjunction by calling out Eisner's "cornball

1. Don McGregor, "Will Eisner: The Artist Who Influenced You When You Didn't Know It," March 7, 2013. Accessed online.

histrionics": "his characters rub their hands, tear their hair, and, if they happen to fancy something, slaver."[2] Schjeldahl has few kind words for the graphic novel in general, and this assessment captures one aspect of Eisner's work that can be a hard sell for modern readers: sentiment and melodrama. In an age where irony and detachment are often privileged and where melodrama and the didactic are anathema, the emotional immediacy and expansiveness of Eisner's work can seem old-fashioned.

Yet a closer look at the graphic novel in the twenty-first century reveals many texts that share Eisner's interest in expansive emotions and theatrical energy. For example, today's graphic memoirs bear strong influences of Eisner's work in the '70s and '80s. Alison Bechdel's *Fun Home* (2006), David Small's *Stitches* (2009), and Carol Tyler's *Soldier's Heart* (2015), each of which wrestles with the narrative challenges of intergenerational memory and understanding, are deeply influenced by Eisner's emotional style and narrative structures. We can also see Eisner's influence in fictional graphic narrative works such as Jason Lutes's graphic novel *Berlin* (2018) or Gilbert and Jaime Hernandez's multigenerational epic *Love and Rockets* (1982–present)—works that, like the Eisner stories collected here, explore the relationships between human lives and lived environments. For Eisner that environment was often Dropsie Avenue, his fictional neighborhood in the Bronx, based on his childhood home. In bringing Dropsie Avenue to life in various projects across two decades, Eisner opened up possibilities for the graphic form that are only now being fully explored by a new generation.

II

Eisner's storytelling consistently emphasizes bodies and faces expressing a broad range of emotions in and through bounded environments. This emotive storytelling finds its origins in the New York City Yiddish theater district, where his father worked as a scene painter in the 1920s. As Eisner recalled: "Among my first experiences is the memory of visiting Second Avenue Jewish theatres where I could see the men working on backdrops. I have a feeling for theatrics. I did some in high school too—some stage design."[3] The theater taught Eisner the art of visual storytelling not only because it was an artistic mode that incorporated script and image, but because his backstage view on a process that included lighting, staging, set design, painting, and costume suggested the range of visual tools that could be manipulated on the page. Even more than the art classes he would briefly attend several years later, this special access was Eisner's education as a visual storyteller.

To modern eyes Yiddish theater might seem the epitome of all that is past and outmoded—a pre–mass media entertainment performed in what is often (and wrongly) perceived to be a "dying language." At the time Eisner first encountered it, however, Yiddish theater was seen as uniquely modern. Writing around the time young Eisner started frequenting his father's workplace, the journalist Samuel Max Melamed described the Yiddish theater

2. Peter Schjeldahl, "Words and Pictures: Graphic Novels Come of Age," *The New Yorker*, October 10, 2005.
3. *Will Eisner: Conversations*, ed. M. Thomas Inge (Jackson: University Press of Mississippi, 2011), p. 51.

scene on 2nd Avenue as "Jewish cultural life in New York . . . in full flower."[4] What made the Jewish theater so special for Melamed is also what made it so important for Eisner: it allowed him to see the people and the city around him for the first time. As Eisner recalled, "The big city has always intrigued me as a place of great theater with a huge amount of story material constantly available, an environment I know and understand."[5] In fact, initially Eisner imagined a career in theater as the ideal avenue for exploring and telling the stories of his city, but larger forces intervened, as they had for his father before him.

Family legend has it that his father, Shmuel (Samuel) Eisner, was born in a shtetl not far from Vienna, Austria, in 1886. As Eisner recounted the story in 1973, "My father was born in a little village just outside of Vienna, so I am Austrian, I guess—although I understand that the municipality kept changing hands over the years, so I might be Hungarian or Polish by extraction."[6] Eisner's uncertainty here is familiar for many descendents of Jewish immigrants. The borders and powers of Europe changed often in the late nineteenth and early twentieth centuries, and most European Jews were marginal citizens (at best) with little access to official record-keeping institutions. Americans descended from Jewish immigrants who arrived during the period of mass immigrations from eastern Europe (myself included) often know only that their relatives came from somewhere in eastern Europe and suffered discrimination and antisemitic violence before leaving for America. Samuel's naturalization papers suggest that, while he was born within the Austro-Hungarian Empire, his birth might have occurred quite far from Austria. This distance would help explain Eisner's understanding that his father was from a predominantly Jewish town or shtetl called Kollmei. While there is no Kollmei in Austria, Kolomyia—in what was then Galicia (part of the Austro-Hungarian Empire, today part of Ukraine)—had a large and thriving Jewish community at the time.

It would not be surprising for Eisner's father to have had a hard time pinning this location down when telling his son the stories that Eisner would retell many years later in his graphic memoir *To the Heart of the Storm* (1991). His father, after all, *was* subject of the Austrian Empire when he left for America, and when declaring for naturalization would have had to renounce allegiance to the emperor. By the time Eisner rendered his father's stories his father was long dead, and the region's geopolitics had been turned upside down by two World Wars and a Cold War.

For Eisner, the one particular that remained poignant was his father's trip to Vienna in the early 1900s. In this romantic voyage in search of the life of the artist, Eisner identifies his own artistic inheritance. Fin de siècle Vienna was the epitome of culture and cosmopolitanism, producing radical innovations in everything from the arts to psychology. It would have been an exciting place for a young man to come of age, and it was there that Samuel found work as an apprentice for a muralist, working in the churches and palatial estates of the city.

4. Samuel Max Melamed, "The Yiddish Stage," *The New York Times*, September 27, 1925, p. 188.
5. *Will Eisner: Conversations*, p. 139.
6. *Will Eisner: Conversations*, p. 24.

Vienna was a city of dazzling possibility; it was also at the center of a growing storm that would soon engulf the continent. The assassination in 1914 of the Austrian archduke Ferdinand by Serbian nationalists culminated in World War I. While Vienna had been welcoming to Jews compared to neighboring states, even before war arrived in Austria there were signs of rising antisemitism in the city, epitomized by Karl Lueger, its mayor from 1897 to 1910, who came to power largely on the basis of an antisemitic campaign. Archduke Ferdinand had promised to protect the Jewish community, so his death meant not only the onset of war but also the loss of a vital protector of Jewish interests in the country. Facing enlistment in the Austrian army and an increasingly precarious future, Samuel Eisner emigrated to the United States shortly before the outbreak of hostilities.

In New York, Samuel found that his talents and culture counted for little. Speaking no English, he managed to find employment in Yiddish theaters. He soon met and married Fannie Ingber, a Hungarian Jewish immigrant—born shipboard during her parents' voyage to America—some five years his junior. Where Samuel was an artist and a dreamer, Fannie was a fierce realist who early in life had been weighed down with family responsibility. It was an unlikely partnership, born more out of necessity than romance, but this combination of visionary and groundedness would shape their son Will's temperament.

William Erwin Eisner was born on March 6, 1917. The family had struggled economically from the start, but their finances deteriorated further after the arrival of sound film in 1927 and the Great Depression two years later, both of which events brought about the rapid collapse of the vaudeville theaters in which Samuel had worked. Fannie pushed her husband to seek out more stable employment. He found work painting finish on metal furniture, but the chemicals made him ill, and he was soon forced to quit. For a time, he set up shop as a secondhand-furniture dealer, but that too failed—as did almost every endeavor he attempted through the 1920s. And each new venture meant another move to a different part of the city. On the 1930 census, the family is listed as living in the Bronx and Eisner's father is identified as a commercial traveler for a wholesale firm. What this "job" entailed is not clear, but it certainly did not support the family. Eisner's mother informed him that "[y]our father isn't making a living," assigning her son the role of man of the house.[7]

Eisner's first job was selling newspapers in Manhattan. This work not only allowed him to begin learning about business, but it also exposed him to the remarkable richness of newspaper comics in the early '30s. He would especially remember being struck by the work of George Herriman (*Krazy Kat*), Milton Caniff (*Terry and the Pirates*), and E. C. Segar (*Thimble Theatre*).[8] He began to imagine a career that would involve his love for art. After all, some of the most successful newspaper cartoonists of the time were making dazzling salaries at this time; Sidney Smith, for example, the creator of *The Gumps*, signed a contract in 1935 worth $150,000 a year.[9]

In 1931 or 1932, Eisner became a student at DeWitt Clinton High School in the Bronx. Here he soon established himself as a creative talent,

7. Michael Schumacher, *Will Eisner: A Dreamer's Life in Comics* (New York: Bloomsbury, 2010), p. 12.
8. *Will Eisner: Conversations*, p. 213.
9. This is in 1935 dollars. Factoring in inflation this would be a little more than 3 million dollars in 2022 dollars.

publishing illustrations in the school's yearbook, literary magazine, and programs for theatrical and talent events. He became involved with theater at the school and increasingly thought about following his father and going into stage design. But with so many of the nation's theaters shuttered or struggling due to the Depression, theater seemed a very risky career. Being a nationally syndicated newspaper cartoonist, however, promised fame and fortune for a talented young artist; and as his sense of his own talents grew during his high school years, this dream started to seem within reach. Pursuing art classes in the evening at the Art Students League of New York, Eisner strengthened his techniques and instincts for anatomy under the tutelage of George Bridgman and Robert Brackman.[1] By the time he failed geometry in his senior year, a class required for graduation, the prospect of spending another semester in high school for a makeup class seemed pointless. It was time to move on, with or without a diploma.

Work, however, remained hard to come by. He found a job at Hearst's *New York American* in the graveyard shift with the advertising department, but it paid poorly and was uninspiring. He found a position in 1936 with a new magazine called *Eve*, marketed to young Jewish women, but it proved a poor fit (not that it mattered—the magazine folded shortly after he was fired). Eisner may have been worrying that his career in art was as doomed as his father's, when he ran into his old classmate Robert Kahn. Having legally changed his name to Bob Kane, Eisner's friend had just sold some of his work to Jerry Iger, founding editor of a new comic book, *Wow, What a Magazine!*

III

Eisner up to this point hadn't thought much about the new medium of the comic book, and there wasn't much to think about it in 1936. The first successful modern comic book had emerged, following a few earlier experiments, only a couple of years earlier with *Famous Funnies*. *Famous Funnies* was entirely made up of reprints of popular syndicated newspaper comics, and its success on the newsstands testified more to the enthusiasm of readers to own newspaper comics in a more permanent medium than to any interest in the new form of the comic book. *Famous Funnies* was quickly followed by titles from rival publishers, all striking deals with newspaper syndicates to reprint popular series. Even the first title entirely dedicated to original material, *New Fun*, was originally conceived as a vehicle to promote new potential strips for newspaper publication. No one had much faith that there was a future in the comic book itself.

New Fun had been the brainchild of Malcolm Wheeler-Nicholson, who realized it would be cheaper to pay for original art than to license from newspaper syndicates. He formed National Allied Publications (which later would become DC Comics). But he was no businessman, and he was soon heavily in debt to his distributors, who forced him out and took over the company. Despite Wheeler-Nicholson's failure, the model he envisioned proved successful. Newspaper syndicates were skeptical of the

1. George Bridgman taught figure drawing and anatomy at the Art Students League for 45 years. Robert Brackman had migrated from what is now Ukraine around the same time as did Eisner's father. In addition to teaching at the Art Students League, Brackman would go on to be a celebrated portrait painter.

upstart comic book business, with its seedy associations with cheap pulp fiction and pornography. They started demanding a bigger cut of the financial pie, and comic books dependent on reprints were proving unsustainable.

Other comic book publishers picked up on Wheeler-Nicholson's idea of looking for original comic art and thereby avoiding the increasingly expensive costs of syndicated cartoons: Iger's *Wow, What a Magazine!* was one such venture. Many artists and writers—including Eisner, desperate for work—signed on to contribute. Eager to make the most of this opportunity, Eisner produced a remarkable amount of work in short order. In the first issue of *Wow* he had two stories, followed by three in the second, and another three in the third along with the cover. But the fourth issue was to be the last. Just when Eisner got a glimpse of what comic books could be, this project was already over.

The failure of *Wow*, however, alerted Eisner to a business opportunity. Having inherited his mother's hard-nosed pragmatism, Eisner realized that among the many problems facing *Wow*, a major one was that Iger was forced to hustle for content. Time and money were lost as he negotiated with artists individually to purchase the work. Eisner's brainchild was to eliminate this inefficiency by creating a packaging house that could supply camera-ready content for publishers eager to get into the growing comic book market.

To start such a business, Eisner also needed a seasoned partner. While Iger might not have been ideal (his first title was, after all, a flop), he was fourteen years the teenage Eisner's senior, and Iger had the industry connections Eisner sorely lacked. The partnership occasionally proved challenging, but neither Iger nor Eisner had many choices at the time. Iger was broke and facing a potentially ruinous divorce, while Eisner had literally no other prospects. Eisner and Iger Studio was a marriage of convenience.

Initially, Eisner did most of the art for the new company himself (with Iger lettering and selling the work to publishers) under a series of pseudonyms (including "Rensie," his name spelled backwards). As demand for the studio's work grew, Eisner began hiring other artists. Like Eisner, many of these artists were the children of Jewish immigrants: Jack Kirby had been born Jacob Kurtzberg to Austrian parents; Lou Fine was born to Russian immigrants; and Bob Kane was born to eastern European Jewish parents.[2] Along with Iger and of course Eisner, all of these artists would later be inducted into the Will Eisner Award Hall of Fame.

Others in the studio included Bob Powell (born Stanley Robert Pawlowski), who struggled often unsuccessfully to contain his own resentment at being forced to work for Jews; the artist Alex Blum and his daughter Toni (at the time the only woman as the studio); George Tuska; Rafael Astarita; Gill Fox; Mort Meskin; and Chuck Mazoujian. Eisner would later recall these exciting and daring years as the dawn of the new comic book industry in his semiautobiographical graphic novel *The Dreamer* (1985).

2. Jack Kirby created or cocreated many of today's most recognizable superheroes, including the X-Men, the Fantastic Four, Captain America, and, late in his career, the Eternals. Lou Fine was a widely admired and prolific comics artist in the 1940s. Bob Kane is credited as the creator of Batman (1939), although it is now widely understood that other artists—especially Bill Finger—contributed at least as much as did Kane.

At his studio, Eisner created or cocreated several enduring characters, including Sheena, Queen of the Jungle (1938), Uncle Sam (1940), Black Condor (1940), and Blackhawk (1941). Eisner had passed on a pitch from two young men from Cleveland, Jerry Siegel and Joe Shuster, but even after DC made their character Superman the hit that launched the superhero boom, Eisner remained cool on superheroes. His skepticism was only deepened by the undisguised plagiarism of Siegel and Shuster's idea he saw everywhere. In fact, he himself was tasked by one of his clients to create for them a superhero clearly designed to resemble Superman; it was no surprise when Wonder Man's one-and-only appearance promptly elicited a lawsuit from Superman's owners. The remarkable success of his former classmate and employee, Bob Kane, with the creation of Batman, only deepened Eisner's growing suspicion. In addition to finding Kane personally annoying, Eisner also rightly believed Kane to be significantly less talented than many others in his studio. That the superhero craze could make a star out of Bob Kane made Eisner doubt the whole phenomenon.

While working with Iger enabled Eisner to own a business, that business depended on appealing to publishers who mostly wanted another Superman, ideally one who could survive the kind of lawsuit that ended Wonder Man's career so quickly. Eisner was forced to produce content for publishers such as Victor Fox, a former accountant and owner of Fox Comics, who liked to stomp around his offices proclaiming himself "the King of Comics." Or Harry Donenfeld at National, who had acquired the company that would become DC by suing its founder, Wheeler-Nicholson. Pleasing these men, who saw comics as little more than a gold rush that was sure to run dry any minute, grew increasingly draining for Eisner, both as an artist and as a businessman. Eisner was ready for something new.

IV

In 1939 an unlikely opportunity presented itself when one of Eisner's clients, "Busy" Arnold of Quality Comics, approached him with an idea. Only a few years earlier newspaper syndicates had been openly contemptuous of the fledgling comic book industry, but following the rise of the superhero boom, the newspaper industry increasingly realized that the popularity of comic books represented a meaningful threat. Arnold's proposal to Eisner was to collaborate to bring comic books *to* newspapers, as supplements in the Sunday papers. In addition to opening up a new marketplace, the project would let Eisner develop comics geared toward more mature readers, whom the comic book industry had not bothered to consider.

This offer was tempting but risky. Eisner's business with Iger was growing; walking away from a steady thing for an untried venture was a terrifying prospect. However, Eisner was hungry for new opportunities and challenges, and the chance to meld the comic book form with the cultural capital of the newspaper proved irresistible.

Extensive negotiations occurred before the venture began, including over Eisner's demand to retain copyright on any characters he created for the new partnership. What Eisner was asking for was virtually unheard of in newspaper comics, where only a handful of cartoonists owned their own characters. In the world of comic books, it was unimaginable.

Eventually a deal was secured, one that guaranteed Eisner would own the characters he created if the partnership dissolved. Eisner had the difficult task of letting his partner know he would be leaving the business. The two came to an arrangement whereby Iger bought Eisner out for $20,000, a nice return on Eisner's original $15 investment; for his part, Eisner agreed to take only a few artists with him to his new studio: Fine, Powell, and Mazoujian.

The newspaper supplement was to be a sixteen-page self-contained comic, featuring each week an eight-page story by Eisner, with supplementary stories by Powell and Mazoujian. Eisner's contribution would prove to be the most famous and enduring creation of his career: Denny Colt, the Spirit. With this barest of nods to the superhero genre he increasingly disdained, Eisner set out to create something unique: a comic book that appealed to children and adults, combining adventure with sophisticated humor and adult sexuality.

The Spirit was distributed by the Tribune Syndicate, reaching around 5 million readers at the height of its popularity. While this work remained popular and recognized as unique, the model of the newspaper comic book supplement did not generate interest in more such supplements. Eisner loved working on *The Spirit*, but as a businessman he could see that there wasn't much room for growth here. And Eisner still had to churn out superhero characters for Quality, even as he wrestled with the new headaches of dealing with angry newspaper editors who often found his content in *The Spirit* too scary or sexy for their imagined young readers.

Despite these frustrations, *The Spirit* provided Eisner an opportunity to experiment, as he had never had a chance to do crafting cookie-cutter work for other publishers. He began to explore the possibilities of the page, playing with dramatic angles and lighting, and with unconventional panels and page layouts. Commercial comics—both in newspaper and comic book form—were by the 1940s highly routinized and increasingly standardized. Eisner's *The Spirit* explored the freedoms and experiments that earlier cartoonists such as Winsor McCay and George Herriman had enjoyed, freedoms that were lost to the industrialization of the form. Thanks to *The Spirit* and its long life in reprints, generations of cartoonists were introduced to the possibilities that emerged when the story—not the industry—determined how the page should look.

V

Shortly after the United States entered World War II in 1941, Eisner was drafted. Since it was only a little more than a year into *The Spirit* and his new business, Eisner was able to secure a deferment until May 1942 to get his affairs in order. It was decided he would continue as long as possible to provide scripts for *The Spirit*, and Fine would take over the art. Eisner and Arnold knew, however, that an overseas deployment would quickly make this arrangement impossible.

As it turned out, there would be no frontline deployment: Eisner's reputation as an artist had preceded him as he made his way from Fort Dix to his initial assignment at the Aberdeen Proving Ground in Maryland. He soon found himself offered a position as a cartoonist at the base's newspaper, the *Flaming Bomb*. It was a dream assignment, as it allowed him to retain a hand in *The Spirit* while serving his country. It also turned out to open up for him a whole new vision on the potential of comics.

First in Aberdeen and later at the Pentagon, Eisner found a new calling: educational comics. This possibility arrived through a life-and-death problem the Army had long struggled to solve. For all the dangers of war for which soldiers trained each day, it proved consistently difficult to get the enlisted men to engage in daily preventative maintenance of equipment and munitions. As a result, numerous accidents and frontline failures occurred that would have been prevented by simply reading the manual and following its detailed instructions. The problem was that the manuals were unreadably dull, and little time was spent in any of the educational material to explain the importance of this work. Eisner realized that comics were the ideal medium for the challenge. To motivate soldiers to perform daily maintenance, Eisner created a new character: Joe Dope, the most inept soldier ever to wear army green. Joe became a lesson in how *not* to be a soldier, and more importantly, a case study in the dangers of not engaging in preventative maintenance. Joe leaves munitions out in the rain, with the result that his fellow soldiers are shooting duds in combat. Joe fires a machine gun without letting the gun cool off, melting the barrel and rendering the gun useless. He fails to secure the turret locks on tanks, so the turrets swing wildly, with gruesome results. Dope was everywhere, doing everything wrong. "Don't be a dope!" Eisner's cartoons warned. "Handle equipment right!"

Not everyone in the military brass was initially sold on Eisner's innovations. As he recalled later, "The military publishing commanders felt that what I was doing was a threat to them. My comics implied that their regular training material was not readable. Which was indeed true!"[3] When Eisner's educational comics were put to the test against the Army's traditional materials, however, Eisner's comics proved uniformly more effective—and more likely to be read by those who most needed the information. Eisner's new faith in the educational potential of comics was confirmed, and he began to imagine postwar horizons beyond the comics industry.

VI

At war's end, Eisner's first task was to revive Denny Colt, who had been growing somewhat anemic during Eisner's absence, despite the talent employed at Eisner's studio. Eisner returned to his character with the December 23, 1945, installment. Within a few weeks, Eisner's passion for his creation was fully rekindled, and a remarkable period of creativity followed, including some of the best-loved stories in its run.

By the end of the 1940s, however, as Eisner's confidence as a visual storyteller reached its height, signs of looming danger for comics were increasingly hard to ignore. What had been scattered criticisms of comic books from ministers, educators, politicians, and parent groups coalesced into an organized movement. With the psychiatrist Frederic Wertham providing the authority of "science," anticomics activists pushed local and national officials for regulation of the comics industry.

3. *Will Eisner: Conversations*, p. 127.

When Eisner had entered the service in 1942, superheroes dominated comic books. By the time of his return to civilian life, the superhero boom was fading fast. Superhero titles began to fold, replaced by an explosion of new genres, including romance, western, science fiction, crime, and horror. These last two were of special concern to critics of the industry, who were troubled both by children's obsession with a medium they saw as worthless and by the increasingly lurid and violent content in crime and horror comics.

Working primarily with newspapers, whose vocal readers and conservative editors naturally kept the content in check, Eisner was not overly worried about the outcry. He noticed, however, that the comics industry's failure to defend itself against the mounting public pressure risked leaving all comics vulnerable to charges of "seduction of the innocent," as Wertham melodramatically framed it. By the early 1950s, Eisner was thinking it might be time to leave comic books behind entirely.

By 1954, the Comics Code Authority was established. This system of internal censorship was designed to ward off government interference and transform the image of comic books into family-friendly entertainment. Hundreds of comics professionals and scores of publishers went under, leaving just a few companies standing, including DC, Dell, and Atlas (later Marvel). Seeing the writing on the wall, Eisner did not hang around for the disaster of 1954, instead bringing *The Spirit* to an end in October 1952. By that point, he already had embarked on other ventures.

VII

In 1948, Eisner had established a new business, American Visuals Corporation—a place for his work in educational and advertising comics. One of American Visuals' earliest clients was the Baltimore City Medical Society, which hired Eisner to create a comic book to convince readers to oppose President Truman's proposal for universal health care. With Eisner writing and producing the covers, *The Sad Case of Waiting Room Willie* (1949) sought to demonstrate the horrors that would emerge should Truman's proposal be realized, amplifying what would become arguments against socialized medicine still used today. Eisner was not alone in producing comics against the universal health care bill, and when Truman's plan was defeated, Eisner was more convinced than ever of the power of comics as a tool to change attitudes and behaviors.

Picking up on his earlier work for the Army, Eisner began working as artistic director for *P*S, The Preventive Maintenance Monthly* in 1951. After the retirement of *The Spirit* he threw himself increasingly into American Visuals, overseeing such titles as *Fire Chief and the Safe Ol' Firefly* (1952) for the National Board of Fire Underwriters, *The Amazing Adventures of Daredevil Davey* (1954) for the American Dental Association, and *More Fun with Your .22 Rifle* (1956) for the NRA. Eisner would remain focused on *P*S* and his promotional and educational comics work at American Visuals for the next two decades.

It was not only the comic book industry's growing problems that had made him decide to walk away. He had married Ann Weingarten in 1950, and a new career out of the public eye in the 1950s and '60s gave him more time to spend with his family. John was born in 1952 and Alice the following year, and the family settled in suburban White Plains, New York. Theirs was a relatively ideal domestic life, and Eisner took such pleasure in his family and his American Visuals work that he rarely missed the world of comic books and paid little attention to the changes happening in the medium over the next two decades.

Tragedy arrived, however, in 1970, when Alice died of leukemia at age 16. The loss devastated Eisner, and it brought about huge changes for the family. John had been heading off to college, but the trauma of his sister's death devastated him and brought to the surface mental health challenges. A few months after their daughter's death, Ann found a needed distraction from the grief when she took a position as director of volunteers for the New York Hospital–Cornell Medical Center in Westchester. Eisner, the bubble of domestic bliss burst, now found himself at sea in search of a new purpose at an age where others might have begun planning for retirement. He did not have to wait long for a new path.

VIII

In 1971, Eisner received a call from Phil Seuling, a young man at the forefront of some dramatic changes in the world of comics. Seuling had founded a comic book shop in Brooklyn and had organized one of the first major comics conventions, the Comic Art Convention in New York. Seuling was calling to invite Eisner to attend the convention as his guest, promising him that the fans in attendance would be very excited to meet him. Eisner had been away from comic books for so long that he had a hard time even conceiving of what such a fandom might look like. The world of comic books he knew in the 1940s was cacophonous and its creators largely anonymous; there had been little interest in cultivating loyal fans or promoting celebrity creators. When modern comics fandom began to take shape in the 1960s, Eisner had been too busy with family, *P*S*, and American Visuals to notice.

What he experienced at the convention at the Commodore Hotel must have made him feel like Rip Van Winkle. In addition to discovering a world of comics fans who knew more about his career than he could have imagined, he encountered for the first time the daring experiments of the underground comix movement. Underground comix had emerged in the mid-1960s and flowered in San Francisco at the end of the decade, offering a radical alternative to commercial comic books of the Marvel and DC variety and a bold refusal of the puritanism of the Comics Code Authority. By self-publishing and distributing outside of newsstands—in record stores, headshops, and conventions—underground comix reimagined the medium without filters of any kind.

Eisner had little interest in the subject matter of most of these comics—acid trips, sexual fantasies, and radical politics were not to his taste. But he was thrilled to see how many barriers underground comix had shattered in such a short time. Through Seuling, Eisner was introduced to a young underground cartoonist, editor, and publisher, Denis Kitchen. The two hit it off immediately, despite their generational and temperamental differences. Eisner talked to Kitchen about the beginnings of the comic book industry and his own experiments with different business models, and Kitchen explained to Eisner how the new direct market for comics functioned.

When Eisner had worked in the industry, comics were all sold through newsstands, where they competed for customers with magazines, pulps, and newspapers. In this system, dealers had the right to collect a return from the publishers on unsold items, leaving them little incentive to market any one publisher's work (and leaving comics publishers always uncertain about their balance sheet). This distribution system had begun to change with the emergence of a network of comic book shops willing to take on comics without the ability to return unsold items. An organized fandom had opened up a new market for back issues, one sufficiently healthy that hanging on to overstock was often a profitable risk for store owners.

While distribution was changing with the emergence of this direct market, within the commercial comic book industry artists and writers continued to be treated largely as they had in Eisner's day: comic book work was work-for-hire, and the writers and artists who created even the most successful characters received no share of the profits or licensing. However, one consequence of the rise of the comic book shop as well as the example of underground comix was that for the first time smaller independent publishers had opportunities to reach customers directly. At these new independent publishers, royalties were often paid and creator copyright was acknowledged. Kitchen had just started one of these new independent presses, and as he described the business, Eisner saw solutions to many of the problems that had so aggravated him when he worked in comics.

Eisner saw in Kitchen a younger version of himself: artist, businessman, and visionary. In addition to their unlikely friendship, they began a business partnership, in which Kitchen was granted rights to reprint *The Spirit*, and Eisner would produce new artwork to help market the comic to a new generation. Eisner retained copyright and received a royalty on sales. All that "Busy" Arnold had found so unthinkable in 1939 was now easily agreed to between the two new partners. While Eisner soon took *The Spirit* reprints to Warren, a bigger publisher, Kitchen and Eisner's business relationship lasted a long time.

Beginning in 1974, Eisner also began teaching classes at the School of Visual Arts in New York, titling his subject "sequential art." Eisner had long believed that the word "comics" had been corrupted by the lousy work churned out for decades by commercial publishers interested only in a quick dime. The young underground cartoonists whose energy had reignited his own felt similarly, coining "comix" for their work. For Eisner "sequential art" carried with it his aspiration for the medium to finally be recognized as an art form, and over the next decade he gathered notes and best practices that he condensed in the first of his books on the craft and theory of comics: *Comics and Sequential Art* (1985).

The same year he began teaching at SVA, Eisner established an independent press of his own, Poorhouse Press, designed to leverage the renewed interest in his work generated by the *Spirit* reprints into a series of novelty books, with titles such as *Will Eisner's Incredible Facts, Amazing Statistics, Monumental Trivia* (1974), and *Will Eisner's Gleeful Guide to Living with Astrology* (1974). Even as he was working on these relatively safe moneymaking enterprises, Eisner was thinking about how he might contribute to the next stage in the form's evolution. With his wife's encouragement, he decided for the first time to take a chance on producing comics that had no built-in marketplace, no promise of sales—in which the financial risks would largely be his alone. After years focusing on the business side of comics, Ann argued, he had earned the chance to let creative ambition take the lead. As he approached age 60, it was reasonable for him to ask (although premature, as it would turn out): if not now, when?

IX

Eisner had already proved comics could entertain, that they could appeal to both children and adults, that they could be a business, and that they could educate and shape public opinion. Now Eisner was ready to turn to his most vulnerable and personal work yet, to try to prove that comics could be literary art. The experience he would draw on was close at hand, as the grief and existential rage that emerged following his daughter's death remained unresolved. *A Contract with God* and, in many respects, the next three decades of his career were born out of the belief that comics could provide a medium to explore and share deeply personal memories—starting with this most painful experience.

As Eisner conceived of a setting for his story of grief and hubris, loss and rebirth, he found himself returning to the world of his youth: Depression-era New York. In this setting, which would provide a recurring backdrop for his work over the next two decades, he was dealing with his daughter's death but also exploring his past and trying to better understand his late parents.

Beyond the personal goals that motivated him in this project, Eisner had something to prove—something that had been nagging at him for decades. In 1941, Eisner had been quoted in *The Philadelphia Record* speaking in especially elevated terms about the potential of the comics form: "The comic strip, [Eisner] explains, is no longer a comic strip but, in reality, an illustrated novel. It is new and raw in form just now, but material for limitless intelligent development. And eventually and inevitably it will be a legitimate medium for the best of writers and artists."[4] Such a statement was unprecedented in 1941, and at the time his colleagues had needled him mercilessly. Thirty-five years later, however, Eisner was meeting younger comics professionals who shared his sense of the possibilities. Now was the time to prove the value of comics, especially to people who had never imagined they would read comics, let alone buy them. He just needed a name for what he was trying to do that was not "comics."

As a teacher he had coined "sequential art," which worked well in the context of an art school. But he needed something more literary and familiar if he was going to fulfill his ambition of seeing his new project in bookstores next to the leading Jewish novelists of the day, such as Saul Bellow, Philip Roth, and Bernard Malamud. The term he settled on was "graphic novel."

While the term had been used earlier—such as by the cartoonist Jack Katz, who first introduced the term to Eisner—Eisner ultimately became

4. Reprinted in *Will Eisner: The Centennial Celebration*, ed. Paul Gravett and Denis Kitchen (Milwaukie, OR: Dark Horse Comics, 2017), p. 32.

most firmly associated with the birth of the "graphic novel." Even though his first "graphic novel" was not in fact a novel, but a sequence of related stories, it was the ideal of the "great American novel" that spurred him on in this work.

Originally called *The Tenement* before being retitled at the suggestion of his editor, *A Contract with God* was published in 1978 by Baronet Books, in association with Eisner's Poorhouse imprint. Larger firms had passed on the idea of publishing a comic in book form, and Baronet was so financially shaky that Eisner lent it money to ensure the press could see the book through. Eisner had Warren's *The Spirit* magazine to heavily promote the book to old and new fans, and through Kitchen and Seuling he had access to fanzines and a small but growing comics press. Promoting the book to readers outside the insular world of comics fandom, however, would be a significant challenge. Bookstores didn't know where to display the title, and Baronet didn't have the prestige to draw in buyers on reputation alone. Under the circumstances, Eisner was not overly disappointed by the weak sales from the first print run. He had learned from his earlier experiences with *The Spirit* that sometimes new readers came to a work much later, and he was in no hurry. He believed in *A Contract with God* and was confident that history, so often trailing him by a few years, would catch up. An invitation to appear alongside Art Spiegelman on an academic panel at the 1978 Modern Languages Association conference on the state of comics—a foundational moment in the early history of academic comics studies—suggested such optimism was warranted. In 1986, Denis Kitchen's Kitchen Sink Press published a new edition of the book, the first of several major new editions in English (alongside numerous international editions). It would not take long for history to catch up.

X

This volume collects the first two stories from the pioneering work *A Contract with God*, alongside selections from other stories set in Dropsie Avenue, the fictional version of Eisner's childhood neighborhood. Eisner would develop this fictional universe over the course of the next two decades, in *Life Force* (1988), *Invisible People* (1992), and *Dropsie Avenue* (1995)—returning to it one last time in 2000 with *Minor Miracles*. Dropsie Avenue began as one building in *A Contract with God*, but over the years it grew to encompass a neighborhood, a world.

While Dropsie Avenue is the focus of the stories collected in this volume, this world represents only a part of a remarkable period of productivity into which Eisner embarked in 1989, resulting in graphic novels ranging from science fiction (*Life on Another Planet* [1983]), to an autobiographical history of the origins of the comics industry (*The Dreamer* [1986]), to, in his final published work, *The Plot* (2005), a nonfiction graphic study of the long-lived antisemitic conspiracy theory known as the Protocols of the Elders of Zion. Between *A Contract with God* in 1978 and *The Plot* in 2005, Eisner published more than twenty books. This would have been a remarkable period of productivity for a young man, but Eisner was in his sixties at its start and was still publishing the year he died, in his late eighties. It remains, in any medium, a remarkable late-career renaissance, one unlikely to be matched in the history of comics.

While *A Contract with God* was originally received with some ambivalence by the small comics press long attached to *The Spirit*, with its rerelease in 1985 and the publication of *The Dreamer*, *Sequential Art*, and *Life Force* within the next couple of years, Eisner received increasingly celebratory attention. He had always been keenly engaged with the reception of his work, and this attention spurred him on to new challenges and new projects.

It also created something of a halo around Eisner, which left him increasingly invulnerable to negative assessment, especially by the comics press (as we will see in the "Reviews and Assessments" section of this volume, more skeptical judgments still emerged in the late '80s from the mainstream press—only then just beginning to attend to comics at all). It was in this context that in 1988 Gary Groth wrote for his *Comics Journal* a famously scathing critique of Eisner's post-*Spirit* work, one that triggered months of responses from readers and comics professionals, outraged by the attack on a man who had by this time taken his place in comics lore as both a founder of the comic book industry and the "father of the graphic novel." Groth's 1988 critique stands out as anomalous within the comics community during this period, so much so that in 2005, when *The Comics Journal* published a memorial issue in honor of Eisner's passing, Groth acknowledged himself "his harshest (his only?) critic."[5]

However, there were other critics along the way. Eisner was keenly aware of his naysayers, and while he rarely if ever responded directly, he took the critiques to heart. As much as the pull of memory, it was almost certainly the original ambivalent assessments of *Contract* (before the book became celebrated as a classic) that brought him back to Dropsie Avenue for four more volumes of tales in this increasingly complex storyworld. And while he never responded directly to Groth's criticisms from 1988, the sweeping historical projects such as *Dropsie Avenue* (1995) and *The Plot* (2005) were motivated in part by a desire to prove Groth wrong. Despite a very healthy ego, Eisner was always fiercely humble about how much he had left to accomplish and how much left to learn about the possibilities of the form. This is perhaps the most remarkable thing about Eisner's career: a master of the craft, a pioneer in the industry, and in his later years a beatified figure in comics history, Eisner remained to the last that Bronx kid in the 1930s trying to figure out what the next thing would be and determined to have a part in making it happen.

Acknowledgments

This volume owes an immense debt to many who have helped along the way, including Lucy Shelton Caswell, Andrew Kunka, Elijah Gardner, Elizabeth Hewitt, Denis Kitchen, Caitlin McGurk, Susan Liberator, Morgan Podraza, Jenny Robb, Paul Williams—and especially to the support of Carl and Nancy Gropper and the infinite patience and editorial vision of Carol Bemis.

5. Gary Groth, "Will Eisner: Chairman of the Board," *The Comics Journal* 267 (April/May 2005): 197.

The Texts of
A CONTRACT WITH GOD AND OTHER STORIES OF DROPSIE AVENUE

A TENEMENT IN THE BRONX

At 55 Dropsie Avenue, the Bronx, New York– not far from the elevated station– stood the tenement.

Like the others, it was built around 1920 when the decaying apartment houses in lower Manhattan could no longer accommodate the flood of immigrants that poured into New York after World War I.

These buildings – called "Tenements" after the 16th century legal term for a multiple dwelling that housed tenants – soon occupied large tracts of Bronx land.

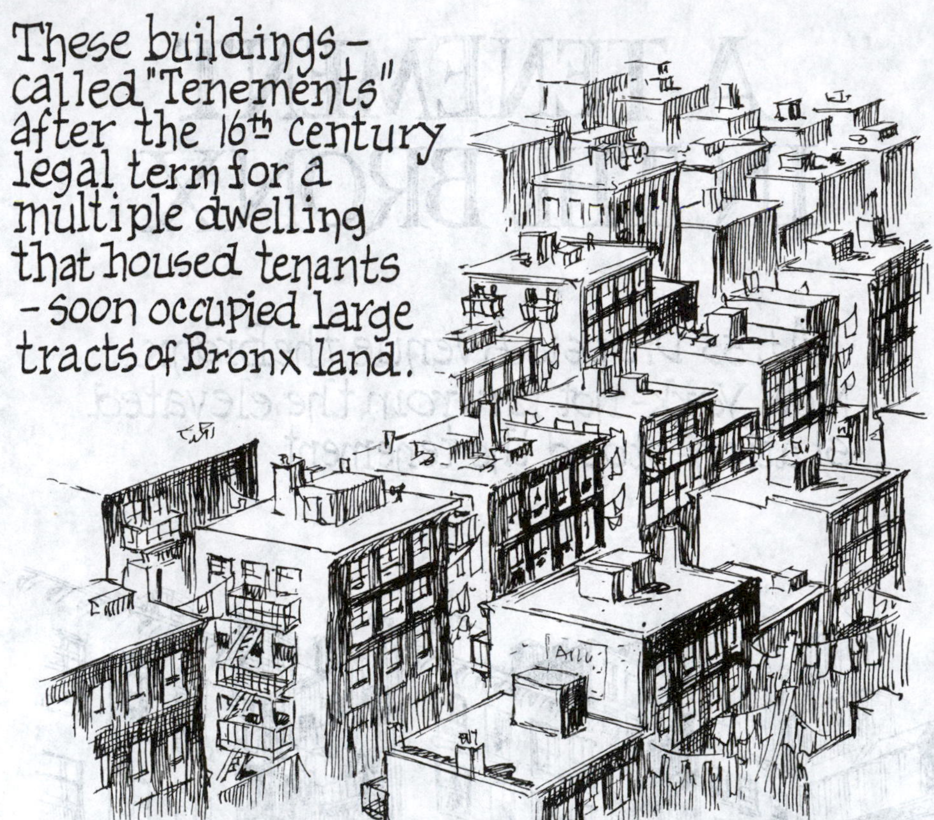

By 1930 they were already part of the roots of a whole new group of first-generation Americans and their foreign-born parents.

Inside – in the "railroad-flat" layouts lived low-paid city employees, laborers, clerks and their families. They teemed with a noisy neighborliness not unlike the life-style the newcomers had left on the "other side." It was a kind of ship board fellowship of passengers in transit – for, they were on a voyage of upward mobility.

They were intent on their own survival, busy with breeding their young and dreaming of a better life they knew existed "Uptown."

What community spirit there was, stemmed from their hostility toward a common enemy – the landlord!

55 Dropsie Avenue was typical of most tenements. Its tenants were varied. Some came and went. Many remained there for a life time… imprisoned by poverty or other factors. It was a sort of micro-village – and the world was **Dropsie Avenue**.

Within its walls great dramas were played out. There was no real privacy-no anonymity. One was either a participant or a member of the front-row audience. "Everybody knew about everybody."

The following stories are based on life in these tenements during the 1930's...the dirty thirties! They are true stories.

Only the telling and the portrayals have converted them to fiction.

Will Eisner

A
CONTRACT
WITH
GOD

All day the rain poured down on the Bronx without mercy.

The sewers overflowed and the waters rose over the curbs of the street.

The tenement at No. 55 Dropsie Avenue seemed ready to rise and float away on the swirling tide. "Like the ark of Noah," it seemed to Frimme Hersh as he sloshed homeward.

Only the tears of ten thousand weeping angels could cause such a deluge!
And, come to think of it, maybe that is exactly what it was...

...after all, this
was the day
Frimme Hersh
buried Rachele,
his daughter.

Not so unusual, a father brings up a child with care and love only to lose her ...plucked, as it were, from his arms by an unseen hand -the hand of God.
It happens to lots of people every day.

...to others, maybe.

... but not to Frimme Hersh.

And why not to Frimme Hersh ??

That's a fair question!

It should not have happened to Frimme Hersh

BECAUSE FRIMME HERSH HAD A CONTRACT WITH GOD!

And
a contract
is a
contract!
It was, after
all, a solemn
agreement of
many years.

HOW LONG AGO WAS IT?
In 1881 Tsar Alexander II of
Russia was assassinated and a
wave of terrible anti-semitic
pogroms swept the country.
In that year also, Frimme Hersh
was born in a little village near
Tiflis, named Piske.
Somehow his family survived the
massacre and Frimmehleh, as he
was lovingly called, grew up.
By the time he was ten, it
became clear that this boy was
special. He was brilliant and
seemed to acquire knowledge
from the air. In a poor shtetl like
Piske, where survival was the main
concern, how else?

Above all, Frimmehleh was helpful and Kind. After his parents died, he became the child of the childless in Piske.
THANK YOU FOR YOUR KINDNESS, FRIMMEHLEH.
GOD WILL REWARD YOU.

In those years, this was said to him often for he performed many, many good deeds.

One day, after a terrible attack, the surviving elders summoned him.

YOU WILL GO WITH REB LIPSHITZ TO THE NORTH. THERE IS A SEAPORT WHERE YOU CAN BUY PASSAGE ON A SHIP!
DO NOT WORRY FRIMMEHLEH, GOD IS WITH YOU. YOU WILL GO TO AMERICA.
...And so Hersh obeyed. Two nights later on the trail deep in the forest...
REBBE... IS GOD JUST?
IF JUSTICE IS NOT IN GOD'S HANDS— WHERE ELSE WOULD IT BE??
IF I AM GOOD WILL GOD KNOW IT ??
WHY NOT?? DOES IT NOT SAY THAT GOD IS ALL-KNOWING !?

THEN I WILL MAKE A CONTRACT WITH GOD!
And that night in the cold forest, he wrote the contract on a small stone.

And with the little stone tablet in his pocket, Frimme Hersh settled in New York City where he found shelter in the Hassidic community. There he took religious instruction and devoted himself to good works.

Faithfully and piously, he adhered to the terms of his contract with GOD.

In time he became a respected member of the Synagogue, trusted with money and social matters. So it was not surprising that it was on Hersh's doorstep that an anonymous mother abandoned her infant girl. What could be clearer? To Frimme, this was part of his pact with GOD.

Since no one wanted a child born of GOD-Knows-what Kind of parents, Frimme Hersh adopted the baby himself.

He named her Rachele, after his mother, and devoted himself to her with all his love.

So, she grew up blossoming in the warmth and nourishment of Frimme's gentle heart and pious ways. She was indeed his child and the joy of his years. Then one day – in the springtime of her life – Rachele fell ill.

Suddenly and fatally.

NO!
NOT TO ME...
YOU CAN'T DO
THIS... WE
HAVE A CONTRACT
!!

That night Frimme Hersh confronted GOD...

...and the old tenement trembled under the fury of the dialogue.

IF GOD REQUIRES THAT MEN HONOR THEIR AGREEMENTS...
...THEN IS NOT GOD, ALSO, SO OBLIGATED ??

I ASK YOU...WERE THE TERMS NOT CLEARLY WRITTEN ?

...DID I IGNORE EVEN ONE TINY SENTENCE - OR PERHAPS A SINGLE COMMA ?

ENOUGH.

CLANK

All during the days of mourning that followed the funeral, the rain fell without pause.
Friends came-each offering Hersh the usual words of comfort which he accepted in stony silence.

At the end of the days of Shiva in the dawn of the eighth day, the sun rose in a clear sky and Frimme Hersh said the morning prayer...for the last time.

Then...with deliberation....he shaved off his beard...
...and walked to the 186th street bank.
SO, MR. HERSH, YOU WANT TO BUY THE PARCEL ON DROPSIE AVE...
YES...YOU KNOW IT- THE TENEMENT AT No. 55.
BANK

WELL, NOW... IT'S AN EXPENSIVE PIECE OF PROPERTY.
WHAT E-X-P-E-N-S-I-V-E? PLEASE, MR. JOHNSON, I KNOW YOU FORECLOSED ON IT TWICE!

SO, FOR THE MORTGAGE I'LL BUY IT!... BELIEVE ME, IT AIN'T WORTH IT... BUT IT'S A START!
HMPFF... WELL, NOW, I THINK WE CAN MAKE A DEAL! ...WHAT IS YOUR FINANCIAL WORTH?

BONDS, I GOT– NO CASH... SO CAN YOU LOAN ME ON THESE?
THEY'LL DO FINE... AMPLE EQUITY THERE. – MR. HERSH, WE HAVE A DEAL!

For the first time, Frimme Hersh lied. For the first time, he committed an act which formerly was unthinkable. The bonds were not his- they had only been entrusted to him for safekeeping by the synagogue.
BANK
...SO, WHAT WAS SO HARD ABOUT THAT? ...HA! WHAT A YOLD!
...AND BESIDES, WHO AM I HURTING?! IN A YEAR I'LL BUY BACK THE BONDS... SO, A BIG TSIMMES!!

So, Frimme Hersh became the new owner of 55 Dropsie Avenue.

YOU WILL ALSO CUT DOWN ON STEAM HEAT 10%. FROM NOW ON THE TENANTS WILL MAKE THEIR OWN REPAIRS...I DON'T WANT TO KNOW FROM NO COMPLAINTS!
ACH... THESE JEWS ...YESTERDAY A POOR TENANT, TODAY THE OWNER! ...HOW DO THEY DO IT ?!

Within a year, Frimme Hersh gleaned enough out of the property to acquire the one next door. Within the next three years, he accumulated the beginning of a real estate empire.

His success appeared to be as much the result of uncanny luck as anything else.

Before long he took a mistress, a 'Shikseh' from Scranton, Pa., and took up a lifestyle he felt more appropriate to his new station.

He traded buildings like toys.

But one building he never sold - the tenement on Dropsie Ave. At least once every week he would come there...just to look at it.

WHY DON'T YOU SELL THOSE CRUMMY BUILDINGS, FRIM?!
WHY DON'T YOU MIND YOUR OWN BUSINESS!!
Y'KNOW, FRIM, YOU GOT, LIKE, A BLACK HOLE INSIDE O' YOU!
YOU DON'T DRINK... YEAH, THAT'S IT-HAVE A DRINK! MY FATHER USED TO SAY IT FILLED THE BLACK HOLE INSIDE HIM... COME ON, BABY, TRY IT!

TRY... COME ON.
AAAH,, Y'R HOPELESS!
...WE NEVER GO NOWHERE, FRIM! WHAT KIND OF LIFE IS THIS?– YOU'RE SO RICH YOU CAN BUY ANYTHING YOU WANT... SO, BUY IT!!
WE DON'T EVEN GO TO NO CHURCH...

HEY! Y'WANT I SHOULD BECOME JEWISH ?
FRIM? FRIM? NOW, WHAT DID I SAY WRONG ?

One evening Frimme Hersh walked from his penthouse uptown all the way to the old Synagogue.
There he called on the wisest of the elders.
DO YOU REMEMBER ME?... I'M FRIMME HERSH.
WE REMEMBER YOU.
I AM VERY RICH NOW. EVERYTHING I TOUCH TURNS TO GOLD- AS THEY SAY.

A FEW YEARS AGO I USED THE CONGREGATION'S BONDS AS COLLATERAL. NOW I CAN REPAY YOU.

SO, I'M RETURNING THEM, WITH INTEREST!
WE ARE ALL GRATEFUL.

NOW, I NEED SOMETHING FROM YOU!
FROM US? ...WHAT CAN WE GIVE A WEALTHY MAN?

Carefully, Hersh recounted the history of his former contract.

THAT CONTRACT WAS WRITTEN WHEN I WAS A CHILD-SO, WHO KNOWS, MAYBE IT WAS POORLY WRITTEN!
BUT MR. HERSH, THIS IS A PRIVATE MATTER BETWEEN YOU AND GOD!!
YOU ARE LEARNED IN THE WORD OF GOD -AND IF YOU KNOW HIS WORD YOU KNOW HIS WILL!

And so the three old men pondered the request.

BUT, REBBE, WOULD IT NOT BE A BLASPHEMY IF WE SHOULD DEVIATE FROM THE LAW?
WE WILL NOT DEVIATE! ...WE WILL ABBREVIATE!

IS NOT ALL RELIGION A CONTRACT BETWEEN MAN - AND GOD?
SO, WHAT IS HERSH ASKING FOR, AFTER ALL??...HE IS ASKING US TO PROVIDE HIM WITH A GUIDING DOCUMENT-SO THAT HE MIGHT LIVE IN HARMONY WITH GOD... CAN WE TRULY DENY HIM THIS??

So in the days that followed, the elders toiled, interrupted only by the Sabbath and certain days of prayer. At last they presented the document to Hersh.

AND NOW, I WILL LIVE UP TO MY BARGAIN– HERE IS THE LEASE TO THE TENEMENT–IN THE NAME OF THE SYNAGOGUE.

FRIMME HERSH, YOU ARE A MAN OF YOUR WORD!

All that night Hersh sat reading the contract. Again and again...he studied every word with great care.

It was bona-fide without question!

I WILL MAKE A NEW LIFE. I WILL GIVE ... I WILL DO CHARITABLE WORK AGAIN ...
... AND, AND AFTER ALL - I AM NOT TOO OLD TO MARRY. I SHALL HAVE A DAUGHTER ... AND I SHALL NAME HER RACHELE, YES, YES !!

THIS TIME, YOU WILL NOT VIOLATE OUR CONTRACT!
THIS TIME, I HAVE THREE WITNESSES!
THIS TIME I
ULP MY CHEST A PAIN IN
GLAK!

At the exact moment of Hersh's last earthly breath... a mighty bolt of lightning struck the city... Not a drop of rain fell.... Only an angry wind swirled about the tenements.

On Dropsie Avenue the old tenements seemed to tremble in the storm. It reminded the tenants of that day, years ago, when Frimme Hersh argued with GOD and terminated their contract.
REAL ESTATE TYCOON DIES
HEAD OF REALTY CO EMPIRE

EPILOGUE

Around midnight, fires started on the roof of a Dropsie Avenue tenement.
Soon the flames, spreading quickly, consumed all the old buildings on the street.
All.... except one!
Miraculously the tenement at 55 Dropsie Avenue was unharmed.

And it happened that a boy, Shloime Khreks, was the hero of the day.

Shloime was a
New Boy .....
And because he was
so different, he became
the object of much
bullying. One day, not
long after the fire, he
was trapped in the
alley of Number 55
by three toughs.

HEY MOIF... LOOK, IT'S THE NEW KID ! LET'S GIVE HIM A NICE E-NEE-SHE-AY-SHUN.
THAT'S SHLOIME KHREKS, HE'S A HASSID-HAW!
HE WEARS A FUNNY HAT!

...THERE IS WRITING ON THIS STONE.

IT'S A CONTRACT A...A CONTRACT WITH GOD!

I WILL KEEP IT!

...And that evening on the stoop of the tenement, Shloime Khreks signed his name below that of Frimme Hersh... thereby entering into a Contract with GOD.

Notes

3. A *Tenement in the Bronx.* In New York City, waves of immigration beginning in the 1840s created a demand for multistory buildings capable of providing cheap housing for the new immigrants. The housing was entirely unregulated and often quickly built, until reforms brought about following the publication of Jacob Riis's *How the Other Half Lives: Studies among the Tenements of New York* (1890). By the early 20th century, little room for affordable housing was left in Manhattan, so new tenements began to spring up in the other boroughs, especially the Bronx. Because of the New York Tenement House Acts of 1895 and 1901, these tenements were now regulated in terms of space provided for each resident and were generally safer and more comfortable than the Lower East Side tenements Riis had documented.
3. *elevated station.* In 1875, the New York Elevated Railway Company began construction of an elevated train line from Battery Park, at Manhattan's southern tip, extending north up Third Avenue. By 1886, the line was extended across the Harlem River, at Manhattan's northern tip, and into the Bronx. The access to public transportation encouraged people to move to the Bronx. Indeed, between 1886 and the period in which *A Contract with God* is set, the population of this borough increased fivefold.
3. *flood of immigrants that poured into New York after World War I.* While there was a lot of immigration after the war, the largest waves of immigration from Europe—especially eastern and southern Europe—peaked in 1907, when 1.3 million people entered the United States through Ellis Island. By 1910, immigrants and their American-born children accounted for more than 70 percent of New York's population. Following a xenophobic campaign in response to the rising population of immigrants in the country, the Immigration Act of 1924 created the first national laws regulating and severely restricting immigration of eastern and southern Europeans. Immigration from Asian countries was entirely blocked by this law.
4. *16th century legal term.* Eisner's etymology is not quite right here. The French term *tenement*, dating to the late 13th century, originally meant simply land or holdings, derived from the Latin *tenementum*, meaning a holding, or fief. "Tenement" as an establishment housing multiple tenants can be traced to late-17th-century Scotland.
4. *"railroad-flat" layouts.* Railroad apartments were laid out such that one room connected directly to the next, like railroad cars. These tenement layouts originally had no hallways, requiring tenants to enter their rooms by passing through the rooms of the other tenants. By the 1920s, when the Bronx tenements of Eisner's fictional Dropsie Avenue were built, railroad flats generally were on the sides of a narrow hallway, with apartment entrances running consecutively off the hall.
10. *"Like the ark of Noah."* This analogy to the Old Testament story (Genesis 6:11–9:19) of the ark, which saved Noah's family and two of each

animal from the floods with which God had inundated the Earth, suggests the protagonist's religious training.

10. *Frimme Hersh.* As is common for Eisner, the protagonist's name contains clues—some ultimately ironic—to his identity. In Yiddish, *frum* (פרום) means pious, and *frimer* means more piously observant. Hersh/Hersch/Hirsch (הערש) is a common Yiddish proper and given name, meaning deer.

12. *Rachele.* Rachele/Rachel is a Hebrew name meaning ewe, or female sheep. In the Bible (Genesis 35:24), Rachel is one of the matriarchs: the favorite wife of Jacob and mother of Joseph and Benjamin. In early drafts of the story, Eisner used his own late daughter's name, Alice.

14. *Missis Kelly.* Mrs. Kelly, a tenant of 55 Dropsie Avenue, is one of the many Irish-American immigrants who had arrived in New York in the second half of the 19th century following the Irish Potato Famine (1845–52) and the generations of systematic discrimination against Irish Catholics in the United Kingdom.

19. *In 1881 Tsar Alexander II of Russia was assassinated.* The assassination—in March 1881, in St. Petersburg—was carried out by members of a radical antigovernment organization, Narodnaya Volya ("People's Will"), which used political assassination in an attempt to destabilize the government and spark an uprising. Alexander had been responsible early in his tenure for some important reforms, including the emancipation of the serfs in 1861 and the removal of some antisemitic laws. Although no Jews were among the conspirators who assassinated the tsar, his death was widely blamed on Jews, and devastating antisemitic violence followed. Alexander III ramped up antisemitic policies during his reign, leading to mass emigration of many Russian and Polish Jews to the United States.

19. *pogroms.* The Russian word *pogrom*, meaning to violently demolish, was used to describe violent attacks on Jewish individuals and communities.

19. *Tiflis.* Tbilisi, the capital and largest city of Georgia, was called Tiflis under the Russian rule, 1801–1917.

19. *shtetle.* Yiddish uses the Hebrew alphabet, so spellings in the Latin alphabet vary. Sometimes transliterated as "stetle," this is the Yiddish word (שטעטל) for town and is typically used to describe small towns in eastern Europe with predominantly Jewish populations.

22. *Reb.* The word is short for *rebbe*, a Yiddish word for spiritual leader of the Jewish community. Both *rebbe* and *rabbi* come from the same Hebrew root, *rav* (רב), which means spiritual guide. While we think of a rabbi as the leader of a particular congregation, *rebbe* has a broader connotation of spiritual teacher and theological scholar.

24. *Hassidic community.* Hasidism, a distinct sect within Judaism, emerged in eastern Europe in the 18th century as part of a larger spiritual revival. It is aligned with Orthodox Judaism and characterized by strict adherence to religious laws. Hasidic communities in the United States have tended to be relatively isolated, providing their own education, shopping, and other services.

35. *Shiva.* In this Jewish ritual of mourning, the family members of the deceased congregate, usually at home, to grieve. The practice is

typically called "sitting shiva" because the grievers sit on low stools or boxes.

35. *morning prayer.* Shacharis is the morning tefillah of Judaism, one of three daily prayers.
36. *shaved off his beard.* A man's having a beard is an act of faith within Orthodox Judaism and Hasidism, following the interpretation of Leviticus 19:27: "You shall not round off the side-growth on your head, or destroy the side-growth of your beard." Thus, when Hersh shaves off his beard, he is literally breaking the contract with God.
39. *yold.* A Yiddish term for a naive or gullible person.
39. *big tsimmes. Tsimmis* is a Yiddish word that means fuss. Hersh is thus saying that what he has done is "no big deal"—that it should cause no fuss.
42. *the El.* The elevated train. See endnote for reference on page 67.
43. *'shikseh.'* This Yiddish term means non-Jewish, or gentile, woman. It frequently has pejorative connotations.

THE STREET SINGER
During the early 1930s, at the depth of the Great Depression, there appeared in the alleys of the tenements, STREET SINGERS.
These wandering street minstrels sang popular songs and segments of operatic arias which, in the acoustics of the place, sounded surprisingly professional.

On warm Summer
afternoons these
victims of the hard times
entertained their
unseen audience
who rewarded their
efforts....

No one knew much about them...

KNOCK
KNOCK
YES...
I'M COMING
I'M COMING

YOUR NOTE-IT SAID FOR ME TO COME UP?!
YES...YES, COME IN...

...DO COME IN, PLEASE! OH, WE HAVE SO MUCH TO TALK ABOUT.

YOU KNOW, YOU HAVE A GOLDEN VOICE - HAVE YOU EVER CONSIDERED A PROFESSIONAL CAREER?
HAVE YOU EVER HEARD OF **DIVA MARTA MARIA** THE SOPRANO?
YOU GOT SOMETHING TO EAT? THIS FRUIT IS WAX!
I...AM... DIVA MARTA MARIA !!

I TRAINED WITH THE GREAT MADAME LA SHTIMME... OF COURSE YOU HEARD OF HER!?
PASS THE SALT.

FOR YEARS I SANG IN CONCERT HALLS AND WITH OPERA COMPANIES ALL OVER THE WORLD...

...THEN, I MARRIED !!

MY HUSBAND WAS A DRUNKARD- HE BEAT ME! HE WAS INSANELY JEALOUS... OFTEN HE WAS SICK! I STOPPED SINGING AND GAVE LESSONS SO I COULD TAKE CARE OF HIM.

FINALLY... IN HOBOKEN ONE WINTER HE DIED — AT LAST!

I TRIED TO RETURN TO MY CAREER— BUT IT WAS TOO LATE !!.... THERE WAS NOTHING LEFT BUT THE DREAM OF WHAT I MIGHT HAVE BEEN.

BUT, TODAY... WHEN I HEARD YOUR VOICE I KNEW THAT A NEW CAREER LAY BEFORE ME ... OURS!! YOUR CAREER AND MINE! ...YOU WILL SING AND I WILL BE YOUR COACH.

FIRST... WHAT IS YOUR NAME ??... OH, NEVER MIND, I'LL GIVE YOU A NEW NAME. HMMM, LET ME SEE...

RONALD BARRY!!! YES, THAT'S IT, YOU'LL BE RONALD BARRY THE GOLDEN BARITONE!

YOU LOOK LIKE QUALITY! Y'KNOW, YOU RESEMBLE JOHN BARRYMORE. HMMM NO... MORE LIKE RONALD COLMAN! YOU ARE VERY ATTRACTIVE... WITH YOUR VOICE AND LOOKS–AND MY EXPERIENCE... WE'LL MAKE IT TO THE TOP–TOGETHER!!
RIALTO

...TOGETHER WE WILL CREATE THE **GOLDEN BARITONE**...

...ANOTHER 'SHEIK OF ARABY' YOU WILL BE A STAR... OH GOD A STAR.

YOU'LL SEE... IT WILL ALWAYS BE LIKE THIS.

AND NOW, MY DEAR, WE MUST START ON OUR CAREER- YOU WILL NEED MANY THINGS... CLOTHES, VOICE LESSONS, BOOKINGS!

HERE IS SOME MONEY—BUY YOURSELF A NEW SUIT! IN THIS BUSINESS YOU MUST LOOK PROSPEROUS!

TOMORROW YOU'LL BEGIN SINGING LESSONS—WITH ME!

COME BACK TOMORROW AT NINE O'CLOCK ... WE START IN THE MORNING EARLY... OH, IT WILL BE HARD WORK, A LOT OF DISCIPLINE AND I SHALL BE A HARD TASKMASTER!

—UNTIL TOMORROW MORNING THEN... ♫RONALD♫

SO MUCH
TO DO

HELLO, MAX? THIS IS MARTA MARIA...
-OH YOU KNOW WHO... THAT'S MY STAGE NAME, REMEMBER? IT'S **SYLVIA**... SYLVIA SPEEGEL!

WAIT- DON'T HANG UP!!!

LISTEN, I HAVE A NEW PROTEGE... A GOLDEN BARITONE, **RONALD BARRY** - OF COURSE YOU NEVER HEARD OF HIM-BUT YOU **WILL**!

I'M GOING TO COACH HIM-MAX, GET HIM A BOOKING... A START, ANYWHERE-WEDDINGS, A BAR MITZVAH-A WAKE, ANYTHING... **MAX**, DON'T TALK DIRTY, HE'S MY PROTEGE... PLEASE, SO MUCH DEPENDS ON THIS... ...MAX... MAX...

MAX ... I'M BEGGING MAX... PLEASE

...YOU'LL DO IT?..OH, GOD BLESS YOU MAX...THANK YOU... I... HELLO HELLO

AT LAST
WE ARE GOING TO BE ON TOP AGAIN!
HELD OVER
RIALTO

HEY, JOE... IT'S ME, EDDIE!
YOU AGAIN?
KNOCK
KNOCK

HERE Y'ARE. Y'GOT MONEY THIS TIME?
PLENTY!

WAAHH

WAHHH
WAHH

WAHHHH
SO, EDDIE, YOU BUM, YER HOME EARLY...'SMATTER, YER VOICE GAVE OUT? ...I HOPE!

WAAA
ALL THAT WHISKEY WOULD KILL A HORSE! EDDIE, Y'GONNA DRINK YERSELF INTO THE GRAVE!
WAAAAAAA
SHADDAP! SHET THAT KID'S MOUTH!!
EEE
WAAAHH

YOU'LL KILL MY BABY! -MURDERER!! DRUNKARD!
SHADDAP
WHERE'D YOU GET THE MONEY FOR ALL THAT WHISKEY... I NEED MONEY FOR THE DOCTOR... YOU KNOW I'M PREGNANT.
SHADDAP
HMPF... IS THIS ALL?? YOU SPEND 20 DOLLARS ON WHISKEY AND YOU GIVE ME ONLY 5 BUCKS- HOW CAN WE LIVE ON THIS ?!
SHADDAP

LOOK AT ME... I WAS SUCH A BEAUTIFUL DANCER... I GAVE UP A CAREER TO MARRY AN ACCOUNTANT!
SHADDAP

BUT NO... HE DON'T WANT A STEADY JOB –HE'D RATHER SING IN STINKIN' ALLEYS FOR PENNIES.
SHADDAP!

YOU DON'T EVEN KNOW HOW TO SING
YOU DIDN'T EVEN WHISTLE BEFORE YOU MET ME!

SHADDAP

BUM BUM
SHADDAP

HALP HE'S KILLING ME AND MY BABY
WAH
SHADDAP SHADDAP SHADDAP SHADDAP
WAHH
WAH WAH
I'M GOIN' TO BED..
...YOU BROKE MY BOTTLE...

EDDIE...IT'S NOON ALREADY—PLEASE, GO OUT AND LOOK FOR A JOB.... PLEASE!
I'M SORRY ABOUT LAST NIGHT, SOPHIE.
THAT'S OKAY, EDDIE! GO, HONEY... DON'T SING TODAY— GET A JOB!

JOE'S

JOE, GIMME A HAIR-OF-THE-DOG ...COUGH... HAD A ROUGH NIGHT.
BEAT IT, EDDIE! Y'R CREDIT STINKS.

ONLY TEMPORARILY! JOE, YOU ARE LOOKING AT THE NEW PROTEGE OF THE GREAT DIVA MARTA MARIA - THE INTERNATIONALLY FAMOUS SOPRANO!
DIVA WHO ?

WHAT DO YOU KNOW ABOUT THE WORLD OF MUSIC..?!

IT'S THE BIG TIME... LOTS OF MONEY... RESPECT, TRAVEL - THE BIG TIME, JOE! NOTHIN' BUT THE BEST!
WHY IS THIS DIVA GONNA DO ALL THIS FOR YOU ?

SHE RECOGNIZES MY SINGING TALENT...... BESIDES, SHE'S SWEET ON ME.

Y'SEE... MY PLAN IS LET HER PROMOTE ME ...THEN WHEN I'M ON TOP–I'LL GO BACK TO MY WIFE AND KID... A SINGING STAR... NOT A CRUMMY ACCOUNTANT.

SEE...YOU, YOU UNDERSTAND JOE?...C'MON JOE....
OKAY, HERE... BOY, EDDIE, YOU'RE ALL HEART!

SAY, WHERE DOES THIS... DIVA LIVE ?

OH, MY GOD

I... DON'T KNOW WHERE... I DIDN'T THINK TO WRITE DOWN THE ADDRESS! I SING IN SO MANY ALLEYS -THEY ALL **LOOK** ALIKE !

NO..NO... WAIT-I'LL SHOW YOU- SHE MUST BE IN THE PHONE BOOK!

NOTHING... SHE'S NOT LISTED.
YOU CONNED ME OUTTA A DRINK AGAIN!

JOE... SHE REALLY.. ...I'M NOT LYING...
GET OUT!

OUT!

Street Singers played a tenement only once.
There were, after all, plenty of alleys...

Notes

71. *the Great Depression.* In fall 1929, the U.S. stock market began a series of declines, culminating in Black Tuesday, October 29, 1929. The severe worldwide economic crisis that followed is called the Great Depression.
81. *John Barrymore.* Of the famous American theatrical family, John Barrymore (1882–1942) was a celebrated stage and film actor.
81. *Ronald Colman.* Ronald Colman (1891–1958) was an actor who began his career on stage and in film in his native England before emigrating in the 1920s to the United States, where he became a movie star.
82. *'Sheik of Araby.'* "The Sheik of Araby," a popular song from the 1920s, was inspired by the silent film *The Sheik* (1921), starring the sex symbol Rudolph Valentino (1895–1926).

AFTER THE CRASH OF THE STOCK MARKET IN 1929
A GREAT DEPRESSION
ENGULFED WESTERN SOCIETY LIKE A GREY CLOUD!
SUDDENLY IT SEEMED,
TO A WORLD WHICH HAD BEEN IN GLEEFUL PURSUIT
OF THE GOOD LIFE,
THAT LIVING HAD BECOME SURVIVAL!
MANY HITHERTO UNQUESTIONED ASSUMPTIONS NOW
CAME UNDER REEXAMINATION.
WHERE THEY COULD, PEOPLE RELOCATED
FROM FARM TO CITY OR CITY TO FARM....
SEEKING GREENER PASTURES LIKE HUNTER-GATHERERS OF OLD.
BUT IN THE BRONX, ON DROPSIE AVENUE,
MOST TENEMENT DWELLERS REMAINED
HOLDING FAST TO THEIR BEACH-HEAD
SIMPLY BECAUSE THEY HAD ONLY JUST ARRIVED
FROM OTHER MORE HOSTILE PLACES.
THEY CARRIED WITH THEM
THE TABERNACLE OF A LIFE FORCE
THEY HARDLY UNDERSTOOD.
IT WAS NOW
THE MIDDLE THIRTIES...
EMPLOYMENT AGENCY
BANK

1934

"... the withered leaves of industrial enterprise lie on every side ... the savings of many thousands of families are gone ... unemployed citizens face the grim problem of existence. ..."

FRANKLIN D. ROOSEVELT
From his first Inaugural Address

ITEMS FROM
THE NEW YORK PRESS

1500 HOMELESS LIVE IN ARMORY

69th REGIMENT HOUSES POOR

FEB. 7, 1934

Sheltered from the cold, over 1500 homeless people have found at least temporary refuge in the 69th Regiment Armory at Lexington Avenue and Twenty-Sixth Street in New York.

These victims of the depression, poorly clothed and dispirited, have been pouring into the huge building filling the drill floor and the mezzanine. Coming from the inclement pavements and wet doorways or dank subway kiosks, they encamp on the polished wooden floors.

SIMPLE GAMES OCCUPY THEIR TIME

In an effort to keep up morale,the men play checkers, jigsaw puzzles and hang around a piano played by a volunteer of surprising talent.

SLUMP CAN AFFECT PEOPLE'S HEALTH

INCREASE IN ILLNESS AND REDUCTION OF INCOME EFFECT.

In an article published on Jan. 14 by the *New York Times,* it was reported that the average annual income of a representative group of American wage-earners dropped from $1700 in 1929 to $900 this year.

The significance of the statistic is that historically an economic depression usually results in sickness and impaired vitality.

RATE OF DEATH SINCE 1929 HAS REDUCED

Strangely enough, the U.S. death rate has fallen despite the drop in living standards.

TWO MEN FAINT OF HUNGER IN CITY HALL WHILE WOMAN SCREAMS

MAYOR LA GUARDIA HALTS CONFERENCE

MARCH 2, 1934

According to the *New York Times,* two men in a group of twenty-two unemployed people besieged City Hall in the belief that the mayor would give them jobs in snow removal work, collapsed in the hall outside the Mayor's Office.

Both men, exhausted from lack of food, were immediately taken to the Beekman Street Hospital at Mayor Fiorello La Guardia's orders.

"WANT JOBS, NOT FOOD"

The men had worked the day before at snow clearing for the Sanitation Department until they were laid off for lack of work.

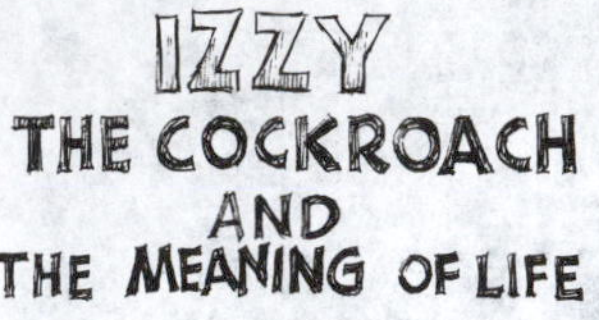

THE TENEMENT AT 55 DROPSIE AVENUE
LAY QUIETLY AT ANCHOR IN ITS SEA OF CONCRETE.
THE SOUNDS OF THE CITY WERE DIMINISHING.
ALREADY ONE COULD HEAR RUSS COLUMBO SINGING
FROM A RADIO IN THE SECOND FLOOR BACK.
IT WAS FRIDAY AND IT WAS SUNDOWN,
AND THE LAST OF THE REGULAR CONGREGANTS
OF THE SYNAGOGUE ON THE NEXT BLOCK
WERE WALKING HOME.

AT THIS MOMENT THREE MINOR EVENTS OCCURRED
...ONE;
JACOB SHTARKAH FINALLY, IT SEEMED, CAME TO THE END OF HIS CAREER.
JACOB, JACOB... PLEASE DON'T MAKE SUCH A BIG TSIMMES ABOUT THIS.
BETH SHOL
BUT BENJAMIN, I GAVE ALMOST FIVE YEARS OF MY LIFE TO BUILD THAT STUDY HALL ON THE SHUL... FIVE YEARS!! IT'S MY NEDOVA!!!
BE REASONABLE, JACOB! FIVE YEARS AGO YOU CAME TO US, IF YOU'LL PARDON ME, AN OLD CARPENTER WITH NOTHING TO DO! SO WE GAVE YOU A 'HOLY TASK'...TO BUILD FOR US A NEDOVA - SO, YOU DID, AND YOU MADE A BIG CAREER OUT OF IT.... WELL, NOW IT IS FINISHED!

WITH MY OWN TWO HANDS I BUILT IT! EVERY NAIL IN THAT BUILDING I HAMMERED! EVEN THE WALLS I PLASTERED!
TRUE, TRUE... BUT WHO PAID FOR IT? MORRIS GOLDFARB! ...IT WAS HIS DONATION THAT PAID YOU A SALARY, BOUGHT THE WOOD, BOUGHT THE LAND, EVERYTHING!
IT WILL BE CALLED, "THE YETTA AND MORRIS GOLDFARB STUDY HALL."
The Yetta & Morris Goldfarb
NO! NO!! IT'S NOT FAIR!
PLEASE, JACOB, PLEASE... ...YOU GOT A FIVE YEARS LIVING FROM IT!

The Yetta & Morris Goldfarb Wing
YOU MUST FACE REALITY JACOB... THE BUILDING COMMITTEE HAS DECIDED ONCE AND FOR ALL! P-E-R-I-O-D!
ME YOU GAVE FIVE YEARS, GOLDFARB YOU ARE GIVING IMMORTALITY !!

TAP
TAP
NU... JACOB.. WHAT ARE YOU STANDING AROUND FOR?? GO HOME! IT'S ALREADY SUNDOWN.
MAYBE YOU GOT ANOTHER BUILDING FOR ME TO BUILD?... SOME BENCHES, A CLOSET, MAYBE, FOR THE TEFILLEN?
NOTHING, JACOB! NO OTHER PROJECTS. EVERYTHING IS DONE... WE DON'T NEED ANYTHING!

GO, JACOB... GO TO LAKEWOOD... TAKE A REST... SIT IN THE SUN... YOU'RE **ENTITLED**... YOU WORKED HARD ALL YOUR LIFE.
FIVE YEARS!

FIVE YEARS! DOESN'T HE UNDERSTAND? IT WASN'T JUST A LIVING... I WAS MAKING A SOMETHING!
A REASON FOR LIVING!
...OTHERWISE, HOW IS A MAN DIFFERENT FROM A COCKROACH ??

A LIFETIME OF WORKING! ...FOR WHAT, I ASK YOU..??!
OY GOTTENOOO! I CAN'T MOVE MY LEGS... MY CHEST HURTS ...OY-VEY I'M DYING!!

TWO...
RIFKA SHTARKAH PREPARED FOR THE SABBATH...
SO, WHERE IS JACOB? IT IS GETTING LATE, ALREADY!

THREE
IZZY THE COCKROACH FELL TO THE FLOOR OF THE ALLEY FROM TWO FLIGHTS UP!

SO?? MISTER COCKROACH, WHAT ARE YOU STRUGGLING FOR?? TO MAYBE STAY ALIVE A FEW DAYS MORE ?

WELL... TO TELL THE TRUTH SO AM I TRYING TO STAY ALIVE!
SO, THEN, WHAT'S THE DIFFERENCE BETWEEN US??
YOU... BEING ONLY A COCKROACH, JUST WANT TO LIVE! FOR YOU IT'S ENOUGH! BUT ME... I HAVE TO ASK, WHY!?

WHY, WHY... WHO KNOWS WHY?! ...GOD??
WELL, THERE ARE ONLY TWO POSSIBILITIES!
EITHER, MAN CREATED GOD...OR, GOD CREATED MAN!

IF... MAN CREATED GOD...

... THEN, THE REASON FOR LIFE IS ONLY IN THE MIND OF MAN !!

...IF, ON THE OTHER HAND, GOD CREATED MAN...

THEN, THE REASON FOR LIVING IS STILL ONLY A GUESS!

...AFTER ALL IS SAID AND DONE...

WHO REALLY KNOWS THE WILL OF GOD??

.....SO, IN EITHER CASE, BOTH MAN AND COCKROACH ARE IN SERIOUS TROUBLE! BECAUSE STAYING ALIVE SEEMS TO BE THE ONLY THING ON WHICH EVERYBODY AGREES!

OY, YOY YOY...
CLOP CLOP
HEY, DON'T
LOOKOUT.. YOU GONNA STEP ON IT ...THAT... COCKA ROACH NO, NO!
WHA? HEY
HEY, LEGGO MY LEG Y'OLD KOKKER !!!
SO, GO AHEAD, HIT ME! ... ONE ZETZ AND... I'M... DEAD.
SO, AT LEAST I'LL DIE FOR A REASON! ... THAT, AT LEAST, I CAN UNDERSTAND ...GO AHEAD, YOU BUM
AAAAAAEHHH OVER A COCK-A-ROACH I AINT GONNA KILL YA... CRAZY OLD FOOL!
CLOP
CLOP
CLOP
CLOP

SIGH
JACOB
JACOB
RIFKA...
WHATTEH YOU DOING IN THE ALLEY COME UP IT'S TIME TO EAT SUPPER
ALRIGHT, ALRIGHT, ALREADY
I'M COMING I'M COMING

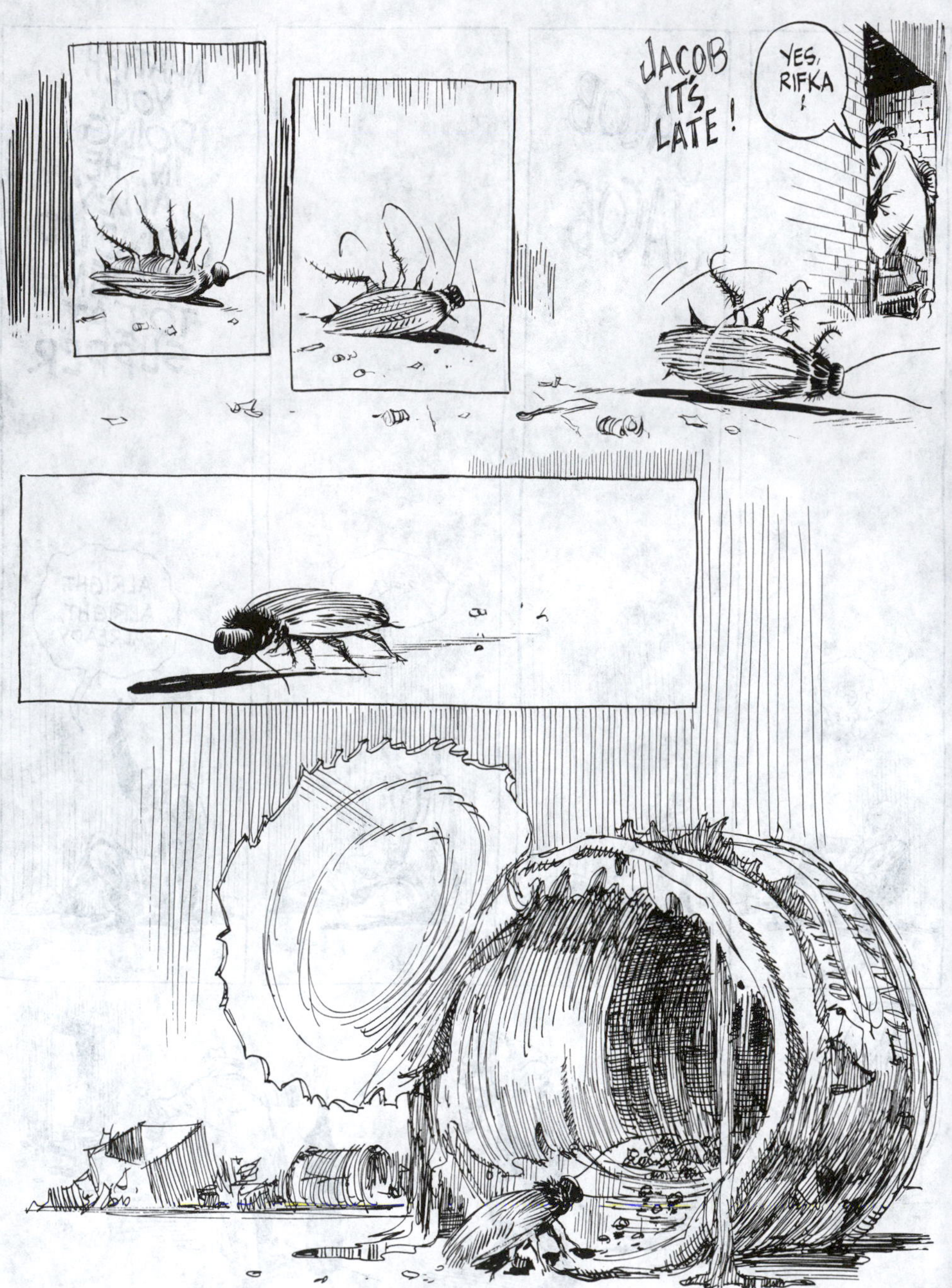
JACOB IT'S LATE!
YES, RIFKA!

JACOB, ARE YOU COMING UP??
YES, YES, I'M COMING... I'M COMING!
BARUCH ATA ADONAI EHLOHEINU MEHLECH HAOLAM ASHER KID'SHANU B'MITZVOTAV V'TZI VANU L'HADLIK NER SHEL SHABBAS
JACOB, DID YOU WASH YOUR HANDS?
NU..., JACOB... SO, HOW WAS TODAY?
TODAY?? TODAY, I SAVED THE LIFE OF A COCKROACH!

Notes

100. *crash of the stock market.* See endnote for reference on page 99.
101. *1934.* The previous year, U.S. national unemployment reached 27 percent, making it the worst year of the Depression in that country. In 1934, Americans waited to see if the New Deal policies of President Franklin Delano Roosevelt (1882–1945) might finally begin to turn things around. This year also saw the German fascist leader Adolf Hitler (1889–1945) consolidate his power.
102. *Russ Columbo.* Ruggiero Eugenio di Rodolfo Colombo (1908–1934), known as Russ Columbo, was a popular American singer, famous for his love ballads.
102. *When the deep purple falls . . .* These are the title lyrics from the song "Deep Purple," written as an instrumental by Peter DeRose in 1931. The song became such a hit that lyrics were added by Mitchell Parish in 1938.
103. *Jacob Shtarkah.* The protagonist in this story (and a unifying character throughout the interconnected stories of *A Life Force*) is named after Jacob, a biblical patriarch (Genesis 25–50) and the husband of Rachel (the name Eisner gave to the lost daughter in *A Contract with God*). *Shtark*, in Yiddish, means strong (שטארק), with a *shtarker* being a strong, powerful person (often idiomatically signifying a thug).
103. *tsimmes.* See endnote for reference on p. 69.
103. *shul.* A Yiddish word (שול) that means school.
103. *nedova.* Yiddish word (כדמה) for donation or gift.
106. *tefillin.* These are small black-leather boxes, which contain written passages from the Torah, that attach to straps. In an important part of Orthodox Jewish practice, men bind the tefillin to both their forehead and arm during prayer.
107. *Lakewood.* Lakewood, New Jersey, was a popular vacation destination for New Yorkers in the 1930s.
110. *Rifka.* Hebrew diminutive of Rebecca, the name translates roughly as to bind or join.
110. *It is getting late.* Shabbat (the Jewish sabbath) requires that candles be lit and prayers intoned just before sundown.
116. *y'old kokker.* In Yiddish, *alte/r kaker/kokker* (אלטער קאקער) is a pejorative term for a crotchety old-timer, or old geezer.
119. *Baruch Ata Adonai . . .* This is a transliteration of the Hebrew prayer for the lighting of the Shabbat candles. In English, the prayer reads, "Blessed art thou, Lord our God, King of the Universe, who has sanctified us with his commandments and commanded us to kindle the Shabbat lights."
119. *Nu.* Yiddish expression (נו) that colloquially means something like "well" or "so" as a question.

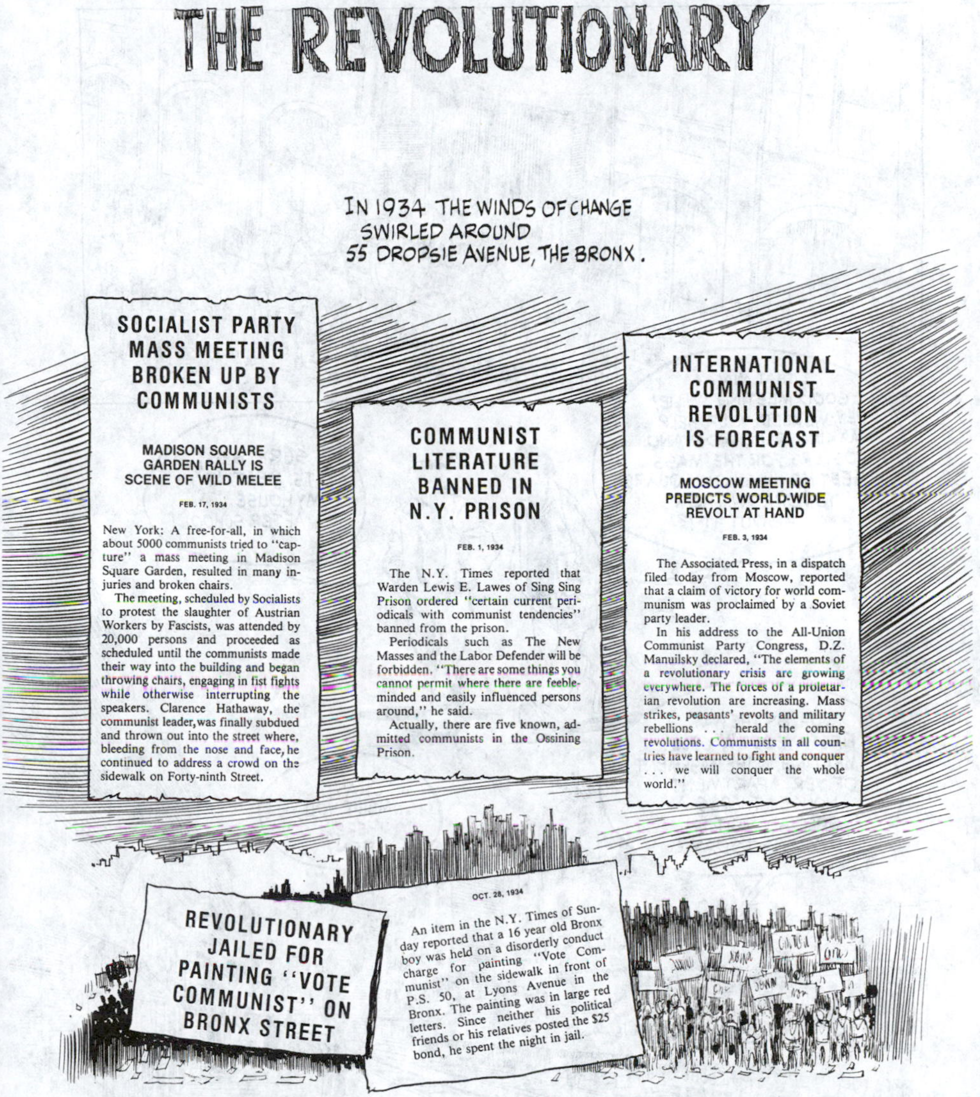

THE REVOLUTIONARY

IN 1934 THE WINDS OF CHANGE SWIRLED AROUND 55 DROPSIE AVENUE, THE BRONX.

SOCIALIST PARTY MASS MEETING BROKEN UP BY COMMUNISTS

MADISON SQUARE GARDEN RALLY IS SCENE OF WILD MELEE

FEB. 17, 1934

New York: A free-for-all, in which about 5000 communists tried to "capture" a mass meeting in Madison Square Garden, resulted in many injuries and broken chairs.

The meeting, scheduled by Socialists to protest the slaughter of Austrian Workers by Fascists, was attended by 20,000 persons and proceeded as scheduled until the communists made their way into the building and began throwing chairs, engaging in fist fights while otherwise interrupting the speakers. Clarence Hathaway, the communist leader, was finally subdued and thrown out into the street where, bleeding from the nose and face, he continued to address a crowd on the sidewalk on Forty-ninth Street.

COMMUNIST LITERATURE BANNED IN N.Y. PRISON

FEB. 1, 1934

The N.Y. Times reported that Warden Lewis E. Lawes of Sing Sing Prison ordered "certain current periodicals with communist tendencies" banned from the prison.

Periodicals such as The New Masses and the Labor Defender will be forbidden. "There are some things you cannot permit where there are feeble-minded and easily influenced persons around," he said.

Actually, there are five known, admitted communists in the Ossining Prison.

INTERNATIONAL COMMUNIST REVOLUTION IS FORECAST

MOSCOW MEETING PREDICTS WORLD-WIDE REVOLT AT HAND

FEB. 3, 1934

The Associated Press, in a dispatch filed today from Moscow, reported that a claim of victory for world communism was proclaimed by a Soviet party leader.

In his address to the All-Union Communist Party Congress, D.Z. Manuilsky declared, "The elements of a revolutionary crisis are growing everywhere. The forces of a proletarian revolution are increasing. Mass strikes, peasants' revolts and military rebellions . . . herald the coming revolutions. Communists in all countries have learned to fight and conquer . . . we will conquer the whole world."

REVOLUTIONARY JAILED FOR PAINTING "VOTE COMMUNIST" ON BRONX STREET

OCT. 28, 1934

An item in the N.Y. Times of Sunday reported that a 16 year old Bronx boy was held on a disorderly conduct charge for painting "Vote Communist" on the sidewalk in front of P.S. 50, at Lyons Avenue in the Bronx. The painting was in large red letters. Since neither his political friends or his relatives posted the $25 bond, he spent the night in jail.

HIGH SCHOOL
...THAT WAS A GOOD MEETING, WILLIE! HEY, WE NEED YOUR HELP MAKING PLACARDS AND POSTERS FOR THE MASS MEETING IN UNION SQUARE TOMORROW... HOW'S ABOUT IT!?
SURE, BEN, LET'S MEET AT MY HOUSE... AFTER SCHOOL!
...OH, BY THE WAY, FIRST WE GOT A 'CELL' MEETING IN THE BASEMENT OF YER APARTMENT HOUSE... THERE'S A SPECIAL VISITOR COMING TODAY!
OKAY, ...MEET YOU THERE, BEN!

...THIS WHERE THEY'RE HOLDING THE MEETING, WILLIE ?
YEAH,... DOWN IN THE 'SOCIAL ROOM'... THE SUPER LET US FIX UP THE CELLAR
HEY, HEY, PRETTY FANCY DOWN HERE!
WE GOT SOME OLD SOFAS FROM THE JUNK YARD!
OKAY... QUIET DOWN! LET'S START THE MEETING...
NOW, AS YOU ALREADY KNOW... WE'RE GONNA HAVE A DEMONSTRATION IN UNION SQUARE T'MORROW AT 3 PM! BEN AND WILLIE ARE MAKING THE SIGNS AND LEAFLETS!
WE'LL RUN OFF THE SHEETS ON THE MIMEO MACHINE IN SCHOOL!
NOW LET ME INTRODUCE OUR GUEST, MR. VOSTROV-HE JUST ARRIVED FROM MOSCOW... HE HAS SOME ADVICE!
...COMRADES, YOUR STRUGGLE IS NOT GOING UNNOTICED BY THE WORKERS OF THE WORLD -TRYING TO THROW OFF THE YOKE OF CAPITALISM!
... TOMORROW, WHEN YOU GO TO THE BARRICADES, REMEMBER: FIRST, THOSE OF YOU WITH BABY BROTHERS AND SISTERS BE SURE THE GIRLS ARE PUSHING THE BABY CARRIAGES UP AT THE FRONT LINE!

NEXT... TOWARD THE END OF THE SPEECHES - A COUPLE OF YOU ACTIVIST AGITATORS START TO PUSH FROM THE BACK! ...THROW A FEW ROCKS AT THE POLICE ...TO GET THINGS GOING!
HEY, THAT'S GONNA FORCE THE COPS INTO A FIGHT!
EXACTLY... ON THE FRONT LINE GIRLS START SCREAMING ABOUT THEIR BABIES... AND THE NEWSPAPER PHOTOGRAPHERS WILL GET PICTURES OF THE POLICE ATTACKING WOMEN AND CHILDREN.
WOW!
I DON'T THINK MY MOTHER WILL LET ME BRING MY BABY BROTHER!
GOSH
AAAH THEY WON'T HIT KIDS.
WHO'S GONNA DO THE FIGHTING?
DON'T WORRY, WE'LL HAVE A FEW MENSHEVIST PROFESSIONALS IN THE CROWD! THEY'LL KNOW WHAT TO DO!
OKAY, ANY LAST QUESTIONS BEFORE WE BREAK UP?
MR. VOSTROV, WHAT ABOUT JEWS IN THE SOVIET UNION?
UNDER COMMUNISM ALL RELIGION IS REGARDED AS A SOCIAL OPIATE... NO CLASSES, NO RELIGION ...THUS NO BIGOTRY!
THEY GOT FREE LOVE IN RUSSIA?
WHAT ABOUT FREE SPEECH?
THERE IS NO NEED FOR DIVERSIONIST DEBATE ...IN A SOCIALIST SOCIETY, THE STATE WILL PROVIDE THE GUIDANCE FOR ALL SOCIAL THOUGHT.
HEY, WE GONNA NEED SIX BABY CARRIAGES.
YAHOO! THE REVOLUTION BEGINS, WILLIE!
OKAY... BEN, LET'S GO UP TO MY APARTMENT, WE CAN WORK THERE.

FACTORY NO ADMITTANCE
DELUX FURS
WHAT DO YOU MEAN...YOU'RE ORGANIZING MY SHOP?!
DELUX FURS
I'M JUST A LITTLE SHOP...WE GOT ONLY THREE WORKERS AND I PAY THEM GOOD WAGES!
YOU ARE A SWEAT SHOP!
LIVING OFF WORKER SWEAT!
FACTORY NO ADMITTANCE
MAX, COME OUT HERE!
MAX IS MY FOREMAN! MAX...THEY WANT TO ORGANIZE US... AM I RUNNING A SWEAT SHOP OR NOT?
WHO NEEDS IT? WE GET THE SAME PAY AS THE UNIONS.
AAAH LISSEN TO THE COMPANY FINK.
GEDADA HERE YOU BUMS. WE DON'T WANTA BE UNION!
STOP SHOVIN' ME!
YOU WANNA BE A DIRTY UNION BUSTER ...SO, HERE'S SOMETHIN' TO THINK ABOUT!!
THE DELEGATE'LL BE COMIN' UP HERE ON MONDAY WITH THE UNION CONTRACT...IF YOU DON'T SIGN UP—WE'LL BE BACK TO GIVE YOU SOME MORE!
MAX... OH! MY GOD... MAX!

GEN HOSPITAL
QUIET
WHAT IS YOUR RELATIONSHIP WITH MAX, SIR?
HE WORKS FOR ME...MY FOREMAN FOR MANY YEARS... LIKE A RELATIVE TO ME, DOCTOR!
WELL...IT'S A VERY SEVERE CONCUSSION. THE X-RAYS SHOW SOME BRAIN DAMAGE BUT HE CAN GO HOME SOON!
OH, MY GOD!
A REPORT WILL HAVE TO BE FILED YOU KNOW!!
IT...ER... WAS AN ACCIDENT IN THE SHOP!

SLAM
MORRIS??...HOW COME YOU'RE HOME SO EARLY...SIT DOWN, I'M STILL MAKING SUPPER...
WHAT'S WRONG? YOU DON'T LOOK SO GOOD, MORRIS.
THEY BEAT UP MAX!
WHO?...WHO WOULD HURT MAX? HE'S SUCH A QUIET, GENTLE MAN.
THE UNION... THEY CAME AND BEAT HIM UP... I TOOK MAX TO THE HOSPITAL!
OH MY GOD, IS HE ALRIGHT?
I DON'T KNOW...THE DOCTOR SAID IT'S BRAIN DAMAGE... THEY HIT HIM ON THE HEAD!
POOR MAX...WHY DO THE UNIONS DO THAT?
THEY'RE GOONS, KILLERS, BUMS!
I TELL YOU, SOPHIE...THEY ARE ALL COMMUNISTS. THEY'RE RUINING THIS COUNTRY!
SHHHH, MORRIS- WILLIE IS IN THE DINING ROOM...HE'S WORKING WITH A FRIEND!

HEY, POPPA, WHAT'S THE MATTER?
THE UNION BEAT UP MAX!

HE WAS OBVIOUSLY BEING AN OBSTRUCTIONIST SIR...
HEH??
HEY, BEN... DON'T DON'T..

UNIONS ARE THE HOPE OF THE WORKING CLASS IN ITS STRUGGLE TO OVERCOME OPPRESSION.
YOU SEE, POPPA, UNIONS ARE THE ONLY EFFECTIVE WEAPON AGAINST THE CAPITALIST EXPLOITATION, TRY TO UNDERSTAND!
WORKERS UNITE
...WHAT EXPLOITATION! SO, AM I A CAPITALIST OPPRESSOR? ?!!!
POPPA... PLEASE... HE DIDN'T MEAN YOU, EXACTLY...

WHAT'S GOING ON HERE ?!
WORKERS UNITE
COMMUNISTS...MY SON A COMMUNIST ORGANIZER?? OY!!
SIR, YOU ARE EXPLOITING LABOR AND AS SUCH, YOU ARE THE ENEMY!
COMMUNISTS, UNION GOONS, RADICALS!! NOT IN MY HOUSE WILL YOU PLOT REVOLUTION !!
POPPA...IT'S ONLY FOR A MASS MEETING, A DEMONSTRATION!
GET OUT OF MY HOUSE!

VERY WELL, SIR... WE'LL FINISH THIS AT MY HOUSE. C'MON, WILLIE.
WORKERS
WILLIE... YOU COMING WITH ME? ... MAKE A DECISION!
WILLIE, HOW MANY KREPLACH YOU WANT IN YOUR CHICKEN SOUP?
IT'S EITHER THEM OR THE REVOLUTION!! WHICH??... CHOOSE NOW! YOU IN OR NOT, WILLIE?
... I'M GOING TO STAY...

Notes

121. *Socialist Party Mass Meeting Broken Up by Communists.* A Socialist Party rally was held at Madison Square Garden (then located at Eighth Avenue and 50th Street) on February 16, 1934, to protest the massacre of 1,000 socialists by the Fascist regime in power in Austria. Roughly 5,000 members of the Communist Party violently disrupted the meeting.
121. *Revolutionary Jailed for Painting "Vote Communist"* . . . This news item inspired the story to follow. The teenager arrested for painting the slogan in front of the public school was named William Newman.
122. *Willie.* Eisner gave this name to his semiautobiographical stand-in in "Cockalein" from *A Contract with God* and in *The Dreamer* (1985).
122. *Union Square.* In the 1930s, this was a sight of major protests and demonstrations.
123. *mimeo machine.* Before the rise of affordable photocopy machines in the 1960s, mimeograph machines—copies that ran ink through stencils—were commonly used in schools and offices for producing small print runs.
124. *Menshevist.* Eisner's use of the term here is confusing; Menshevism was defined in opposition to the militancy of Bolshevism in pre-Soviet Russia, as the Menshevists favored a gradualist approach to revolution. After the Russian Revolution of 1917 and the consolidation of Soviet Marxism, "Menshevist" was often used by Communists to refer to one who was "soft" or even counterrevolutionary.
130. *kreplach.* Small dumplings, filled with meat or potatoes, often served in chicken soup but also served fried. Especially associated with the Jewish holidays of Purim and Rosh Hashana.

INSTINCTIVELY HE UNDERSTOOD THAT BEING UNNOTICED IS A MAJOR SKILL IN THE ART OF URBAN SURVIVAL...

AS PINCUS GREW OLDER HE LEARNED THAT HIDING WAS NOT THE ONLY WAY TO AVOID DANGER.
STEP ON A CRACK WILL BREAK YOUR BACK
BLESS YOU.. YOUR KINDNESS WILL BE REWARDED
I HOPE SO... IT IS SUCH A-A DANGEROUS WORLD.
SOON HE ACHIEVED REAL INVISIBILITY THROUGH WHICH HE WAS ABLE TO AVOID THE RISKS AND THE INVOLVEMENT OF ROMANCE
...WHAT ABOUT THAT GUY YOU WERE TALKING TO AT THE PARTY LAST NIGHT?
OH, HE WAS NICE... BUT, FUNNY, I...I...CAN'T RECALL HIS NAME OR EVEN WHAT HE LOOKED LIKE!
MARKET
YOU WHAT ???
DAMN!! BY MISTAKE I GAVE A GUY A 20 DOLLAR BILL... BUT I CAN'T REMEMBER WHAT HE LOOKED LIKE.
EGGS $1 DOZ
SALE CAKES
OIL OLIVE
EVENTUALLY THE REST OF THE WORLD BECAME INVISIBLE TO HIM! PINCUS HAD LEARNED THE URBAN ART OF AVOIDANCE

IN TIME, PINCUS BECAME A SKILLED CLOTHES PRESSER AND SECURED A STEADY JOB IN ABE SHMOTTER'S DRY CLEANING STORE.
NICE WORK!
I HIRE THE BEST...WE GOT A GREAT PRESSER MISSUS...
YOU'RE A VERY GOOD PRESSER, PINCUS. BUT HONESTLY YOU CAN MAKE MORE BEHIND THE FRONT COUNTER!
NAH... I LIKE IT HERE, ABE... IN THE BACK, WHERE IT'S A LOT SAFER!!
3

EACH EVENING AFTER WORK, WITHOUT FAIL, PINCUS WOULD BLEND INTO THE STREAM OF THE HOMEWARD BOUND AND MAKE HIS WAY TO THE SANCTUARY OF HIS TENEMENT ROOMS, APARTMENT 4B, 55 DROPSIE AVENUE..

...ONE MORNING....
MORNING
THE SUN

HELLO...
HELLO! HELLO! DAILY NEWS? GET ME THE OBITUARY DEPARTMENT
I WISH TO REPORT A MISTAKE. I AM NOT DEAD!

JUST A MOMENT SIR... PSST.. JOE GET ME TO-DAY'S OBIT COLUMN!
NOW, SIR... YOU SAY YOU ARE PINCUS PLEATNIK? ...AH... HERE IT IS... YESS!
Pincus Pleatnik; on Friday, Nov. 14, of a stroke. At 55 Dropsie Avenue. Services at Midtown Memorial
SO, WHAT'S THE PROBLEM, SIR!?
IT'S A BIG MISTAKE I TELL YOU. ...I AM PINCUS PLEATNIK AND I AM NOT DEAD!!
NOW, NOW PLEASE CALM DOWN, MISTER! THIS DOES SAY, "Pincus Pleatnik of 55 Dropsie Ave.."
BUT I'M CALLING FROM 55 DROPSIE!!
MISTER, THERE IS NO NEED FOR HYSTERIA! WE PRINT IT AS IT IS FILED HERE!
SIR, SIR!
A NUT!
HMPF... I NEVER MAKE MISTAKES... BESIDES... MY JOB IS TO EDIT THE LISTINGS AS THEY'RE FILED WITH US... WHO DIES IS NOT MY RESPONSIBILITY!
CLIK
CLIK
CLIK

WHAT SHOULD I DO?
CALL THE POLICE!
WHAT FOR?
IT'S JUST A...A MISTAKE SO, WHAT COULD IT HURT?
I SHOULD CALM DOWN... BE SENSIBLE!
PINCUS...PINCUS, YOU ARE A GOOD PRESSER! YOU GOT A JOB IN ABE SHMOTTER'S STORE... YOU MAKE A LIVING!
SO, WHAT'S TO WORRY?
BESIDES, I AM A BACHELOR WITH NO KIDS...NO FAMILY! WHO WILL CARE?
IT'S MY DAY OFF... I'LL TAKE A NICE WALK IN THE PARK... MAYBE IT'LL CALM ME DOWN!
CLIK
CLIK
CLACK
CLIK
SOME NERVE ... I'VE BEEN WORKING IN OBITUARIES FOR TWENTY YEARS! I DON'T MAKE MISTAKES P-E-R-I-O-D!

AFTER ALL... THERE ARE LOTS OF PEOPLE WITH THE SAME NAME WHO DIE EVERY DAY!
OKAY... SO WHAT IF THE FUNERAL PARLOR MADE A MISTAKE IN THE ADDRESS... IS THAT MY FAULT??
I CAN ONLY PRINT WHAT THEY GIVE ME, RIGHT?
GERTIE, GET ME THE MIDTOWN MEMORIAL CHAPEL!
...I'M SORRY EDNA THEIR OFFICE IS CLOSED! IT'S FRIDAY AFTERNOON!
THANKS, GERTIE!
WELL, I TRIED... SO, WHAT AM I ...GOD??
MODWAY FURNITURE 30-WEEKS TO PAY NO DOWN PAYMENT
HOLY SMOKE! HEY, CHOLLY!

YEH, WOT, BOSS ?
DIDN'T WE DELIVER A CHIFFONIER TO A PINCUS PLEATNIK AT 55 DROPSIE ?
YEAH, THREE DAYS AGO...IT'S A 20-PAYMENT DEAL!
I THOUGHT SO
PINCUS PLEATNIK DIED YESTERDAY!
REALLY? ..UH, OH!
DON'T STAND THERE, REPOSSESS THE CLOSET !!
NOW?
NOW, DUMMY! BEFORE HIS ESTATE GRABS IT!
I'M GOING, I'M GOING! IT'S FRIDAY NIGHT! I'LL BE LATE FOR SUPPER AT MY MOM'S
...BUT PINCUS PLEATNIK IS DEAD! IT'S IN THE PAPERS !!
YEAH, YOU'RE THE SUPER...Y'GOT TO LET US IN. ...WE GOT TO REPOSSESS A CLOSET!
I..I DON'T KNOW
YER SURE PINCUS IS DEAD ??
HERE, LOOK AT THE PAPER!
CAREFUL, DON'T BANG UP THE WALL!

REAL ESTATE
YES, MR SCRUGGS, I KNOW YOU ARE MY SUPER AT 55 DROPSIE! WHAT'S A MATTER ??
ONE OF OUR TENANTS DIED?? SO??...WAS HE BEHIND IN THE RENT??...HMMMM A MONTH?.. AHA YES HE IS LISTED IN THE OBITUARY! ...PINCUS PLEATNIK!
WHADDYA MEAN ONLY ONE MONTH...HE'S BEHIND... SO, YOU KNOW WHAT TO DO! LOCK IT UP!
CHANGE THE LOCK AND PUT OUT A 'FOR RENT' SIGN... AND RAISE THE RENT!
WHADDYA MEAN WE CAN'T? ...WE GOT A LEGAL RIGHT! ...WE CAN HOLD HIS ASSETS... HE OWES US!
DON'T WORRY. I GOT LAWYERS TO HANDLE THAT! ...JUST CHANGE THE LOCK!
WHAT'S GOING ON SUPER ?
HMM IT'S 4B ...WE NEVER SEE HIM COME OR GO!
MR. PINCUS PLEATNIK DIED... I'M CHANGING THE LOCK!

UH, OH, IT'S GETTING LATE... TIME TO GO HOME FOR SUPPER!
HEY!!! MY DOOR IS LOCKED! MY KEY DON'T FIT!! OH... IT'S BEEN CHANGED!
WHAT'S THE BANGING OUT THERE MANNY ?
SOMEONE IS TRYING TO GET INTO PLEATNIK'S APARTMENT! ...DON'T LOOK OUT...MIND OUR OWN BUSINESS!
MR. SCRUGGS! MY DOOR IS LOCKED...I CAN'T GET IN!!
WHO YOU?
I'M PINCUS PLEATNIK OF 4B...MY DOOR IS
NAHH HE'S DEAD!
GIT OUTTA HERE... BUM!
GRRRRR!

SQUAD ROOM 14 PRECINCT
HEY, CASEY! CAN YA HANDLE THIS... I'M BUSY!
YEH!
MY NAME IS PINCUS PLEATNIK. I LIVE AT 55 DROPSIE ... I'VE BEEN LOCKED OUT!
YOU GOT ANY IDENTIFICATION MISTER?
YES, HERE, MY UNION CARD!
HMM SO YOU HAVE.
WHY WOULD YOU BE LOCKED OUT, NOW ?
THE SUPER THINKS I'M DEAD!
NOW, WHY WOULD HE THINK THAT ?
THE NEWSPAPER ...IN THE OBITUARY, SEE... IT'S A BIG MISTAKE!
H'LO DAILY NEWS?...THIS IS SERGEANT CASEY 14TH PRECINCT... I'M CHECKING ON AN OBITUARY...A PINCUS PLEATNIK... OH, YOU GOT A COMPLAINT FROM HIM... WELL, COULD IT BE A MISTAK- ?! HEY!
LOOK, LADY! NO REASON TO GET SO MAD... I JUST WANT TO VERIFY YER SURE NOW? OK, OK, OK, OK, OK,... G'BYE!
NOW, NOW LOOK HERE MISTER ...WHY DONTCHA BE NICE AND GO HOME!? ...THERE'S A GOOD MAN!
14
14

HOT DOGS 5¢
I AM NOT DEAD!
TELEPHONE

RING RING RING RING RING RING
SHMOTTER TAILORS
LADIES 25¢
MENS 50
HAALO??
HELLO!
HELLO?! ABE SHMOTTER'S ...WHO ARE YOU? ...OH???... THE CLEANING LADY??
...WELL THIS IS PINCUS PLEATNIK! I'M THE PRESSER! ...LISTEN I MUST TALK TO
CLICK!
BZZZZZZZZZZZ
TELEPHONE

RING RING
HELLO? YES...THIS IS MISSIS SHMOTTER. ...YES?
WHAT? WAIT, I'LL GET ABE!
OY!
REBA, LOOK AT THIS...MY PRESSER, PINCUS DIED YESTERDAY! DAMMIT!
ABE. ABE.. YOU GOT A CALL
A CALL FOR ME.??? WHO IS IT?
IT'S THE CLEANING LADY FROM YOUR STORE, ABE!
SHE SAYS, PINCUS, YOUR PRESSER, JUST CALLED THERE AND....
HANG UP!
SURE, BUT... BUT...
DON'T SAY ANYTHING.. JUST HANG UP!!
OH, MY GOD! THEY DID IT!
WHO DID WHAT?
THAT CALL WAS THEIR WAY OF WARNING ME... THEM UNION GOONS MUSTA KILLED POOR PINCUS!

I DON'T UNDERSTAND, ABE...
PINCUS BELONGED TO THE MEN'S SUIT UNION... NOT THE PRESSER'S UNIOIN .. DON'T YOU SEE?
SO, HE'S UNION! WHAT'S A DIFFERENCE ??
TWO LOCALS ARE FIGHTING FOR CONTROL OF MY SHOP!!
THE PRESSERS WANT TO PUT THEIR MAN INTO MY SHOP!
...I SEE... TO DO THAT THEY GOT TO MAKE A VACANCY!
OH, MY GOD!
EXACTLY!! THE DIRTY ROTTEN GOONS!
WHAT ARE YOU GOING TO DO, ABE?
...HELLO, VITO! THIS IS ABE.... OKAY, YOU WIN!! THERE'S A-A-ER VACANCY.... SO, YOU CAN SEND YOUR PRESSER IN FIRST THING MONDAY!

MOVE ALONG, BUM... NO LOITERING HERE... C'MON, C'MON!
OFFICER, I'M NOT A BUM. I'M A VICTIM OF THE CITY!
MOVE!
DOES ANYONE CARE? DO YOU?
BEAT IT!
...NO!! VAGRANTS ARE A SOCIAL NUISANCE... DEBRIS... TO BE SWEPT ASIDE BY A MINDLESS AND CRUEL SYSTEM... WE ARE INVISIBLE PEOPLE!
...JUST DOING MY JOB!
HAH... YOUR JOB, YOUR JOB! WHAT ABOUT THE LIVES YOU TOUCH ???!!
AAAAAH!
TO YOU IT'S JUST MOVING ONE BUM FROM A BENCH! BUT TO THE BUMS IT IS SURVIVAL!!!
?

WELL, LOOKEY HERE... ANOTHER PIECE OF DRIFTWOOD!
YOU, BUDDY..Y' ARE IN MY OWN PLACE... HMMM I AIN'T SEEN YOU 'ROUND HERE!
EXCUSE ME... I'VE GOT NO PLACE TO GO!
PLEASE I GOT A TEMPORARY PROBLEM! I DON'T KNOW WHERE TO GO OR WHAT TO DO ABOUT IT!
ALL OF LIFE IS TEMPORARY BUDDY! TELL ME ABOUT IT!
I'M LISTED AS DEAD IN THE OBITUARY! ...SINCE THEN I'VE BEEN LOCKED OUT IT'S LIKE I DO NOT EXIST!
HAH!! YET ANOTHER VICTIM OF THE SYSTEM!
LISTEN... I'M ONLY TRASH! I GOT NO WAY TO BEAT 'EM! BUT YOU?...YOU CAN FIGHT BACK!
YES, YES... YOU'RE RIGHT! MONDAY, FIRST THING I'LL GO TO MY JOB... I'LL PRESENT MYSELF. ...MY BOSS, ABE SHMOTTER WILL HELP ME OUT!

GUSSIE, DID YOU SEE THE OBITUARY IN THE PAPER FRIDAY!?
PINCUS PLEATNIK DIED! HE'S A RELATIVE, NO??
YES! ...TOO BAD!
SO?? WAS HE WORTH ANYTHING?? I MEAN WE SHOULD LOOK INTO IT, NO?
OH, HERB, THIS IS VERY EMBARRASSING! PINCUS ONLY DIED FRIDAY. ...I HARDLY EVER SAW HIM!
DON'T BE DUMB, GUSSIE! HE MAY HAVE LEFT A BUNDLE! ...YOU ARE HIS COUSIN!
VERY DISTANT... IN THE OBITUARY THEY DIDN'T EVEN MENTION MY NAME!
DID HE HAVE ANYBODY??
NO! HE WAS A SOLITARY MAN, I HEARD!
THAT IS JUST THE POINT
IF PINCUS LEFT ANY MONEY YOU SHOULD BE FIRST IN LINE!
I..I FEEL LIKE A VULTURE.
CALL OUR LAWYER!

YE-ES...UH HUH...YES... OKAY, GUSSIE I UNDERSTAND! NOW, THE FIRST THING WE MUST DO IS GET TO THE PINCUS' WILL...DID HE HAVE ANY MONEY!
JAKE GOLD
LAW OFFICE
HMMMMMM WELL HE MUST HAVE HAD A BANK ACCOUNT, A UNION PENSION...AN INSURANCE POLICY MAYBE? ANY BENEFICIARIES?? ...YOU...DON'T...KNOW?? OK, OK, OK?
IT'LL PROBABLY GO TO PROBATE...AS HIS ONLY KNOWN RELATIVE YOU SHOULD FILE NOW. ...THERE'LL BE LEGAL FEES OF COURSE!
JAKE GOLD
LAW OFFICE
SO... WHAT DO WE DO NOW?
GO THRU HIS EFFECTS! HIS PAPERS... THEY MUST BE IN HIS ROOM!
OOOH, THAT IS TOO GHOULISH FOR ME?
YOU DON'T HAVE TO! I'LL DO IT!!
I'LL BET OL' PINCUS HAD A BUNDLE STASHED AWAY!

A. SHMOTTER
TAILORS
DRY CLEAN 25¢
DING
WHO'S THERE
A. SHMOTTER
TAILORS
DRY CLEANING
IT'S ME PINCUS! HAS ABE COME IN YET?
NO, HE'S COMIN' IN LATE TODAY!
FEH, FEH...I'M SOME MESS... BEEN SLEEPING IN THE PARK ALL WEEKEND! ...BOY, HAVE I GOT A PROBLEM!?
SO, WHO ARE YOU?
I'M TONY, THE PRESSER HERE.

WHAT PRESSER? I·AM THE PRESSER HERE!
YOU?...Y'CAN'T BE... HE DIED...THE UNION SENT ME TO REPLACE HIM!
I AM NOT DEAD!
CALM DOWN! CALM DOWN! ER...I'LL BE RIGHT BACK.
HELLO... GIMME JOE, THE DELEGATE!! ....THIS IS TONY, AT SHMOTTER'S TAILOR SHOP ...YEH, YEH...
I GOT A GUY HERE WHO CLAIMS HE'S PINCUS, THEIR REGULAR PRESSER!
...WHAT? OH...HE LOOKS LIKE A..A..BUM!
NATIONAL UNION PRESSERS
LOCAL 507
LOCAL 507
OKAY, TONY! NOW... JUST KEEP HIM THERE...WE'LL TAKE CARE OF IT! ...YOU GO BACK TO WORK!
HOW D'YA LIKE THAT...THE DAMN SUIT UNION SENT THEIR MAN DOWN CLAIMING HE'S A PRESSER... IT'S A MUSCLE!
WOT NERVE!
OKAY, WE'LL PLAY IT THEIR WAY...HEY, GUIDO BRING BENNO IN HERE WITCHA!
SHOO BOSS!

...WE GOT A LITTLE PROBLEM BOYS... GO DOWN TO SHMOTTER'S STORE AND PICK UP A GUY. ...HE'S GIVING OUR MAN, TONY, A HARD TIME!
SO, Y'WANT WE SHOULD WORK HIM OVER?
NO, NO, NO! HE'S JUST A PLANT FROM THE SUIT UNION ...A NOTHIN'
SO?
SO, WE DO A LITTLE TRICK BACK ON THEM!
JUST TAKE HIM OUT TO JERSEY... SAY, SECAUCUS... AND DROP HIM OFF OUT THERE!
NO ROUGH STUFF. ...BUT BY THE TIME HE'LL GET BACK IT'LL BE NIGHT HAW, HAW!
...BY THEN, LOCAL 406 OF THE SUIT UNION WILL GET THE MESSAGE AND LAY OFF OUR TURF!
YOU GOT IT!
YER BODDERING ME, MISTER! GO'WAY!!
THIS IS MY JOB!

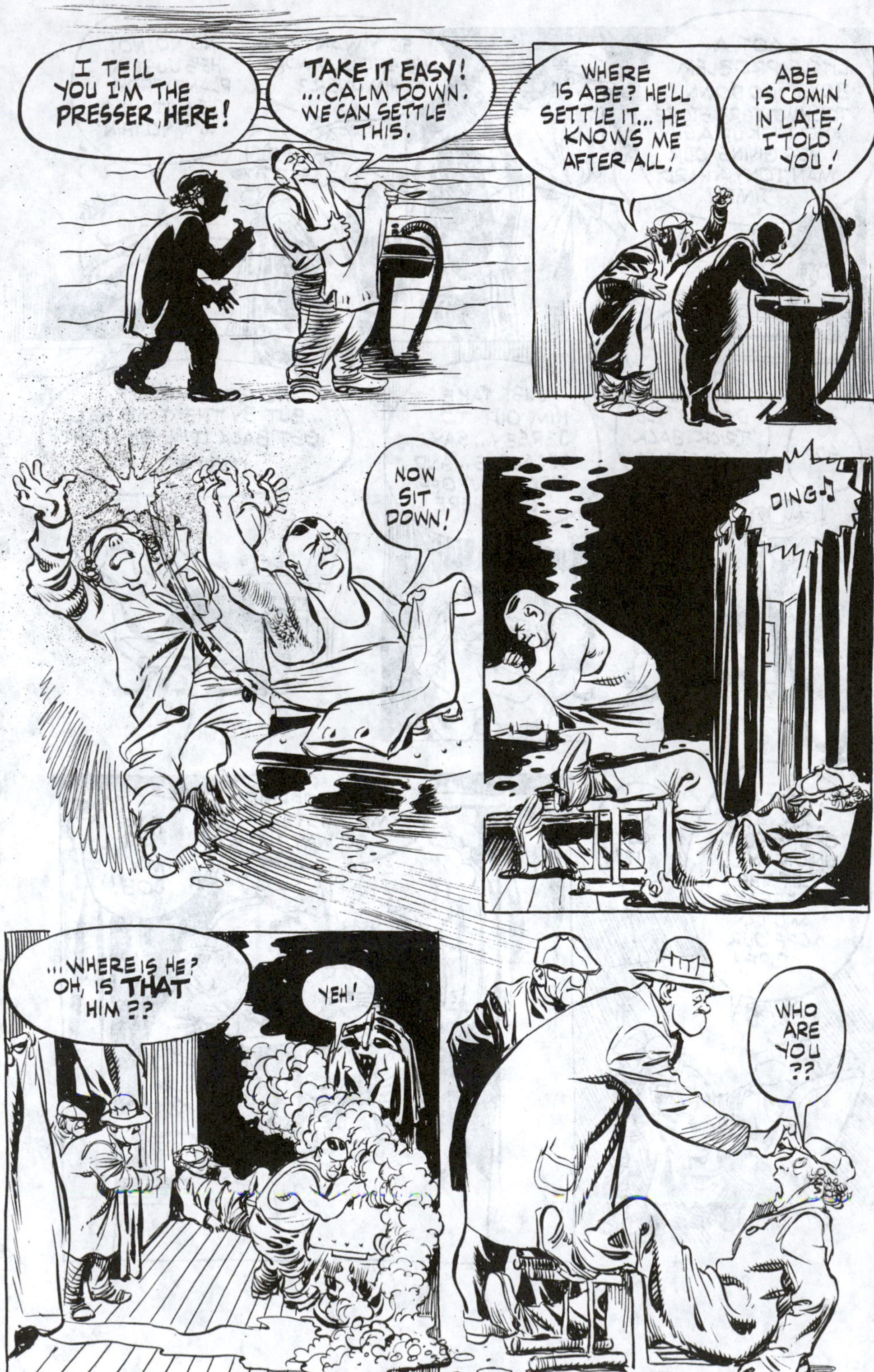
I TELL YOU I'M THE PRESSER, HERE!
TAKE IT EASY! ...CALM DOWN. WE CAN SETTLE THIS.
WHERE IS ABE? HE'LL SETTLE IT... HE KNOWS ME AFTER ALL!
ABE IS COMIN' IN LATE, I TOLD YOU!
NOW SIT DOWN!
DING♫
...WHERE IS HE? OH, IS THAT HIM??
YEH!
WHO ARE YOU??

LET ME GO!
SHHHH
NOW, BE NICE. DON'T MAKE NO TROUBLE!

JUST STAY PUT AND SHUT UP! WE'RE JUST GOIN' FER A LITTLE RIDE!
WE DON'T WANT NO TROUBLE!

YOU DON'T EVEN KNOW WHO I AM! LET ME OUT!!
SURE WE DO!! YOU'RE A PLANT FROM LOCAL 406! NOW, SIT BACK AND YOU WON'T GET HURT!

YOU DON'T UNDERSTAND...I'M NOT DEAD! Y'SEE IT'S A MISTAKE!
JUST SHUT UP!
WHERE ARE YOU TAKING ME?
I TOL' YOU WE DON'T WANT NO TROUBLE!

HE'S NICE AND QUIET NOW.
GOOD!! KEEP HIM THAT WAY... WE'LL BE HITTING THE BACK ROADS IN A MILE OR TWO!

SCREECH
HOLY SHIT! HE JUMPED OUT ON US!!
YER GODDAM RIGHT... HE'S DEAD DOWN THERE!
WOT'LL WE DO BENNO?
KEEP OUR MOUTHS SHUT! WHO'S GONNA KNOW? LET'S GET OUTTA HERE...LET'S GET OUTTA HERE!
HIGH TIDE
5
4
3
2
1

HIGH TIDE
...IT WASN'T OUR FAULT! WE JUST DROVE HIM OUT HERE!
RIGHT!
HIGH TIDE
HIGH TIDE
5
4
3
2
1

POSTMORTEM

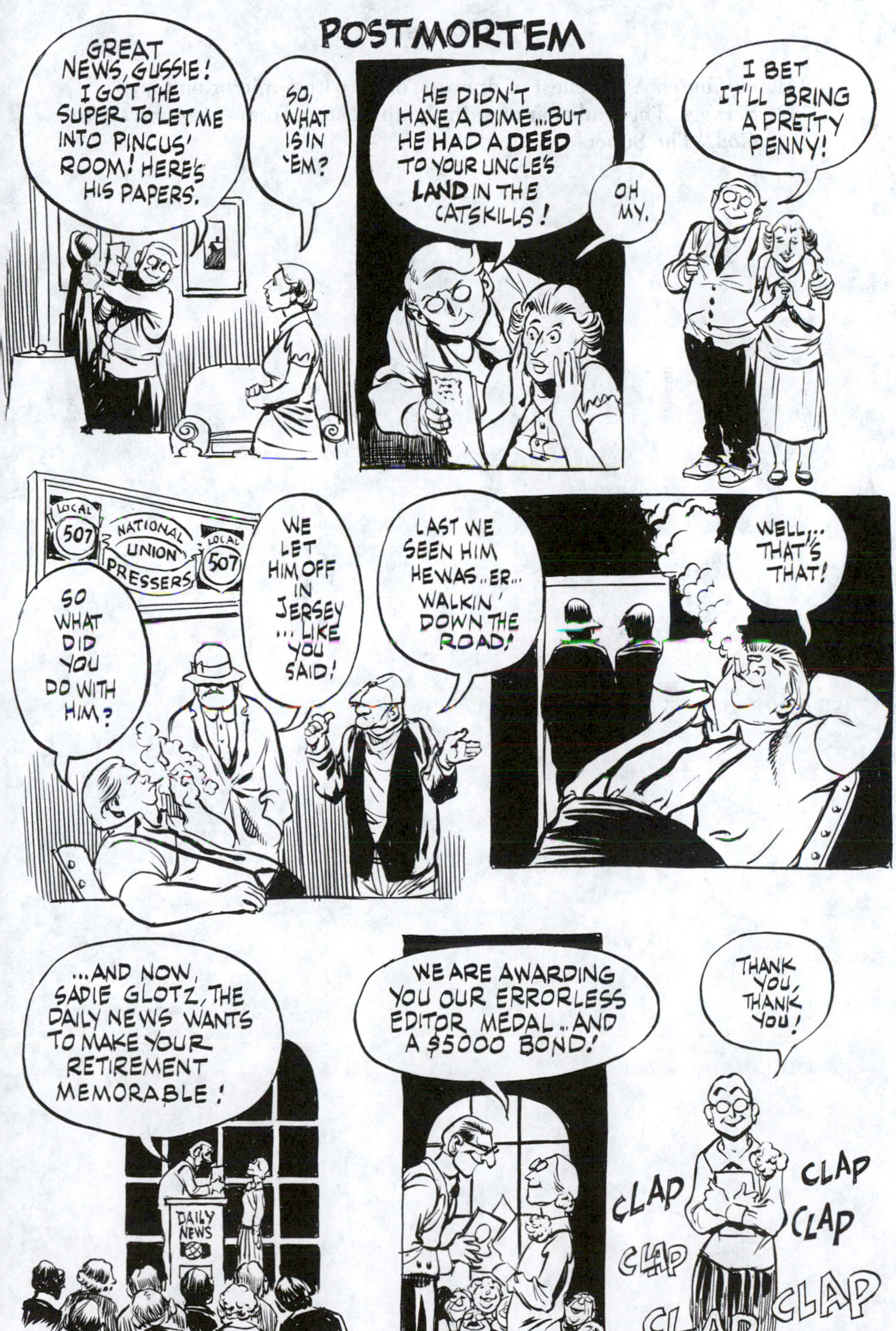
GREAT NEWS, GUSSIE! I GOT THE SUPER TO LET ME INTO PINCUS' ROOM! HERE'S HIS PAPERS.
SO, WHAT IS IN 'EM?
HE DIDN'T HAVE A DIME...BUT HE HAD A DEED TO YOUR UNCLE'S LAND IN THE CATSKILLS!
OH MY.
I BET IT'LL BRING A PRETTY PENNY!
LOCAL 507
NATIONAL UNION PRESSERS
LOCAL 507
SO WHAT DID YOU DO WITH HIM?
WE LET HIM OFF IN JERSEY ... LIKE YOU SAID!
LAST WE SEEN HIM HE WAS..ER... WALKIN' DOWN THE ROAD!
WELL,... THAT'S THAT!
...AND NOW, SADIE GLOTZ, THE DAILY NEWS WANTS TO MAKE YOUR RETIREMENT MEMORABLE!
DAILY NEWS
WE ARE AWARDING YOU OUR ERRORLESS EDITOR MEDAL...AND A $5000 BOND!
THANK YOU, THANK YOU!
CLAP
CLAP
CLAP
CLAP
CLAP
CLAP

Notes

141. *chiffonier.* A tall chest of drawers, often with a mirror on top.
142. *Scruggs.* The lead character in the third story from *A Contract with God*, "The Super."

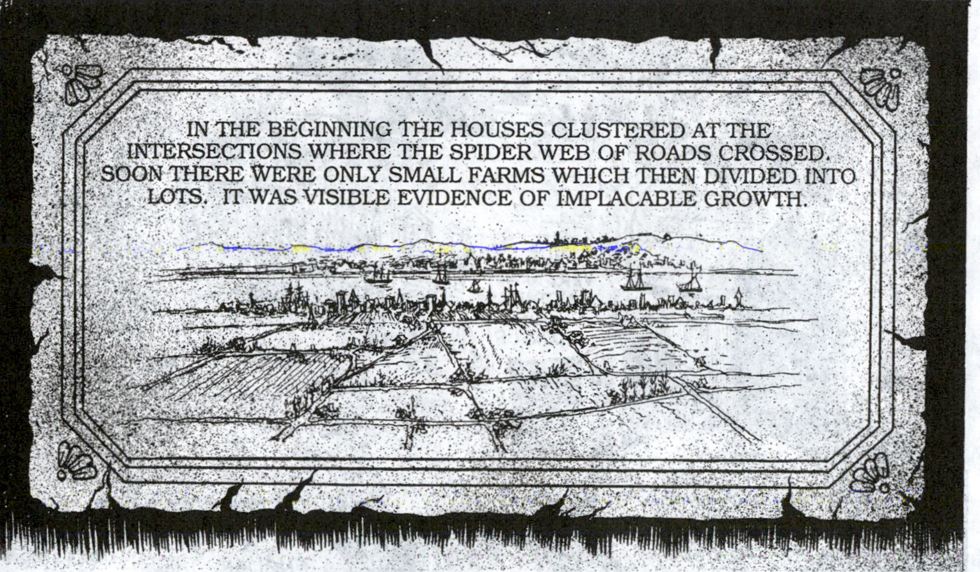

THE NEIGHBORHOOD
BEGAN TO FORM EVEN WHILE A FEW OLD DUTCH FAMILIES STILL CLUNG TO THE HOLDINGS THEY INHERITED...

IT WAS 1870

AND STILL THERE WERE FARMS IN THE BRONX.

HUT VERDAMMIT ANOTHER HOUSE GOING UP!
RIGHT ALONGSIDE OUR PROPERTY! SOON IT VILL BE A TOWN HERE!
YAH, HENDRIK, IT WAS ALL OPEN LAND VEN FATHER VANDROPSIE BUYS THIS PLACE FROM VAN BRONK!
AAACH!! THE ENGLISH... THE ENGLISH.. THEY ARE BUYING UP EVERYTHING! ...SOON THE DROPSIE NAME VILL MEAN NOTHING HERE!

THEY ARE NOT SUCH BAD FARMERS, THE ENGLISH!
NOW, NOW, DIRK!
THEY MAKE THINGS BAD FOR US...WE ARE NOT SELLING OUR CROPS SO WELL THESE DAYS!
AND... THEY ARE GETTING HIGHER PRICES THAN WE DO!
!
IT IS BECAUSE YOU ARE TOO LAZY TO WORK.. YOU ARE A SLOTH... AND THAT IS THE TRUTH OF IT, DIRK!
HENDRIK! DO NOT TALK TO MY BROTHER THAT WAY!
YAWWWWN... VERY WELL MARGOT, NOW COME TO BED! YOU GO TO SLEEP NOW TOO, HELDA!
YOU SHOULD GO TO BED TOO, UNCLE DIRK!

DAMN ENGLISH! YOU DON'T BELONG HERE!
WE WERE HERE FIRST!
UNCLE DIRK!

BURN THEM OUT, YAHHH
UNCLE DIRK!
THEY THINK THEY ARE OUR BETTERS... EH?
WHAT ARE YOU DOING UNCLE?
HEE HEE HA HA!
YOU'RE SPILLING WHISKEY ON MY DRESS!! EEEEE!

HEE HEE HELDA, SEE HOW IT BURNS!!
UNCLE DIRK HELP ME!

THAT'S THE OLD DROPSIE PLACE! OUR NEIGHBORHOOD HAS GROWN UP AROUND THEM ...BUT THEIR HOUSE STILL STANDS!
THE ORIGINAL DROPSIES STILL LIVE THERE...QUITE ALONE ...NO ONE EVER SEES THEM!
THEY SAY IT WAS THE DEATH OF THEIR DAUGHTER, HELDA, THAT MADE 'EM HERMITS!
BUT THAT WAS THIRTY YEARS AGO!
...WELL, IF YOU ASK ME, IT WAS A MURDER! ...HARDLY APPROPRIATE TO THE REPUTATION OF OUR NEIGHBORHOOD EH, MY DEAR!?
HENDRIK

TIME FOR BED, HENDRIK!
YAHH SOON...
IS THIS THE PLACE?
YES...'TIS THE OLD DROPSIE PLACE... BEEN UNTOUCHED SINCE IT BURNED DOWN IN THE SPRING OF '90... THE LAST OF OPEN LOTS IN THE GOOD NEIGHBORHOODS!

LEMINADE
1¢
TRAFFIC IS SURE GROWIN' IN THIS NEIGHBORHOOD.
MODERN TIMES IS HERE!

ROWENA FLOWERS

AHEM...
TELL THEM, FATHER O'LEARY!
HAVING TODAY JOINED YOU, ROWENA, AND YOU, PRINCE, IN HOLY WEDLOCK ...AND BEFORE THIS GATHERING OF YOUR NEIGHBORS... I WANT TO EXTEND OUR...
C'MON FATHER! ...GET TO IT!!
YESS...YES, NOW SEEING AS HOW YOUR GRANDMOTHER SOLD THIS HOUSE UPON HER DEATH ...AND SEEING AS HOW YOU'VE BOUGHT A NEW ONE IN WESTCHESTER...
WE...YOUR GOOD NEIGHBORS, IN OUR APPRECIATION FOR THE YEARS OF BEAUTY YOUR FLOWERS HAVE BROUGHT TO DROPSIE AVENUE...
...HAVE COLLECTED A LITTLE CASH AND SOME SEEDS TO HELP YOU PLANT A NEW GARDEN THERE.
CONGRATULATIONS!
I HEAR THAT YOUR NEW HOUSE HAS TWO ACRES... MY, MY, YOU CAN GROW ALL KINDS OF THINGS!!
WE'RE GOING T'MISS YOU!
YOU MADE DROPSIE A REAL WARM NEIGHBORHOOD FOR US.
THANK YOU, THANK YOU.

GOODBYE!
'BYE
OH, FATHER, MY DREAM HAS COME TRUE... AND YET I'M SAD ABOUT LEAVING.
WE OFTEN PAY FOR GOD'S GIFTS WITH WHAT WE GIVE UP FOR THEM.
C'MON, MISS ROWENA, WE GOTTA GET ROLLING IF WE'RE TO MAKE WESTCHESTER BEFORE DARK!
NOW RENTING APARTMENTS 2,3 ROOMS HEAT, ELECTRIC, WATER MARIO MARONI BUILDER
WHO'S THE BUILDER?
SOME EYE-TALIAN!
SO... THE WOPS WILL BE MOVIN' IN ON US!
NEXT THING YOU KNOW WE'LL GET JEWS... LIKE ON CRESTY STREET!
IT'S OUR NEIGHBORHOOD!!
WE GOTTA KEEP IT THAT WAY!
... ELSE THEY GONNA OUT-NUMBER US!

I ♫ CASH ♫ CLOTHES ♫
?
SMASH TH' GODDAM SIGN!
YAHHHH
NOW RENTING APARTMENTS
WHAT'S GOING ON, OFFICER SWEENEY ?
JUST TH' LOCAL ROUGHNECKS TRYIN' TO PRESERVE THE NEIGHBORHOOD.
I SEE... SO THEY OBJECT TO THEM WRECKERS TAKING DOWN THE FLOWER HOUSE!?
NOT QUITE, IZZY.
THEY'RE OBJECTING TO WHAT'S COMING IN!
WE DON'T WANT NO WOPS ON DROPSIE AVENUE!!
WOPS KEEP OUT!
NO FORRINERS IN OUR NEIGHBORHOOD!
I CASH ♫ CLOTHES ♫

FOR RENT
MARIO MARONI
PROPERTIES
NEW BUILDING
SCUSI!
HAW... EYETALIANS ...THEY LOOK LIKE THEY JUST CAME OFF THE BOAT, O'MALLEY!
YEAH?? OKAY...NOW WHO YOU LOOKIN' FER FOLKS?
MORONI, MORONI!
SI, SI!
WELL, NOW... THAT'S THE MORONI BUILDING RIGHT THERE!... HE RENTS TO ALL THE EYETALIANS THAT COME 'ROUND!
GRAZIE!

FOR RENT
MAMMA ROSA
PASTA FAMILY COOKING
MAMMA ROSA
RISTORANTE
MAMMA ROSA
FINE
ITALIAN FOOD
PIGEONS ON OUR ROOF!! SHEEEET THEM DIRTY WOPS!
WOTTAYER GONNA DO? ...WELL, WE ARE MOVIN' TO JERSEY...I DON'T GIVE A DAMN NO MORE!
PHEW... THE WHOLE BUILDING STINKS OF GARLIC NOW!
IT AIN'T FROM OUR PEOPLE'S COOKING, GRACE!
...AHH, FATHER O'LEARY... IT MUST BE HARD FOR YOU TO BE LEAVING THE NEIGHBORHOOD AFTER SO MANY YEARS!
AYE...IT IS, FATHER GIANELLI. I WAS BORN ON DROPSIE AVENUE!
MOSTLY YOUR PEOPLE HERE NOW. THEY'LL NEED A PRIEST OF THEIR OWN KIND!

HOORAY... YOU BEAT IRISH MIKE!! ...YOU'RE THE NEW PRIDE OF THE NEIGHBORHOOD, POLO!!

MAMMAROSA
RISTORANTE
MAMMAROSA
FINE
ITALIAN FOOD
DROPSIE AVENUE
IS PROUD OF
POLO PALERMO
BOROUGH CHAMP
O SOLE MIO

DROPSIE
MARKET CRASHES
WPA PROGRAM PROVIDES WORK
DESTITUTE FIND JOBS
HEY, THAT LADY IS GIVIN' AWAY FREE COFFEE!
THAT'S THEM EYETALIANS. ...LET'S GET US A CUP!

SINCE MORONI BUILT HIS TENEMENT THEM PEOPLE HAVE BEEN MOVIN' IN ON US LIKE FLEAS!
WELL, THEY ARE REALLY NEIGHBORLY FOLKS!
HEY, AIN'T YOU FROM AROUND HERE?
...BORN AND BRED ON DROPSIE AVENUE!
YEAH, YEAH! AINT YOU THE STOCKBROKER FROM NUMBER 30 DOWN THE BLOCK?
I WAS... BUT THE MARKET CRASH PUT AN END TO THAT!
SO... NOW YER SHOVELING SNOW F'R WPA AT 25 CENTS AN HOUR.
HARD TIMES!
YEAH... LOOK AT ALL THEM F'RENT AND F'SALE SIGNS ON THE BLOCK!
FOR SALE
SHIT! THE WHOLE NEIGHBORHOOD IS GOIN' DOWNHILL!
SO'S THE WHOLE COUNTRY!!
PEOPLE ARE MOVING OUT... TIMES ARE-A-CHANGING!

I CASH CLOTHES
I CASH CLOTHES
I CASH CLOTHES
I CASH CLOTHES
NIZE DAY, IZZY!
HELLO, TONY!
5¢ I
ICES
FOR SALE
BOROUGH BANK
The BOROUGH BANK FOR SAVINGS
The BOROUGH BANK FOR SAVINGS

IZZY CASH CLOTHES TO SEE YOU MR. MASON.
GET RID OF HIM!
I TRIED TO... BUT...
LISTEN IZZY, WE DON'T HAVE ANY OLD CLOTHES TO SELL.. WE ARE A BANK!
I KNOW, I KNOW! BUT YOU DO FORECLOSE ON REAL ESTATE...NO?
WE HAVE TO! THESE ARE HARD DAYS.
PEOPLE CAN'T PAY RENT... SO THE LANDLORD CAN'T MEET THE MORTGAGE PAYMENTS!
SO... YOU GOT A BUILDING FOR SALE?
YES!! NOW LEAVE PLEASE..I AM BUSY!
SO, ARE YOU TOO BUSY TO SELL ME THIS BUILDING?
THAT'S THE MORONI BUILDING! HA, HA, HA, HA, HA THE PRICE IS $5000!
NOW, GO!!
DO YOU MIND IF I PAY CASH?
I HOPE YOU'LL EXCUSE IT... THE MONEY IS A LITTLE WRINKLED!
SIR... IZZY HAS JUST BOUGHT OUR PARCEL ON DROPSIE AVENUE!
HMPF?

COULD YOU PLEASE DIRECT ME TO THE LANDLORD?
IZZY CASH, FIRST FLOOR.
$25-A-MONTH RENT? IT'S A ROBBERY!
LISTEN GREENIE! ... HERE IN AMERICA WE GOT SUPPLY-AND-DEMAND!
IZZY CASH GIVES GOOD VALUE FOR THE MONEY! A TWO-MONTH CONCESSION ...AND HEAT FROM OCTOBER TO APRIL!
CLANG CLANG
MISSIS NERO... STOP UP THERE KNOCKIN' ON THE RADIATOR... IT AIN'T OCTOBER YET!!
SO... TAKE IT OR LEAVE IT! ... TENANTS I GOT PLENTY!!
... ALRIGHT!
GONNIF!
OH, HERMAN, DON'T COMPLAIN! ... WE'RE SAFE IN AMERICA!!
IT'S NOT A BAD NEIGHBORHOOD. ... AND OUR ABIE CAN GROW UP HERE, SAFE FROM WHAT WE LEFT! YOU KNOW... WHAT IS HAPPENING ON THE OTHER SIDE!

* * *

IS THIS WHAT YOU WANT TO BUY, MISS ROWENA?
YES... ALL THAT'S LEFT OF DROPSIE AVENUE!
MY HOUSE WAS RIGHT THERE. ...IN THE BACK WAS MY MAGIC GARDEN!
PLEASE, MISS ROWENA, IT IS TOO EXERTING FOR YOU!
OH SHUT UP, DOCTOR! ...SO, WHAT DO Y'THINK, ED?
HMMM IT'LL HOLD ABOUT 250 SINGLE FAMILY UNITS
PRICED AT, SAY, $125,000 EACH
LAND, UTILITIES, BUILDING... OH, I'D GUESS IT'LL TAKE ABOUT 15 MILLION TO HANDLE IT!
NO PROBLEM FOR ROWENA CORPORATION. IT CAN HANDLE IT EASILY!
IT WOULD BE A VERY PROFITABLE INVESTMENT.
PUT ME BACK IN THE CAR NOW, DOCTOR!

CITY PLANNING COMMISSION
YOUR PROPOSAL SOUNDS GOOD, BUT THE CITY WILL NEED TO KNOW MORE ABOUT YOU.
OF COURSE... OUR OWNER, MISS ROWENA, HERE, IS A VERY SUBSTANTIAL CITIZEN... AS YOU'LL SEE.
SHE WAS BORN ON DROPSIE AVENUE... AS AN ORPHAN SHE WAS REARED THERE BY HER GRANDMOTHER!
IN THIS HOUSE.
SHE LEARNED HORTICULTURE IN THE BACK GARDEN.
SHE MARRIED AND MOVED TO A FARM UPSTATE.
THERE SHE AND HER LATE HUSBAND BUILT A HUGE BUSINESS IN GIFT PLANTS.
TODAY THEY HAVE 13 FACTORIES ACROSS THE COUNTRY! THE ROWENA PLANT CORPORATION IS THE LARGEST OF ITS KIND IN AMERICA!

YES...THE CITY WILL SELL YOU THE LAND! BUT THERE'LL BE FORMALITIES ...PROCEDURES!
NOW, YOUNG LADY...DON'T WASTE MY TIME WITH THAT BUREAUCRATIC BABBLE!
THE ROWENA CORPORATION HAS OVER 500 MILLION IN ASSETS...IT IS TRADED ON THE STOCK EXCHANGE! WE'RE NOT A FLY-BY-NIGHT OPERATION!
RUBY BROWN DIRECTOR
OH, STOP MEALYMOUTHING GEORGE...NOW, MISS RUBY BROWN, YOU LISTEN TO ME!
MY DROPSIE AVENUE HOUSING WILL RECREATE A NEIGHBORHOOD! ...SINGLE FAMILY HOMES...NOT GRIMY TENEMENTS, SEE!
COOL IT LADY...I TOO GREW UP ON DROPSIE AVENUE!
THEN YOU UNDERSTAND WHAT THIS MEANS...OKAY, TELL ME WHAT IT WILL TAKE TO MAKE IT HAPPEN!
ALL RIGHT! PUBLIC HEARINGS, ZONING BOARD...EASEMENTS...YOU'LL NEED A LAWYER WHO KNOWS THE AREA!
CLARA... GET ABIE GOLD! ...TELL HIM I HAVE A CLIENT FOR HIM!
YES MA'AM

So...you're Abie Gold, eh? Well, we're both Dropsie alumni! ....a few years apart!
Yes... but we may have different memories of it!
Rowena Plants Corporation
But... we do have our own memories...one doesn't forget one's roots.
You're too late with too much!!
Where were you with your money when it began to decay?
Who can mark the point at which neighborhoods start to die?
Abie, will you handle my bid?
Of course I will!
Mr. Gold...I'm Irving Milker... of MK Properties! ...we hear you are representing the Rowena bid.
Abie Gold Attorney at Law
Your father was a finisher years ago!
My family wants that land...we'll put in an opposing bid to get it and tie you up!
Really??
Now if you drop the bid we can make a deal.
No way! ...that's illegal bid rigging!

YES, MR. MILKER... I AM THE DECIDING VOTE ON THE REVIEW BOARD!
HOW MUCH DO YOU WANT?
WELL MR. GOLD OFFERED ME.. AH.. $25,000.
I'LL DOUBLE IT!
YOU'VE GOT A DEAL SIR!
MR. GOLD AND MISS RUBY BROWN TO SEE YOU, MR. MILKER!
MILKER & SON
I'LL BE BRIEF...WE HAVE THE AFFIDAVIT OF A REVIEW BOARD MEMBER ...THAT YOU BRIBED HIM!
THAT RAT... HE TOLD ME YOU TRIED TO BRIBE HIM FIRST. ...I JUST TOPPED YOU!
EXACTLY WHAT I HAD HIM TELL YOU!
YOU SET ME UP!
WE'LL DROP CHARGES...IF YOU WITHDRAW YOUR BID, MILKER!
STUPID!
YOU'LL NEVER LEARN THE REAL ESTATE BUSINESS

MR. GOLD... WE CONGRATULATE YOU ON YOUR SUCCESS IN GETTING OUR BID THROUGH THE COUNCIL! ...YOU ARE QUITE SKILLFUL!
ROWLEN
PLANT
CORPORAT
THERE IS JUST ONE PROVISION... THE IZZY CASH ESTATE, OF WHICH YOU ARE COUNSEL, MUST DO THE DEVELOPING!
BUT I THOUGHT ROWENA WANTED TO DO IT!
WE ARE DEPOSITING 15 MILLION INTO YOUR CLIENT'S ACCOUNT.
BUT... ..WHY?
MISS ROWENA DIED LAST WEEK!

SHE FELT THAT YOU HAD A BETTER UNDERSTANDING ABOUT WHAT TO DO ABOUT DROPSIE AVENUE.
SHE LEFT THIS NOTE FOR YOU.
you were right, abie. Dropsie avenue as we knew it is gone
only the memory of how it was for us remains
In the end buildings are only buildings
but people make a neighborhood

DROPSIE GARDENS
A
Residential
Community
OF
AFFORDABLE
MODERN HOMES
IMMEDIATE OCCUPANCY
2 BDRMS AND 3 BDRMS
ROWENA/CASH
FOUNDATIONS
DEVELOPERS

HEY, GEORGE... YOU HAPPY WITH WHAT IS GOING ON HERE IN DROPSIE GARDENS?
WHY... WHAT DO YOU MEAN?
I'LL SHOW YOU... COME ON!
OKAY, LOOK AT THAT THERE!
I SEE GARBAGE PAILS LEFT ON THE STREET! MESSY LAWNS.
...WE SHOULD TALK TO THEM AS NEIGHBORS, FRED.
AW... THEY'RE FOREIGNERS ...THEY WON'T EVEN SPEAK OUR LANGUAGE!
...GUESS THEY WANT TO PRESERVE THEIR CULTURE.
PRESERVE WHAT CULTURE? THEY CAME HERE FROM A BACKWARD LAND-ON LEAKY BOATS...
WE ALL CAME HERE ON LEAKY BOATS...
AAAH... THEY MOVE INTO A GOOD NEIGHBORHOOD LIKE OURS AND START TRASHING THE PLACE!

BESIDES... SEE HOW THEY DECORATE THEIR HOUSES ...WEIRD COLORS, DINKY ORNAMENTS. YEEECH
WELL, IT ADDS VARIETY TO OUR NEIGHBORHOOD, FRED.
VARIETY?? IT'LL CHANGE THE WHOLE CHARACTER OF DROPSIE GARDENS! ...BETWEEN THEIR ETHNIC TASTE AND NEGLECT... THEY WILL RUIN THE WHOLE NEIGHBORHOOD!
REALLY? HOW??
PROPERTY VALUE, GEORGE! IN A FEW YEARS YOU'LL SEE THESE PLACES GOING AT HALF PRICE!
THEN WE'LL GET A LOWER CLASS OF PEOPLE COMING IN HERE!
MMMM I'M THINKING MAYBE I SHOULD TAKE THAT JOB OFFER IN FLORIDA!
FOR SALE

Notes

166. *Van Bronk.* Jonas Bronck (ca. 1600–1643) was an immigrant who arrived from Europe in the Dutch colony of New Netherland in 1639, during a period in which the Dutch West India Company was trying to bolster claims to the land in the face of growing English settlement. The Bronx and the Bronx River are named after him.
177. *Westchester.* This is the county immediately to the north of the Bronx. By the 1930s, Westchester had emerged as an affluent and desirable suburb to New York.
179. *Wops.* A derogatory slur directed against Italian-Americans. Between 1880 and 1924, more than 4 million Italians immigrated to the United States.
180. *Scusi.* Italian for "excuse me."
180. *Grazie.* Italian for "thank you."
181. *Jersey.* Short for New Jersey, the state to the west of New York, just across the Hudson River.
183. *O sole mio.* Neapolitan song written in 1898. It has been recorded many times, including by Enrico Caruso in 1916. "*O sole mio*" translates as "my sunshine."
184. *Market Crashes* and *WPA Program Provides Work.* The two headlines in the snow conflate events a few years apart. For the first, see endnote for reference on page 99. The WPA, or Works Progress Administration, was established by the administration of Franklin Delano Roosevelt in 1935 (see endnote for "*1934*" on page 120).
188. *Gonnif.* Yiddish (גנבֿ) for "thief."
193. *finisher.* Someone who buys buildings in order to strip them of anything of value, after which the building is sometimes burned down for insurance money.

EISNER ON THE GRAPHIC NOVEL AND COMICS

During the decades in which he worked on the stories in this volume, Eisner was also exploring his own approach to comics theory and pedagogy. In correspondence, interviews, essays, and two major works—*Comics and Sequential Art* (1985) and *Graphic Storytelling and Visual Narrative* (1996)—Eisner developed an increasingly sophisticated account of how comics work and of his own ambitions for and in the medium.

WILL EISNER

After several larger publishers turned down *A Contract with God*, it found a home at Baronet Publishing. Baronet's president, Norman Goldfind, had recently come from Pyramid Publications, where he had been involved with launching a series marketed as "America's First Adult Graphic Novel Review."

Letter from Will Eisner to Norman Goldfind (1978)†

Norman Goldfind, Pres.
Baronet Publishing Co.

Dear Norman—

The Contract with God which you've agreed to publish is at long last finished and ready for publication.

It represents two years of work and many many more years of thought and preparation.

I've yielded to the nagging thought that there is much more to be said in the comic book medium than I have done so far: It is an experiment to see whether themes other than cops and robbers can be successfully dealt with in this art form.

My first effort undertakes to explore the world of the Tenements in the Bronx, N.Y. during the 30s . . . often called the "dirty thirties—" and to share the drama I witnessed while passing over the threshold into manhood.

Sometime around 1919 when the number of decaying tenements in lower Manhattan could no longer accommodate the influx of immigrants that poured into New York City these buildings began to spring up in the boroughs—Brooklyn, Queens and the Bronx. By the late 20's tenements had already disintegrated into seedy communities with the noisy neighborliness of greenhorns intent on making their way in America.

I have selected a quartet of stories which for want of a better description is "eyewitness fiction." That is to say that they are compounded of events & people I have known at first hand.

I am grateful for your faith in this effort and I hope your courage in publishing these will be rewarded.

Sincerely
Will Eisner

† Transcribed by the editor from the original provided by The Ohio State University Library.

WILL EISNER

This is Eisner's first major interview following the publication of *A Contract with God*. yronwode would go on to become an important editor and publisher in and around the world of comics, including serving as editor-in-chief for Eclipse Comics.

Interview with cat yronwode (1978)†

YRONWODE: You've got some new projects in the works; one of these is being published by Kitchen Sink in *The Spirit* magazine . . .

EISNER: The thing for Kitchen Sink is an idea—to see if I can develop it into a new dimension of a novel in comic book format within the framework of the paperback size. I've always been fascinated with this. I think comics—well, let's say I think that's where comics have to go.

YRONWODE: Paperbacks rather than the large "coffee table" size?

EISNER: It's not *size* so much—there's a lot of things happening right now. Comic books, the old ten-cent comic book, are of course changing, and the old standards are disappearing. We know where some of it is going—some of it's becoming *Heavy Metal*, some of it's fractioning off into things like *Howard the Duck* and that kind of stuff.[1] There have been a few attempts made, several times, in fact, to bring off a paperback—which is the logical successor, in my opinion, to the comic book format. So far, paperbacks have never done well with comics in them, with the exception of those which have been reprints from cartoons or magazines like *Mad* . . .[2]

YRONWODE: There were those EC and Warren reprint books too . . .

EISNER: I don't know how well those have done—but most of the distributors tell me that they haven't sold all that well.

YRONWODE: Do you think that's because of the small size? People are used to having comics a certain size . . .

EISNER: Well, I think there are many reasons. People think of comics as kid stuff and also they are used to seeing comics in a larger format—but more important than that, people regard paperbacks as an inexpensive reprint or a bargain, if you will. From a big novel which they would normally pay $10.00 for, they can get a paperback for $1.95. So it's a reprint, they think. Secondly, there's a phenomenon that occurs in the bookstore—people pick up a paperback and if it's filled with cartoons or with a cartoon story that doesn't seem to have the kind of permanence of a collection, say, of *Peanuts*—and those sell very well in

† From *The Comics Journal* 46 (May 1979): 35–49, and 47 (July 1979): 41–48. Reprinted by permission of catherine yronwode. Notes are by the editor of this Norton Critical Edition.

1. *Howard the Duck:* an American comic book character first introduced by Marvel Comics in 1973, with his own title beginning in 1976. Created by Steve Gerber and Val Mayerik, *Howard the Duck* brought to mainstream comics a ribald and dark humor of the kind associated with underground comics. *Heavy Metal*: an American comics magazine founded in 1977; in its early years its material was dominated by translations from the French comics magazine *Métal hurlant*, which had begun in 1975.
2. *Mad* was a satirical comic magazine founded by Harvey Kurtzman in 1952, publishing its last issue in 2018. Its cutting humor and celebration of nonconformity inspired many cartoonists who grew up with the magazine in the 1950s and who helped found the underground comix movement in the 1960s.

paperback—or a reprint from *Mad* Magazine, which contains classic jokes by some of the best talent there is—they tend to read it in the store and put it down and not buy it. Most of the booksellers that I've talked to tell me that. At this point there has been no real market developed for comic books in paperback format. Several people have tried—Gil Kane, with his *Blackmark*, Warren's *Vampirella*, and so forth—and now they're attempting to do classic stories in the paperback format. I believe that we just haven't found the right formula yet. It's there. So one of the things I'm going to do now is attempt a series of stories in *The Spirit* Magazine which will be a pull-out section—you can pull it out and fold it up and you get a paperback. Since I can't sit down and write and draw a two-hundred-page story in one issue, I'm going to do it in serial form which will be gathered together maybe and be cut to one big novel.

YRONWODE: What's the name of this?

EISNER: It's called *Life on Another Planet*. It does not deal with mutants or people living in other galaxies—we never get into another planet. It's going to explore a very realistic, serious theme, one which has occupied my thinking for a long time, which is what would happen on *this* planet, on planet Earth, if we were to discover that there is intelligence on another planet only ten years away. The idea is very exciting to me—the possibilities are tremendous—and while it doesn't have a lot of visual potential—that is, I won't be dealing with mutants, aliens, and clones, with spaceships flying around and blasting each other into nothingness—I *will* be more concerned with character study and so forth. The first chapter goes rather slowly because I tried to get a great deal of the story into it all at the same time and I'm trying to develop a character, a man called Cim Blud—an astrophysicist turned detective. He'll be a space detective—the first space-sleuth.

YRONWODE: [Laughter] Is this an extension of "Denny Colt in Outer Space"?

EISNER: I would suppose, yeah, it's Denny Colt without a mask, I guess.

YRONWODE: Does he have gloves?

EISNER: [Laughter] No—no gloves, no mask. He wears a hat and has a hawkish nose. Actually, I haven't really centered on him—I'm gonna' let it happen, just do it and let it happen. For me this is the real fun and excitement. Aside from the preliminary plans I did for Denny Colt, most of the characters I've created just happened, they arose in answer to a given problem. I don't know what the second chapter is going to be yet, but I'll do that very shortly. The first chapter [appeared] in *The Spirit* #19.

YRONWODE: And then there's the book . . .

EISNER: Ah yes, that's the other project. I worked on that for two years and it's also out now—the book is called *A Contract with God*. This is what I've devoted my major serious efforts of the last few years to. It's something that I've wanted to do for a long time. In the foreword of the book I explain why I did it and how it came to be, so there's really no sense in repeating that—hopefully people will buy the book and read the foreword and then they'll know what my reasons were. For the purpose of this interview I must say that I am still the same Will Eisner of 1942–43, trying to expand the horizons of my medium, my medium being a sequence of pictures on paper. I believe that sequential art is the oldest communicating art form, I think it has the validity of any other art form—and while it may not have the breadth and dimension of motion pictures and it may not have the ability to cover abstracts the way lines of words do, and it may not be able to do a *lot* of things—it has served humanity since early man because it has the ability to transmit a story. So I am at work now, hopefully not singlehandedly—I'd like to be joined by other artists—in an effort to produce literature in sequential art form, or what you would call "comic art." I've been struggling with the word "comic book" for thirty years now . . .

YRONWODE: It's a bad word . . .

EISNER: It's a *terrible* word—but every time I try to change it, I find that people force me back into it. I had finally settled on the term "graphic novel" thinking that would be an adequate euphemism, but the class I teach is called "sequential art"—and of course that's what it is—a sequence of pictures arranged to tell a story.

YRONWODE: You say you're the same Will Eisner and that's exactly what I thought of when I read *A Contract with God*—in some ways it strikes me as the story of what was going on in the streets on which The Spirit wasn't chasing criminals. The atmosphere is the same—the tenements, the rain, the poverty, and without the use of crime per se—without the almost metaphoric use of crime as a vehicle for social commentary which you developed in *The Spirit*—the themes are even more clearly expressed. *A Contract with God* deals with the ideas you would bring out in the more "realistic" Spirit stories—like the ones about Bleak and Sparrow or the ones which follow some little man as he becomes trapped in societal forces beyond his control. And of course, in the introduction you state that the work is in some ways autobiographical . . .

EISNER: *A Contract with God* is drawn from life. Keep in mind that all the work I've done is done within the frame of what I knew about. I'm not writing fantasy. If I were writing about life on Mars, that would be something else again. But here I'm writing, as I did in *The Spirit*, about an area which I knew first-hand. Over 90 percent of the artwork—and perhaps I shouldn't say this because it might defeat the impression which the artwork should have—but over 90 percent of it was done from memory. I *know* buildings by heart. I *know* how an elevated structure works. I *know* what a fire hydrant looks like—I know it by *feel*. When I was selling newspapers in New York, I used to *sit* on a fire hydrant [laughter]—I know it from the seat of my pants. The city is my territory as much as another artist might know the West. Remington[3] knew the rivers and the streams and the Indians and the horses of the Far West as well as any man did—and he drew it that way.

So anyway, *A Contract with God* talks about an era which I think has been somewhat overlooked. This is the '30s, in the Bronx during and after the Depression period—1932, '35, all the way up to '38. That period was a very exciting time from the point of view that it was a time which produced a lot of very important people—the Danny Kayes, the

3. Frederick Remington (1861–1909), artist who specialized in romantic representations of the American West.

important people in American literature. *Marty*, by Paddy Chayefsky,[4] was of that era—and I know that era very well. At any rate, I've always believed, as any teacher of writing will tell you, that you should write about the things you know about—and I do know about that era. The city is what I know. My drawings are affected by my life in the city. My lighting is a result of living in a city where lights always came from single sources, from above or from below. My perspective was learned looking out the window of a five-story tenement building. Everything you see in the city as a little boy is in sharp perspective, going up or down.

YRONWODE: And your well-known use of stark artificial lighting . . .

EISNER: . . . and the artificial lighting. Sunlight only came down through the openings of buildings above you. Had I been born in Montana, in the wide open spaces, my thinking might have been different.

YRONWODE: I certainly haven't seen you draw many trees.

EISNER: Well, there weren't very many trees to draw. But I do love trees now, of course, and I do think of trees—but I think of them as gnarled human beings. I think of trees as humans.

YRONWODE: The style of inking you use in *A Contract with God* is quite different from what you did in *The Spirit*—you're not using the coarse brush that you used to use—there's a lot of fine pen lines. In fact, and this is sort of off-the-wall, I don't know if you're into Winsor McCay at all . . .[5]

EISNER: Of course I know his stuff very well.

YRONWODE: . . . Well, he started off with a relatively simple inking style in *Little Nemo* in 1905, but when he got older and began to do those editorial cartoons during the last ten years of his life, he got into an *extremely* fine crosshatching style—he avoided solid blacks altogether at that point . . .

EISNER: Yeah, sure—we all seem to go that route. Michelangelo too—in his later years he began to have a looser approach to his carving. The unfinished statues that you find in Florence are an example of that. And Milton Caniff[6]—look at the change in his work over the years. As one gets older, as one matures, the tight line, the finely constructed line, loses its value. Perhaps one gets more interested in the theme than in the technique.

People don't remain the same, they change over the years. The only features that never altered their structural line are features like *Mickey Mouse*. Even Al Capp[7] changed—although he never loosened up to the point of sketchiness. When you have a strip that's very very personal to the artist, a strip which isn't drawn by formula, you'll find that the art will change. Usually it will tend to get looser. There's a lack of patience

4. American playwright, screenwriter, and novelist (1923–1981), born in the Bronx to Jewish immigrants. Chayefsky won three Academy Awards as a screenwriter, including for *Marty* (1955). *Danny Kayes*: Danny Kaye (1911–1987), American actor and comedian. Like Eisner, Kaye was the son of Jewish immigrants who worked his way up to stardom.
5. Pioneering American cartoonist and animator (c. 1866-71–1934), most famous for his long-running newspaper comic, *Little Nemo*, and for his breakthroughs in the art of animation with characters such as Gertie the Dinosaur.
6. American newspaper cartoonist (1907–1988), most famous for his work in the adventure genre with titles such as *Terry and the Pirates* and *Steve Canyon*. *Michelangelo*: Italian painter, sculptor, and architect (1475–1564), arguably the most talented and influential artist of the Italian Renaissance.
7. American newspaper cartoonist (1909–1979), most famous for his long-running strip, *L'il Abner*.

with having to retain that heavy line. In *The Spirit* that heavy, very controlled line was an effort to retain color, color which had to be applied after all by someone else. We had to give them what we used to call "trap areas." Now that's not necessary—the technology has advanced, color can be applied in other ways. Besides, I *like* that loose line—and I think it looks nicer . . . more expressive.

YRONWODE: In all the work you've ever done, you've struck what I see as an uneasy balance between tragedy and humor. In *A Contract with God* this balance is again expressed, to even greater levels of extremity than you did in *The Spirit*. Also, and I've glossed over this, you've put out a lot of straight humorous books through the years, the *Gleeful Guides, Star Jaws,* and the like . . .[8]

EISNER: *Why* did I do that? Is that what you're asking?

YRONWODE: Not exactly. I think to phrase it *that* way would be to let you know my preferences in too partisan a way. Let's just say that I want a little glimpse into your mind. I want to know what you see as the cutting edge between humor and tragedy and I want to know why you seek that balance, why you carry it to those extremes. On one page innocent victims may be littering the landscape and on another page you may be parodying a singing commercial. You take it from extremes of really gut-wrenching despair on the one hand and then you turn around and just yuk it up.

EISNER: Aren't those two things really the very essence of life? Really—between extreme tragedy and extreme humor—what *is* there? I suppose I never think about it that way until I'm interviewed, I've never really sat down and analyzed it, but I think satire is a form of rage, an expression perhaps of anger. There is kindly humor and there's bitter tragedy. There is a relationship between the two in my mind—I can't keep them separate. Every time I do a very tragic scene, I can see a humorous scene within the same frame and it can be *converted*. A man walking down the street and falling into a manhole can be a very tragic thing—or it could be very funny. So much depends on what else is involved. I see humor as an incongruity. There are lots of definitions of what humor is—some think it's man's inhumanity to man, some think people laugh because they're glad it isn't happening to them, some people laugh because of happiness, or kindness, or even fear—but I see humor as a kind of incongruity. There are a lot of things which do seem peculiar to me and funny to me. I think it requires perspective to see humor as well as tragedy. When you step back, almost the way a painter does in front of a canvas, to look at the humor of something or the tragedy of something, you see it in a kind of clear focus. I don't think you see it if you're up close. If I'm walking down the street and someone drops water on me, it depends on how I see it at that moment whether it's a funny thing or a tragic thing. A good example of that very often is to look out the window, down on the street in New York, and see all the people milling about—and suddenly it seems to you that you're watching a whole scene or act of some kind—and it could be tragic, or it could be serious, it

8. In the early 1970s, Eisner's Poorhouse Press published a series of "Gleeful Guides" to everything from astrology and "occult cookery" to houseplants and death. In 1978, with Baronet Books, Eisner published *Star Jaws*, a series of comic strip parodies of *Star Wars* (1977).

could be very funny. Walk down 42nd Street some time and you can find anything you want—tragedy or whatever. I can't go beyond that with philosophy—but I enjoy humor, I enjoy *doing* humor, and I don't think it's less worthy of me than doing the stories I did in *A Contract with God* . . .

YRONWODE: . . . which is by no means a humorous quartet of stories.

EISNER: No. Well, *A Contract with God* is a group of stories about the '30s in the Bronx. It's all built around a tenement which I named 55 Dropsie Avenue for want of a better name. I think there was a Cropsie Avenue in the Bronx and I took it from that. The tenement is as typical as I could get it—and I built all the stories around that one old structure because in one tenement you could have as many stories as there were families—and that's another fact which has always intrigued me.

YRONWODE: The last of the four stories, "Cookalein," seems to be highly autobiographical—there's a character named Willie in it . . .

EISNER: *Really?!* How *clever* of you! [Laughter]

YRONWODE: [Laughter] Yeah.

EISNER: Every one of the people in those stories is either me or someone I knew, or parts of them and me—but like any other writer of stories I suppose I—well look, in *Death of a Salesman*, Willie Loman was Arthur Miller's father.[9] A lot of these characters were people I've known intimately, or me, or people like me. How can you *not* be autobiographical if you're writing about something that you've seen. In the character Willie—well, I was called Willie when I was a kid, so I guess you might say it was autobiographical, yeah. I *did* go to the country, to a cookelein[1] like Willie does—and I *did* see many of the things that he sees there. And I must say that it took a lot of determination, a kind of courage, to write that story.

YRONWODE: I was personally very affected by that last story—it has a universal quality, at least it reflects some events in my life . . . all of them do, but the last three stories hit me closer than the first one did.

EISNER: That's very interesting because the first story, "A Contract with God," rather than "Cookalein," was the one I treated as seriously as I could. Well, they're all serious stories as far as I'm concerned—there is humor in them but they were all very seriously done. It will be interesting to me to hear the reactions from people who have never lived in this area of New York, or during that era of time—to see whether they find any relevancy to it at all.

YRONWODE: Right—that's why the first story doesn't affect me as much, even though it is a very well told story—it relies too much on the idiosyncrasies of Judaism for its punchline, if you can call it that—whereas "The Street Singer," "The Super," and "Cookalein" deal with some of the common horrors and joys in almost anyone's life. The *setting* is ethnic but the emotions are universal.

EISNER: That's an interesting reaction. You see, when I did it, I wasn't certain that the subject matter of the plots would be of any interest to anybody beyond Hoboken.[2] * * *

9. *Death of a Salesman*; a 1949 play by Arthur Miller (1915–2005), portraying a traveling salesman, Willy Loman, as he contemplates his life and his death.
1. This word is a hybrid of English ("cook") and Yiddish ("aleyn" or אלײן)—or "cook-alone." These were small resorts, usually located on a farm, where the guests cooked for themselves—much more affordable than the Catskill resorts where the middle-class vacationers stayed.
2. A city in New Jersey, directly across the Hudson River from lower Manhattan in New York City.

YRONWODE: * * * [T]here's a lot more overt sexuality in this book than in anything else you've ever done . . .

EISNER: Yes. I realize that. I found it difficult to keep it out. Even though my women at least have always had strong sexual overtones, I struggled with the problem of inserting it—I didn't *want* to get into the sex thing but no way I could avoid it.

YRONWODE: In three of the stories it's actually the major turning point of the plot.

EISNER: Well, how could I avoid it? In "The Street Singer" that scene is essential to the kind of man he is. At one point in early roughs I had eliminated the scene in which he has sex with the old singer, largely because—well, I guess I was almost embarrassed by doing it—it was an intimate thing. But it was the only way I could show this man's relative impotence—really, that sex act had to show her strength. She was using sex as a kind of power. So I redrew those panels three or four times—I enlarged 'em and I reduced 'em, then I had just one scene, then I had two—and it didn't seem honest—so finally I decided I was just gonna let it hang out and *do* it. In the case of "Cookalein," the discovery of sex was what it was all about—going to the country. In a sense that was what it was all about. Now that's my statement—maybe other people will not agree. The relationships in tight families stem from a kind of sex relationship. In the case of the first story, "A Contract with God," there was no sex because there was no need for it to tell the story. Sure, he had a mistress—but there was no need to demonstrate any sex between them. I don't like putting intimate sex into a comic book, visualizing it unless there's a reason for it—unless it belongs. When it's absolutely essential I will put it in, regardless of how explicit it gets.

* * *

YRONWODE: In this new book as well as in *The Spirit*—and I'm referring here to most of the male characters in *The Spirit*—the men are seen as victims of the women for the most part. The women are stronger, more aggressive—they make sexual advances to the men . . .

EISNER: In *A Contract with God?*

YRONWODE: The little girl in "The Super" . . .

EISNER: Yeah, well in that . . . yeah . . .

YRONWODE: . . . The woman, Maralyn, who comes to Willie in the night . . .

EISNER: Yeah, but *that* . . . well, yeah . . .

YRONWODE: The old singer . . . and of course women are always coming on to The Spirit—everyone from P'gell down to Ellen Dolan . . .

EISNER: Do you think that possibly there's some significance—that maybe it's a clue to my own attitude toward sex?

YRONWODE: Well, that's for you to say, isn't it? But I do think it's interesting because several people have accused you in print of having a "sexist" attitude toward women.

EISNER: Well, I was brought up as a male chauvinist.

YRONWODE: By that do you mean that you think that men are innately superior to women?

EISNER: No. When I say I'm a male chauvinist I say it with some tongue in cheek because it's now a trigger word. But remember that I was brought up to believe that manhood was somehow synonymous with sexual prowess and wealth. It was the man who *did* things and the women who were dependent wholly on men. This was my early indoctrination.

YRONWODE: But you rarely do a story about women like *that*. The women you draw are . . .

EISNER: They're strong—because it's women like *that* that I admire. Obviously everybody "does" women that they admire—Frank Frazetta does big busted, solid fleshed women and Rich Corben[3] does big busted . . .

YRONWODE: . . . bigger *busted* . . .

EISNER: . . . solid fleshed women. I go for the skinny, neurotic [laughter] *sexy* woman who's got an intellectual problem. I don't know—incidentally, I didn't marry such a woman—I married someone entirely different from P'gell.

YRONWODE: Was she like Ellen?

EISNER: No, not at all—as a matter of fact she's not like any one of my heroines. But in the case of *The Spirit* I was drawing the kind of women that I thought were attractive to see.

YRONWODE: A lot of them are based on movie stars.

EISNER: Yeah—Lauren Bacall was a *tremendous* influence on me—I was *fascinated* with her and very attracted to her kind of woman. There was a whole series of women like Lauren Bacall and Katharine Hepburn in the movies at that time, during the Bogart era.[4]

* * *

YRONWODE: Well, having disposed of sexism and sex . . .

EISNER: Have we? [Laughter]

YRONWODE: [Laughter] No . . .

EISNER: I hope not!

YRONWODE: [Giggles]

EISNER: What more can we say about sex? I mean, I just admit that it deserves a long discussion. I just want to point out, before we let it go, that I am conscious of the fact that I'm not associated with it in the mind of the public—I mean, I've never before shown any explicit sex acts in anything I've ever drawn—especially in *The Spirit*—even though they might be suggestive, they only kiss . . .

YRONWODE: They certainly are suggestive kisses though . . .

EISNER: They're very sexy and very suggestive . . .

YRONWODE: They're more sexy than a Jack Kirby kiss . . .[5]

EISNER: Oh yes . . . oh yes. I hope Jack Kirby will not take offense at that.

YRONWODE: [Laughter]

EISNER: I've never kissed Jack Kirby, by the way.

YRONWODE: [Hysteria deleted] None of your work has ever been subject to the Comics Code and it doesn't look like any of it ever will be . . .

3. American illustrator and comic book artist (1940–2020), most famous for his work for *Heavy Metal*. In 1976, Corben published a pioneering graphic novel, *Bloodstar*, based on a story by Robert E. Howard. *Frank Frazetta*: American illustrator and comic book artist (1928–2010), whose work greatly influenced the look and feel of modern fantasy art.

4. *Lauren Bacall*: American film actress (1924–2014), perhaps best remembered for her performance alongside her husband, Humphrey Bogart, in the film noir *The Big Sleep* (1946). *Katharine Hepburn*: American actress (1907–2003), working in film, theater, and television over a career that spanned almost seven decades.

5. American comic book artist (1917–1994), who began his career working in Eisner's first studio before founding his own studio. Over the course of a long career, Kirby created many of the most lasting characters in comics, including Captain America, Black Panther, and the Fantastic Four.

EISNER: That's right—I have no contact with it in any way . . .

YRONWODE: Do you think it's unnecessarily restrictive?

EISNER: Well, actually I don't know how restrictive it is—I've not seen their editing. The administrators of the Comics Code are very conscientious people—I know the people who are involved with it. The Code was formed to provide the comics field with freedom from legal restrictions which would have been imposed on them had the Code not appeared. So really I see them not as an enemy but as a policeman who stands in front of your house to keep you from being attacked. He's there and he gets in the way and he's a nuisance—but he's a necessary evil.

YRONWODE: Do you think that comics should be censored in this way?

EISNER: I don't believe in censorship. I don't think there is such a thing as pornography. I think there is *obscenity*—one man killing another man is obscenity. We see it on television all the time and I can't say in my mind that it's all right to show one man stabbing another man or shooting another man or causing the death of somebody while at the same time not allowing a sex act to be shown.

WILL EISNER

In 1985, Eisner collected his best insights and lessons from his teaching at the School of Visual Arts into *Comics and Sequential Art*, published by his Poorhouse Press. Over the next two decades, he continued to write about the theory and practice of comics in various forums, including a companion volume, *Graphic Storytelling and Visual Narrative.*

From Comics and Sequential Art†

'Comics' as a Form of Reading

For more than a century, modern comic book artists have been developing in their craft the interplay of words and images. They have in the process, I believe, achieved a successful cross-breeding of illustration and prose.

The format of the comic book presents a montage of both word and image, and the reader is thus required to exercise both visual and verbal interpretive skills. The regimens of art (eg. perspective, symmetry, line) and the regimens of literature (eg. grammar, plot, syntax) become superimposed upon each other. The reading of a graphic novel is an act of both aesthetic perception and intellectual pursuit.

* * *

In its most economical state, comics employ a series of repetitive images and recognizable symbols. When these are used again and again to convey similar ideas, they become a language—a literary form, if you will. And it is this disciplined application that creates the "grammar" of sequential art.

As an example, consider the final page from the *Spirit* story, "Gerhard Shnobble," the story of a man who is determined to reveal to the world

† From *Comics and Sequential Art* (New York: W. W. Norton & Company, Inc., 2008), pp. 2–5, 39–42. One figure caption has been omitted. Notes are by the editor of this Norton Critical Edition.

AND SO... LIFELESS...
GERHARD SHNOBBLE FLUTTERED
EARTHWARD.

BUT DO NOT WEEP
FOR SHNOBBLE...

RATHER SHED A TEAR
FOR ALL MANKIND...

FOR NOT ONE PERSON IN THE
ENTIRE CROWD THAT WATCHED
HIS BODY BEING CARTED AWAY...KNEW
OR EVEN SUSPECTED THAT
ON THIS DAY GERHARD SHNOBBLE
HAD **FLOWN.**

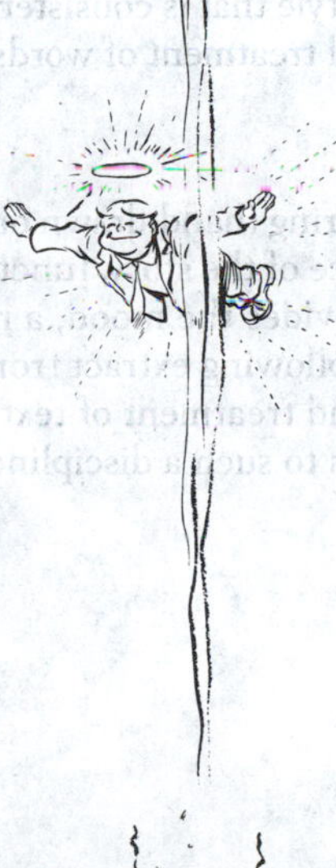

his ability to fly, only to be shot down by a stray bullet, his secret sealed forever by his pointless death. * * *

This concluding page depicts the death of Gerhard, as he is hit by a stray bullet from a shoot-out on a rooftop. The first panel presents the reader with the climax of the story. A description of the action in this panel can be diagrammed like a sentence. The predicates of the gun-shooting and the wrestling belong to separate clauses. The subject of "gun-shooting" is the crook, and Gerhard is the direct object. The many modifiers include the adverb "Bang, Bang" and the adjectives of visual language, such as posture, gesture, and grimace.

The second panel concludes the subplot, and again uses the language of the body and the staging of graphic design to delineate the predicates.

The final transition requires the reader to break from the convention of the left-to-right sequence. The eye follows the air stream down past a nebulous background, onto the solid body on the ground, and then bounces back upward to view the half-tone cloud in which Gerhard is resurrected. This bounce is unique to the visual narrative. The reader must implicitly use his knowledge of physical laws (ie. gravity, gases) to "read" this passage.

The accompanying text adds some non-illustrated thoughts hand-lettered in a style that is consistent with the sentiment that its message conveys. The visual treatment of words as graphic art forms is part of the vocabulary.

TEXT READS AS AN IMAGE

Lettering (hand-drawn or created with type), treated "graphically" and in the service of the story, functions as an extension of the imagery. In this context it provides the mood, a narrative bridge, and the implication of sound. In the following extract from my graphic novel, *A Contract With God,* the use of, and treatment of text as a "block" is employed in a manner which conforms to such a discipline.

All day
the rain
poured
down on
the Bronx
without
mercy

The sewers overflowed
and the waters rose
over the curbs of the street.

Here, the lettering is employed to support the "climate." Designing the typeface to permit it to be drenched by the rain, converts the normally mechanical aspect of type into supportive involvement in the imagery.

I CAME TO YOUR HOUSE AS A FRIEND AND YOU MURDERED ME!!... FOR THIS MAY YOUR PEOPLE BE PARALYZED BY THE STAIN OF MY BLOOD

The meaning of the title is conveyed by the employment of a commonly recognized configuration of a tablet. A stone is employed—rather than parchment or paper, for example, to imply permanence and evoke the universal recognition of Moses' Ten Commandments on a stone tablet.[1] Even the mix of the lettering style—Hebraic vs. a condensed Roman letter—is designed to buttress this feeling.

Another example of how text rendered in concert with the art shows how the 'reading' of it can be influenced. In the following page from *The Spirit's Case Book of True Ghost Stories,* the dialogue executed in a certain manner tells the reader how the author wishes it to sound. In the process it evokes a specific emotion and modifies the image.

The Frame

The fundamental function of comics art to communicate ideas and/or stories by means of words and pictures involves the movement of certain images (such as people and things) through space. To deal with the *capture* or encapsulation of these events in the flow of the narrative, they must be broken up into sequenced segments. These segments are called panels or frames. They do not correspond exactly to cinematic frames. They are part of the creative process, rather than a result of the technology.

As in the use of panels to express the passage of time, the framing of a series of images moving through space undertakes the containment of thoughts, ideas, actions and location or site. The panel thereby attempts to deal with the broadest elements of dialogue: cognitive and perceptive as well as visual literacy. The artist, to be successful on this non-verbal level, must take into consideration both the commonality of human experience and the phenomenon of our perception of it, which seems to consist of frames or episodes.

If, as legendary magazine editor Norman Cousins[2] points out, ". . . sequential thought is the most difficult work in the entire range of human effort," then the work of the sequential artist must be measured by comprehensibility. The sequential artist "sees" for the reader because it is inherent to narrative art that the requirement on the viewer is not so much analysis as recognition. The task then is to arrange the sequence of events (or pictures) so as to bridge the gaps in action. Given these, the reader may fill in the intervening events from experience. Success here stems from the artist's ability (usually more visceral than intellectual) to gauge the commonality of the reader's experience.

ENCAPSULATION

It should surprise no one that the limit of the human eye's peripheral vision is closely related to the panel as it is used by the artist to capture or "freeze" one segment in what is in reality an uninterrupted flow of action. To be sure, this segmentation is an arbitrary act—and it is in this encapsulation that the artist employs the skill of narration. The rendering of the elements within the frame, the arrangement of the images therein and their relation to and association with the other images in the sequence are the basic "grammar" from which the narrative is constructed.

1. The biblical story is recounted in Exodus 20:2–17.
2. American author, editor, and professor (1915–1990).

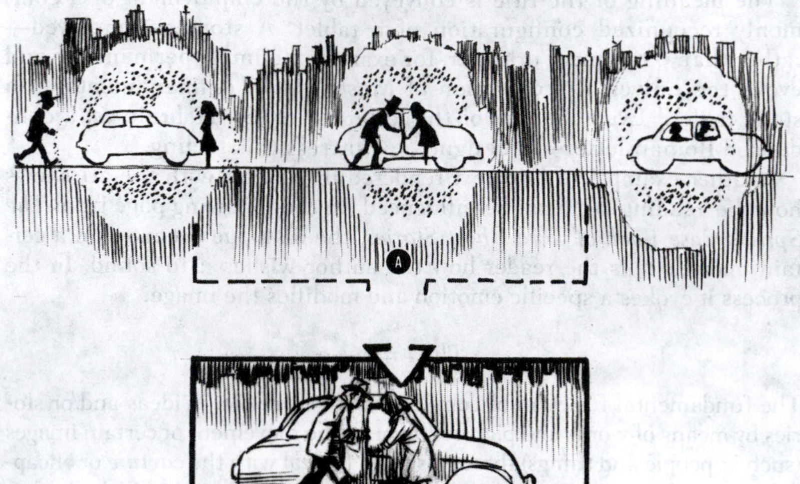

A. The scene viewed through reader's eyes . . . seen from inside reader's head. **B.** Final Panel selected from sequence of action.

In visual narration the task of the author/artist is to record a continued flow of experience and show it as it may be seen from the reader's eyes. This is done by arbitrarily breaking up the flow of uninterrupted experience into segments of "frozen" scenes and enclosing them by a frame or panel.

The total time elapsed may be minutes in duration and the periphery of the stage very wide. Out of this, the position of the actors in relation to the scenery is selected, frozen and encapsulated by a panel frame. There is an unquestioned relationship here between what the reader perceives as the flow of events and what is frozen in time by the panel.

THE PANEL AS A MEDIUM OF CONTROL

In sequential art the artist must, from the outset, secure control of the reader's attention and dictate the sequence in which the reader will follow the narrative. The limitations inherent in the technology are both obstacle and asset in the attempt to accomplish this. The most important obstacle to surmount is the tendency of the reader's eye to wander. On any given page, for example, there is absolutely no way in which the artist can prevent the reading of the last panel before the first. The turning of the page does mechanically enforce some control, but hardly as absolutely as in film.

The viewer of a film is prevented from seeing the next frame before the creator permits it because these frames, printed on strips of transparent film, are shown one at a time. So film, which is an extension of comic strips, enjoys absolute control of its "reading"—an advantage shared by live theater. In a closed theater the proscenium arch and the wings of the stage can form but one single panel, while the audience sits in a fixed position from which they view the action contained therein.

* * *

The viewer sees (reads) a film only one frame at a time. He cannot see the next (or past) frames until they are projected by the machine.

Still, even given these technical advantages, in all forms of comics the sequential artist relies upon the tacit cooperation of the reader. This cooperation is based upon the convention of reading (left to right, top to bottom, etc.) and the common cognitive disciplines. Indeed, it is this very voluntary cooperation, so unique to comics, that underlies the contract between artist and audience.

In comics, there are actually two "frames": the total page (or screen, in digital comics), on which there are any number of panels, and the panel itself, within which the narrative action unfolds. They are the controlling devices in sequential art.

The (Western culture) reader is trained to read each page independently from left to right, top to bottom. Panel arrangements on the page assume this. In Japanese *manga*,[3] the opposite reading sequence is employed, and most translations of Japanese comics retain this right-to-left configuration.

One of these arrangements, then, is ideally the normal flow of the reader's eye. In practice, however, this discipline is not absolute. The viewer will

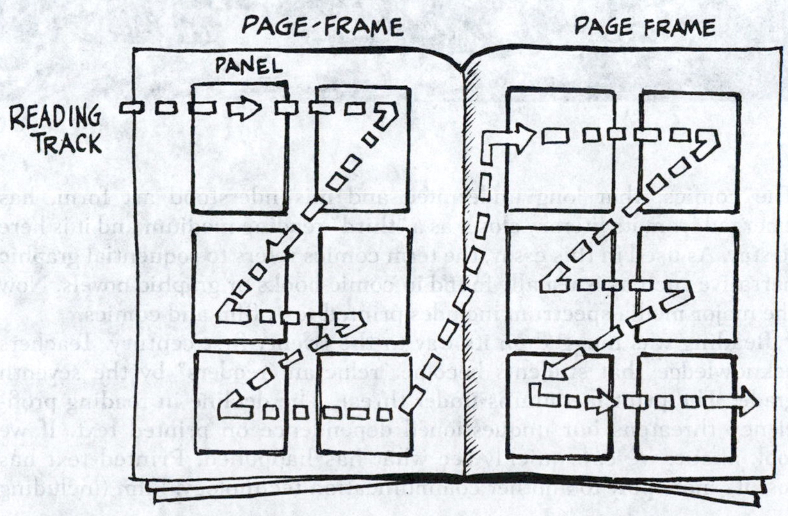

3. Japanese comics. As Eisner discusses on p. 227, in his later career he grew fascinated by the diversity of manga in terms of genre and audience.

often glance at the last panel first. Nevertheless, the reader finally must return to the conventional pattern.

WILL EISNER

Comics and the New Literacy: An Essay[†]

The comics, that long underrated and misunderstood art form, has emerged from its literary closet as a "third" reading medium and it is here to stay. As used in this essay, the term comics refers to sequential graphic narrative such as is usually found in comic books or graphic novels. Now the major media spectrum includes printed text, film and comics.

Reading was mugged on its way to the twenty-first century. Teachers acknowledge that students become "reluctant readers" by the seventh grade. The print medium is under threat. The decline in reading proficiency threatens our unquestioned dependence on printed text. If we look about, we can quickly see what has happened. Printed text has lost its monopoly to another communication technology. Film (including

† From "Comics and the New Literacy: An Essay," *INKS: Cartoon and Comic Arts Studies* 1.2 (1994).

video) has become the major competitor for readership and is the communicator of choice. With its limited demand on a viewer to acquire skills, film makes the time-consuming burden of learning to read seem obsolete. What has happened?

Clearly the drift has been toward electronic instruments that provide information, entertainment, and artificial experience through a combination of sound and imagery. But let us not waste time on ways of controlling its patronage. We have no choice but to accept it. Television, the primary disseminator of film, has become the major source of information for many and it will soon become the electronic library in most American homes. Evidence shows that television-watching has increased as literacy has decreased. Clearly film and video are influencing reading habits.

How we read has been changing. Viewers "live" through countless lifelike experiences of ordained duration as they watch TV where artificial situations and contrived solutions become integrated into the audience's mental inventory. The actors become "real" people. Most importantly, watching film establishes a rhythm of acquisition. It is a direct challenge to print. The reader, accustomed to the pace of film, grows impatient with long text passages. He or she is used to acquiring stories, ideas and information quickly. As we know, complex concepts become more easily digested when reduced to imagery.

But electronic dominance is not total. Printed communication is still a viable and necessary medium. In fact, it is responding to the challenge of electronic media by accommodation. A partnership of words with imagery has become the logical permutation. The resulting configuration is called comics and it fills the gap between print and film.

Comics are admittedly a mutant based on the earliest form of written communication. Their mix of text and image neatly satisfies the current reader's need for accelerated acquisition of information. They are capable of dealing with both instruction and storytelling. Comics are a formidable teaching tool and can cope with subject matter of considerable sophistication.

The impact of comics on literacy or the process of reading is worth examining. Because of their intelligent conventions and flexible structure, they are a valid reading vehicle in the traditional sense, and with the addition of their universal visual ingredient, they become a cross-cultural medium that transcends language barriers. Learning how to read a comic is an easily acquired skill. Comics are a disciplined arrangement of words and images which require reader participation and involvement. Comics employ both image and text interdependently and require a reasonable word vocabulary. The fundamental difference between comics and illustrated text is that the imagery in comics is intrinsic to narrative content and employs analogous images in sequence as a language. Unfortunately this ease of reading gave comics a reputation for usefulness confined to people of low literacy and limited intellectual accomplishment. Encouragement and acceptance of this medium by the educational establishment has been less than enthusiastic. For a long time comics were not employed for much more than simple entertainment. The predominance of art and the traditional comics format bring more attention to its form than its literary content. It is hardly surprising, therefore, that comics as a reading form were always assumed to be a threat to literacy, as literacy was defined in the pre-visual/electronic era.

* * *

Today comics attempt to deal with sophisticated subject matter. One major element of comics that has always provoked resistance to its acceptance as serious reading is imagery. I believe, however, that images are a reflection of experience. Because experience precedes analysis, the intellectual digestive process that results from reading comics takes place at a more rapid pace.

Narrative imagery has had a long history. Primitive images evolved into a symbol-code alphabet which ultimately became written language. Later images were sidelined to serve as supporters of text. The technology of set type made printed books a universal medium. Historically pictures in books were employed to make printed prose more attractive. But when the image is isolated and required to function as a narrative, another standard for it arises. Its employment must conform to a discipline tied to traditional reading. An image does have limitations. Images do not easily articulate abstractions and are not easily employed in the expression of complex thought. An image does, however, have the advantage of defining in absolute terms. It shortcuts the process of delineation that occurs when words are translated and converted into imagery in the brain. Images do transmit with the speed of sight.

Reading a comic requires a certain contract between the reader and the author. Intellectual participation by the reader is mandatory. The comic begins with the concept of sequentially arranged images and words printed to emulate in structure the written sentence of text. The reader must then contribute the intervening action, time, place and ideas that are implied between the images. Words, in the form of dialogue or descriptions of time and place, are read within the image flow.

Comic art is a form of impressionism. It relies on images that are reduced to extreme simplicity. Usually the cartoonist employs an economy of realism to convey emotion, evoke humor, or, by exaggerations of anatomy, to simulate heroic action. For adventure stories, the art is often more realistically rendered. The text, mostly dialogue, seeks to emulate real speech and is encapsulated in balloons, a necessary device to deal with space and sound. Comics depend on the stereotype and cliché to evoke comprehension drawn from common experiences. Their actors must be caricatures if they are to be recognized. The sequence of events is shown by selected segments taken from a seamless flow of action. The comic book reader quickly digests the suspended animation implicit in an ongoing action that gives intellectual meaning to the whole. The frames (or panels) punctuate the flow and provide the sense of time. Drawing style and skill of draftsmanship have an effect on the transmission of the idea and on the impact of its content. Because of the amount of space normally employed by this medium, the content must often be accommodated to it by a certain brevity.

A critical fact is that the reader is expected to supply the intervening action implied by the images which depict either the start or the end of an action. This problem can be compared to the one facing a playwright who depends on stage setting, dialogue, and the skill of the actor—with the advantages of sound, live action, and real time. The playwright enables the audience to witness reality. With film, the viewer is a passive spectator of recorded reality. In comics, the audience views implied reality and the reader must interpret the meaning of postures and gestures, which, despite the limitation of a "frozen" image, try to convey subtle internal feelings. The arrangement of these postures and gestures in accordance with a common reading convention is the cartoonist's control over telling the story and the progression of reading.

Comics are not a text-reading substitute. They will not make words obsolete. In fact, text is an integral ingredient of comics and complexity of content often determines the ratio of pictures to words. The graphic treatment of letters and words often reinforces their partnership in the cognitive process. This is a reading experience in every sense. Comprehension of the message is, of course, impaired by the inability to read the text of a dialogue or narrative, but the skilled deployment of images generally provides clues to word meaning. Success in teaching foreign languages via comics testifies to this. No one really knows for certain whether the words are read before or after viewing the picture. We do know that they are not read simultaneously. While modern comics begin with a typewritten script, the process of composing each page gives a certain primacy to the image or visual elements. Obviously the skill of the artist has a great deal to do with the product. Modern comics are most often produced by a writer and artist team, and a failure in coordination sometimes affects clarity and readability. Nevertheless, most teams have grown more secure in their craft and the scope of subject matter and quality of content have expanded.

From works relying heavily on text with static pictures to strongly evocative pictures with limited or no text, comics have matured to address more sophisticated experiences and dramatize complex themes. Comics have now established a niche in the library of printed communication and are a testimony to the durability of printed reading material. In the United States alone, the number of specialty comic book shops grew from one hundred to four thousand between 1970 and 1992. This growth and the huge volume of titles published and bought annually are ample evidence that comics are a reading medium whose time has come. Comics belong to the new literacy.

WILL EISNER

In 1985, Eisner collected his best insights and lessons from his teaching at the School of Visual Arts into *Comics and Sequential Art,* published by his Poorhouse Press. Over the next two decades, he continued to write about the theory and practice of comics in various forums, including a companion volume, *Graphic Storytelling and Visual Narrative.*

The Reader†

To whom are you telling your story?

The answer to this question precedes the telling because it is a fundamental concern of delivery. The reader's profile—his experience and cultural characteristics—must be reckoned with before the teller can successfully narrate the tale. Successful communication depends on the storyteller's own memory of experience and visual vocabulary.

Empathy

Perhaps the most basic of human characteristics is empathy. This trait can be used as a major conduit in the delivery of a story. Its exploitation can be counted upon as one of the storyteller's tools.

Empathy is a visceral reaction of one human being to the plight of another. The ability to "feel" the pain, fear or joy of someone else enables the storyteller to evoke an emotional contact with the reader. We see ample evidence of this in movie theaters where people weep over the grief of an actor, who is pretending while in an event that is not really happening.

Wincing with vicarious pain when observing someone being hit is, according to some scientists, evidence of fraternal behavior, the work of a neural psychological mechanism developed in hominids from very early on. On the other hand, researchers argue that empathy results from our ability to run through our minds a narrative of the sequence of a

† From *Graphic Storytelling and Visual Narrative* (New York: W. W. Norton & Company, Inc., 2008), pp. 47–49. Two illustrations have been omitted.

particular event. This not only suggests a cognitive capacity but an innate ability to understand a story.

There is a whole body of clinical studies to support the conclusion that humans learn from infancy to watch and learn to interpret gestures, postures, imagery and other non-verbal social signals. From these, they can deduce meanings and motives like love, pain, and anger, among others.

The relevance of all this to graphic storytelling becomes even more apparent with the claims by scientists that the evolution of hominids' ability to read the intentions of others in their group involves their visual-neural equipment. This was possible, they contend, because as the visual system evolved it became more connected to the emotional centers of the brain. It helps, therefore, for an image maker to understand that all human muscles, in one way or another are controlled by the brain.

Based on the understanding of empathy's cause and effect, we can then come to the fashioning of a reader-storyteller contract.

The "Contract"

At the outset of the telling of a story, whether oral, written, or graphic, there is an understanding between the storyteller and the listener, or reader. The teller expects that the audience will comprehend, while the audience expects the author will deliver something that is comprehensible. In this agreement, the burden is on the teller. This is a basic rule of communication.

In comics the reader is expected to understand things like implied time, space, motion, sound and emotions. In order to do this, a reader must not only draw on visceral reactions but make use of an accumulation of experience as well as reasoning.

TOM HEINTJES

Heintjes cofounded the magazine *Hogan's Alley* in 1994 after serving as a writer and editor at *The Comics Journal* during the previous decade. This interview first appeared in *Hogan's Alley*.

[Interview with Tom Heintjes]†

TOM HEINTJES: What challenges do you see cartoonists facing that they traditionally haven't had?

WILL EISNER: Before we can discuss any challenge facing a cartoonist, we've got to decide what we're talking about: Are we talking about his art form, or are we talking about the publication that will carry his work? Cartoonists have always worked for publication, as opposed to painters, who work for galleries. It's the final vehicle that often determines "the challenge," as you put it. A painter's vehicle is the gallery. The painting he makes is "the product." The cartoonist, however, is creating something for reproduction. This has an effect on the challenge.

Let me step back here and answer the question in two parts. The cartoon art form—the art of treating an image impressionistically—will not fade. It will keep growing in popularity, because a cartoon is able to convey an idea as an image, and images are the means of communication that are proliferating. Communication in the future will be based on imagery, the transmission of ideas by images. The vehicle of transmission is changing under our noses and will influence how the artist deals with the medium. He'll configure his work to suit the method of transmission. Historically, print has been the major vehicle. The arrival of the Internet has provided the cartoonist with another vehicle of transmission, which has a different set of requirements. The relationship with the reader, which is primary to the entire business of communication, has to be accommodated. In print, you can count on the fact that the reader will either glance at your work or dwell on it for a great length of time. You therefore can develop what I call a "contract with the reader" during the time he or she has it in their hands. In electronic transmission, we have no way of knowing how long a reader stays with you or what their retention time is. We're dealing with a totally different relationship.

* * *

HEINTJES: One of the pleasures I get from enjoying cartooning is a tactile one, and I miss that on the computer screen.

EISNER: I have the same reaction. I enjoy the brush work, and I enjoy inspecting the pen-and-ink techniques. But I've been in debates with some younger cartoonists who argue that the day of the paper cartoon is coming to an end. They believe there will come a time when readers will have lost the experience of looking at things on paper, so they

† "Eisner Wide Open," from *Will Eisner: Conversations*, ed. M. Thomas Inge (Jackson: University Press of Mississippi, 2011), pp. 196–204. Reprinted with permission of Tom Heintjes. Notes are by the editor of this Norton Critical Edition.

won't have the same frame of reference that we do today. They'll only have looked at things on a screen. I argue that the tactile experience of holding a book will be very hard to diminish, but it is an argument that a lot of Internet-oriented cartoonists do not easily accept. I was having this very same sort of discussion last year at a panel at the San Diego comics convention, and one of the cartoonists told me I sounded like a medieval monk who sneers at the future of this guy Gutenberg with his movable type.[1]

The bottom line is, technology is doing something to the comic-book business. Comic books as we knew them in the 1940s, 1950s, and 1960s are experiencing a continuing drop in sales.

* * *

HEINTJES: What effect do you think today's media have had on the way people perceive stories?

EISNER: The media have had a tremendous effect on storytelling. A young reader's sense of wonder is very quickly satisfied by electronic media. It will generate things that a more limited medium like comics can only allude to. For example, a comic strip about space travel cannot compete with the experience delivered by the film *Star Wars*. So you have to deal with this generation in terms of its own experience, and part of that experience is MTV. I've been trying to watch MTV to figure it out, but I can't watch too much of it or my eyes bump into each other. What they're doing is using visual clichés over and over. You can connect into their message by using the experiences you've had watching other films or videos. The message doesn't come from your own real-life experience. It comes from artificial experience. But those of us who are trying to tell a story must pay attention to that.

HEINTJES: Historically, when comic books entered periods of slumping sales, one survival technique was to have a broad appeal, so you had material geared toward a variety of demographics: funny animals for children, romance comics for girls, teenage comics for young teens, as well as the usual superheroes, monster, western, war, and science fiction material. Now, with a few exceptions, mainstream comics have given themselves over almost entirely to superheroes.

EISNER: Perhaps that may explain the malaise. It's interesting to look at Japan. Some of their comic books sell at the rate of 8 million copies a week, and the subject matter is enormously diversified. They have comics for expectant mothers, comics for adults, boys and girls, all different ages. It's a huge industry, but their culture has grown up with a language that is basically pictorial.

* * *

HEINTJES: After all you've accomplished in your career, what continues to drive you?

1. In 1439, the German printer Johannes Gutenberg (c. 1400–1468) developed the first Western system for printing movable type, ultimately sparking the print revolution that swept Europe in the 16th century.

EISNER: Oh, there's so much that is undone in this medium. I want to do it. I've got a book coming out called *Last Day in Vietnam*[2] in which I eschew the use of balloons altogether. It's a collection of true incidents that happened to me in my visits to Vietnam and when I was in Korea. But it's done with a totally different approach. I only used this once in *The Spirit*, where the reader is a participant, and the characters are talking to the reader. At the time, I felt it was successful, but I never followed it up. I'm constantly experimenting. As we're talking, I'm dummying up another book that has to do with folk tales back in Dropsie Avenue.

Glenn Miller[3] used to say he was still looking for "the sound." That's how I feel. Actually, I'm still looking to achieve what I set out to do fifty years ago: to achieve a literary level in this medium. One of the problems is in marketing. Maybe one of the problems is that the adult reader is turned off by the form. He sees a lot of pictures, and he sees balloons, and he sees a book that he pays fourteen dollars for, which gives him maybe a half-hour's worth of reading time. For that same money, he can get a book by Stephen King or John Updike[4] that would give him hours and hours of reading time. Perhaps the solution is not in form but in content. This is something I'm struggling with, trying to seize the adult reader.

HEINTJES: What trends do you see in the work of today's aspiring cartoonists?

EISNER: A preoccupation with special effects. A lot of them are preoccupied with creating new superheroes. Recently some young black creators showed me a new ethnic superhero. What a waste of creativity! We don't need another ethnic superhero—we've got plenty of them. Show me something about ethnic life in America today. That's what we don't have enough of. But they're thinking of where the money is at, and they know they're not going to get anywhere fast by doing my kind of stuff. They're going to get instant money by doing superheroes of some kind.

HEINTJES: Looking back at your body of work, which are you proudest of? By the way, you're not allowed to say, "My next one."

EISNER: You intercepted me [laughter]. It's hard to say, but . . . I guess *A Contract with God* is like my first child. "Gerhard Shnobble" in *The Spirit* is a favorite story, because it was the first time I attempted a philosophical point. From a technical point of view, I think *A Life Force* was well structured. *Dropsie Avenue* was, for me, a technical tour de force because I attempted something I didn't think was possible in this medium, and that is to do a proper history of a neighborhood. In each case, I've always attempted to climb a hill, and sometimes I succeed and sometimes I don't.

2. A 2000 book by Eisner, collecting stories of the end of the war, some of them based on experiences he had or heard of during his visit as part of his ongoing work with the U.S. Army on maintenance manuals.
3. American musician and bandleader (1904–1944), wildly popular during his short career.
4. American author (1932–2009), whose fiction tended to focus on white middle-class American life. *Stephen King*: American author (b. 1947), most famous for his many contributions to the horror genre.

REVIEWS AND ASSESSMENTS

Until recently, comics and graphic novels were not reviewed in mainstream magazines and newspapers. As comics fandom organized in the 1960s and '70s, a network of fanzines and semiprofessional periodicals emerged to fill this gap, providing critical assessment of new works in the field.

RICHARD KYLE

Kyle coined the term "graphic novel" in the fan-critic newsletter *CAPA-alpha* in November 1964. He was an influential early champion of the artistic possibilities of comics in such venues as his "Graphic Story Review" column in *Graphic Story Magazine.*

To Baronet Publishing Company†

March 21, 1978

Baronet Publishing Company
509 Madison Avenue
New York, NY 10022

Sirs:

* * *

We're particularly anxious to receive the hardcover edition of Will Eisner's A CONTRACT WITH GOD. This is a *very* fine book—in my judgement (and that of many of my customers) the finest "straight" work yet done in the graphic story format. And it's an extremely handsome book in the paper format. (Frankly I was concerned that the title might mislead our customers. To an extent, I believe it did. But when they saw the real nature of the book, we had no dificulty in selling it.) We've had many requests for the hardback edition. I hope it's available.

Best wishes,
WONDERWORLD BOOKS

Richard Kyle

† Transcribed by the editor from the original provided by the Ohio State University Library. Reprinted with permission of the author's estate.

MIKE FRIEDRICH

Friedrich is an influential comics editor and writer who published the groundbreaking independent comic *Star*Reach* (1974–79), seeking to provide an alternative for mature readers to underground comix.

To Will Eisner†

STAR*REACH PRODUCTIONS
Box 2328
Berkeley, CA 94702

15 Nov 1978

Dear Will,

I go to bed early, feeling a bit down. I start reading A CONTRACT WITH GOD. I can't put it down. I stay up till past Three A.M.

I wake up this morning with a terrible sore throat and cold. Oy.

Well, Will, there could be nothing further apart than The Bronx, 1930's, and my own life. The immigrants in my family are three or more generations back. I'm a post WWII baby boomer, raised in a very middle class California suburb. Catholic (though not of the oppressive kind). I met my first Jew when I was 18. How much further can I go?

But you're an artist, my man. You make it real, you make it breathe, you make it bleed. You touch me.

A lot of guys, they go from the Bronx to White Plains, they forget. Or worse, they don't forget, but paper it over with A Big House, A Nice Car, More Than I Ever Had. The children of such people are *my* generation, I must deal with them all the time and *their* angers, *their* repressed spirits.

Your book opens a door that perhaps will show the people of my time where some of their parents came from, opening up perhaps new channels of communication and understanding.

For others (and I more number myself among these) you've added new chapters to my proud heritage as an American and as a human being, for now The Bronx lives in me and is part of my life. I can't thank you enough.

* * *

Thanks for sending me this book; it's enriched my life.

Best,
Mike Friedrich

† Transcribed by the editor from the original provided by the Ohio State University Library. Reprinted with permission of Mike Friedrich.

MIKE VALERIO

Valerio would go on to become an award-winning filmmaker, but in the 1970s he was an active member of the burgeoning fan-critic community. *CAPA-alpha* first started publishing in 1964 at the beginning of modern comics fandom, collating various fan-critics' newsletters into a regular fanzine.

Review of *A Contract with God* in *CAPA-alpha* 172 (1979)†

Remember all those great SPIRIT stories that Will Eiser and company did way back when that hardly had the Spirit in them at all? The ones where either the Spirit was the narrator or just a casual observer?

Well, that what this is. A CONTRACT WITH GOD is a collection of four SPIRIT stories without the Spirit. These are not reprints—they are four brandy-new stories by one of the most talented men ever to work in the comic book medium.

The stories in A CONTRACT WITH GOD all revolve around the residents of a tenement—55 Dropsie Avenue in the Bronx—in the Depression years of the 1930's. Despite the cover-claim that this collection is a graphic novel, the four stories are not interlocked in any way other than that they share a common backdrop.

The first story—A CONTRACT WITH GOD—tells of an immigrant Jew who makes a contract with God only to have God go back on his word. With the original contract null and void, the Jew—Frimme Hersh—strays from his old ways of kindness and gentleness and becomes a slum-lord. He attains great wealth through deceit and lying and it is only when he sees his life coming to an end that he attempts to strike up another contract with God. The story of Frimme Hersh is the longest in the collection—and the most touching and thought-provoking.

* * *

If my descriptions of the stories seem a bit thin, that's because they are. I don't want to give away too much of Eisner's fine tales. Unlike his Spirit work, the stories in A CONTRACT WITH GOD are short on plot. This is more than made up for, however, by Eisner's sense of mood and superb characterizations. The residents of 55 Dropsie come alive—if living in a tenement in the 1930's can be called living. The stories are draped in a shadow of despair and hopelessness that works well. When all is said and done, A CONTRACT WITH GOD is a work to ponder.

Eisner's artwork, too, is at least comparable to his old stuff. It is obvious that this work meant a great deal to him and the effort shows. Purists will protest that the Spirit is the definitive work and there can be no argument there. A CONTRACT WITH GOD, however, gives us a different Eisner, an Eisner without his tongue in his cheek, an Eisner who has created four remarkable little tales of tenement life called A CONTRACT WITH GOD.

Do yourselves a favor, friends, and check it out.

† From *CAPA-alpha* 172 (February 1979). Reprinted with permission of Mike Valerio.

JAMES VAN HISE

Van Hise, a popular-culture historian and occasional comics writer, was at this time editor of the influential fanzine *Rocket's Blast Comicollector*, which, like *CAPA-alpha*, traced its origins to 1964. In addition to reviews, columns, and information on collecting comics, *RBCC* regularly featured fan art and comics by individuals who would go on to long careers in comics.

Review of *A Contract with God* (1979)†

This is a book of four stories written and drawn by Will Eisner in a free form comic strip format (panel borders are used as often as not). The stories all center around an area of tenements in the Bronx and concern the people therein as they lived in the 1930s.

The first story, "A Contract With God", is the most ambitious as it tells the story of a man's entire life. The man is Jewish and the story deals with a contract he makes with God (a figurative one, although it seems real enough to him) when he is a child. The man feels the contract has been violated when his daughter dies, whereupon he changes his entire life-style and becomes a business tycoon. At the conclusion he makes another contract with God which he feels cannot be violated this time, whereupon he drops dead of a heart attack. The story seems to do a lot of thrashing around as it attempts to come to grips with this idea. It even has an epilogue which seems to point to life being cyclical. There are contrasts which show that while he lived by the contract he was selfless, while afterwards he became selfish, but this is just the old chestnut of the bitter tycoon who became a success after turning his back on everything but his own desires. The story is apparently supposed to be ironic but it could have done a lot more with the idea than it did.

The other three stories, "The Street Singer", "The Super" and "The Cookalein" are pretty much just slice of life stories and don't have any real solid plot the way "A Contract With God" did.

* * *

Eisner was apparently trying to take the step from comic books into more realistic adult fiction, while at the same time straddling both tracks. The main flaw in this book is that it lacks a true direction. We really don't know what he was trying to say with all of this other than seeing his recreations of life in the depression era tenements. While reading this I had the feeling I was reading the background for events which were probably a lot more interesting. His character portrayals are only sometimes successful and seldom even approach what he achieved in, for instance, the Spirit strip "Ten Minutes" and the character of Freddy.

I know what Eisner was trying to do in this book, and to some degree he is successful, but not to the degree he could have been.

† From *Rocket's Blast Comicollector* 148 (April 1979): 1–2. Reprinted with permission of James Van Hise.

BILL SHERMAN

Sherman was and remains an active fan-critic, first in fanzines and then increasingly for the emerging professional comics, such as *The Comics Journal*.

Review of *A Contract with God* (1979)†

SEPIA SENTIMENT

I had hopes for Will Eisner's first "adult" project, but they weren't very robust ones. All those snippets of recent comic work—the weak one-pagers in Krupp's early SPIRIT title, the slight non-Spirit tales in the recent Krupp series, not to mention the comically out-of-step SNARF cover[1]—seemed to indicate an artist locked in a manner of comic book storytelling that was no longer viable, at least as it related to Eisner's new sense of purpose.

Make no mistake: I love the Spirit. But not when Eisner "modernizes" him and gives us a hard-broiled lesbian P'Gell (*sans* any of her original charm) as a villain like he did in Krupp's SPIRIT #2. I like realistic comics, too. But not when they're consistently tempered with early Hollywood sentimentality.

* * *

A CONTRACT WITH GOD is Eisner's graphic "novel," a series of four stories set in the depression era Bronx. Drawn to fit the format of a 6-by-9 in. book (looks as if Eisner discovered his page limitations as he went along: the first pages look especially gimmicky and weak), Eisner's stories were written with no pre-supposed page limit. ". . . each story was written without regard to space and each was allowed to develop its format from itself," Eisner writes in his introduction. A pity. For say what you will about the restrictiveness of the original "Spirit's" seven-page format, the fact is it forced Eisner into a certain kind of economy. Too much of CONTRACT is bloated. Thus we get six pages of full-panel rain images in the title story where two would suffice, a laughable bit of inconsistent character description in "The Super" that seems to have been written more for sound than sense, illogical full-page panels all over (eg. the poker party panel in "Cookalein"). It's no accident that the two most successful tales are the shortest, "The Super" and "The Street Singer." Flawed as they are, both tales have a consistency and singlemindedness that raise them above Eisner's more ambitious—that is to say: pretentious—offerings here.

"Contract" is the worst offender. The story of Frimme Hersh, Hassidic immigrant whose devoutness dissolves on the death of his adopted daughter, "Contract" alternates between the mawkish and the true. (Lamest moment: when Hersh's mistress—after he's renounced the faith to become a landlord—asks with dumb blond tactlessness: "Y'want I should become

† From *CAPA-alpha* 175 (May 1979). Reprinted with permission of Bill Sherman. Notes are by the editor of this Norton Critical Edition.

1. *Snarf* is a rare example of an underground comic that transitioned into a modern alternative comic. First published as a stand-alone by Denis Kitchen in 1969, it was published infrequently until 1990.

Jewish?") Eisner's dealing with the Big Theme here: Man's Presumptuousness in Trying to Dictate to God. But the trappings are too heavy, too obvious. Frimme can't just argue with God, he has to do it in the midst of a furious storm. His mistress can't just be dumb, she has to be wide-eyed and cartoony next to Frimme's *angst*-wrinkled old man. The intent, it seems, was to achieve a sort of operatic *Faust* feel,[2] but it doesn't come off. Eisner keeps undercutting it with flashes of realism, with inconstant art.

DENNIS O'NEIL

O'Neil was an influential comics writer and editor, at the time most famous for his work with artist Neal Adams on *Green Lantern/Green Arrow* and *Batman*.

Review of *A Contract with God* (1979)†

When I agreed to do this review, I planned to cheat. Instead of actually assessing *A Contract with God*, I thought I'd pay tribute to the astonishing anomaly that is its author, Will Eisner: the creator of a self-described "middle class hero" who has himself been a professional nonconformist; the rebel who has prospered working within that epitome of the Establishment, the Department of Defense; the hard-working, unpretentious deadline-meeter who, nonetheless, produced his genre's best art. There is a major critical work to be written about Will Eisner and I hoped to use this space to begin sketching at it, and, incidentally, to confess my own admiration and envy for the man. (I have tried on at least 20 different occasions to write a "Will Eisner story" and haven't yet come close.)

But I wanted to avoid dealing with *A Contract with God* because I didn't think I'd like it and I didn't care to publicly dump on a continuing source of enjoyment and inspiration; better to avoid the issue. I'd glimpsed the book at a lecture Eisner had given a week prior to publication and I wasn't impressed. It seemed that not even Eisner had accomplished what comics professionals are forever talking about: transcending the limitations of commercial comic books and using the medium for something other than simplistic morality tales, baby science fiction and, in the case of the undergrounds, scatological satire—which are the things comics have been at their best, and not to be scoffed at. Still, isn't there *anything* else?

The answer is yes, as of the publication of *A Contract with God*. After reading the book five times, I am convinced it needs no apologia. Goethe's[1] critical dictum remains the best: the critic can only decide what the

2. Based on the legends that gathered around the historical Johann Georg Faust (c. 1480–c. 1541), an alchemist and magician who traveled widely during the German Renaissance and who was said to have made a pact with the Devil for knowledge. Many versions of the Faust myth have been told in literary history, including Christopher Marlowe's play *The Tragical History of Doctor Faustus* (c. 1604) and Johann Wolfgang von Goethe's play *Faust* (1808–1832).

† From *The Comics Journal* 46 (May 1979): 52–53. Reprinted with permission of the publisher. Notes are by the editor of this Norton Critical Edition.

1. Johann Wolfgang von Goethe (1749–1832) was a German playwright, poet, novelist, and scientist. Although his contributions are numerous, he is perhaps most famous for his novel *The Sorrows of Young Werther* (1774) and his play *Faust* (see previous note).

artist was trying to accomplish, and whether he succeeded. By that standard, *A Contract with God* is a near-masterpiece.

However, for me to appreciate Eisner's achievement I had to resolve two problems—problems which may bother you, too. The first was a preconceived notion of what a comic *is*: I've written over 700 comic book stories and read tens of thousands and so, despite pretentions to perception and objectivity that accompany a reasonably fancy degree in Eng. Lit., I pick up a comic with reflexive anticipations. Action, movement, extravagant locales, a certain kind of pacing and—may the ghost of Henry James[2] forgive me—a broad drama of crime and punishment: those are my expectations from anything with pictures and word balloons, and they are catered to very little in *Contract*. The second difficulty is that, being from the Irish-Catholic Midwest, I am largely unfamiliar with the Jewish milieu that forms Will Eisner's memories.

What he has given us here are those memories, as tales, and realized in a fusion of image and copy. They are simple and they are harsh: there are no easy morals to be gotten from them. The Good Guys don't win and the Bad Guys don't lose because there are no good guys and bad guys. Instead, there are lonely, frightened, and ambitious people, immigrants seeking relief from poverty, despair, and the dread that, unhappy as the present is, the future may be worse. A man remembering in that way is not likely to depict heroes and villains; rather, he will be compassionate toward everyone, winner and loser alike, and compassion is the pervading, unstated theme of Eisner's work. His sympathetic recognition of human frailty and folly is most evident in his representations of sex: not the smirking T and A prurience that usually passes for the erotic in comics (and in many other arenas of popular culture) but the pleasures of the body as a palliative for misery and as manifestations of a raging libido—performed, incidentally, by individuals not particularly beautiful.

Of course, such autobiographical reminiscence is common in modern writing; it is the raw material of the stories of Bernard Malamud, Philip Roth, and Isaac Singer,[3] to name three of dozens of Jewish writers. But Eisner's presentation *is* unique: with the fusion of image and copy I mentioned earlier, he mimics the operations of memory itself, perhaps as well as they can be imitated on paper. The prologue which relates the background of the Bronx tenement that is the setting of the stories and a brief digression explaining the plight of Jews in Tzarist Russia correspond to the gestalt of the consciousness—information a bright child would acquire from his environment without anyone specifically teaching it. The scenes he could not actually be remembering, the scenes he was not present at, are the adult's attempts to make whole his childhood recollections, to fill in the gaps, a process akin to psychoanalysis. Eisner writes in the past tense, a departure from normal comics technique; these are, after all, past events. Yet his dialogue, presented in the familiar balloons,

2. American author (1843–1916), who helped guide the novel from realism into the modernist movement of the 20th century.

3. Isaac Bashevis Singer (1903–1991), Polish-born American writer, who wrote in Yiddish and was a central figure in the Yiddish literary movement in the first half of the 20th century. *Bernard Malamud*: American writer (1914–1986), who played a central role in the renaissance of Jewish American literature in the 20th century. *Philip Roth*: American writer (1933–2018), who along with writers such as Saul Bellow and Bernard Malamud helped bring Jewish American fiction into prominence.

is present tense; one remembers words in the mode they were spoken. There is no contradiction here: Eisner is using the resources of the language exactly as a novelist uses them, to combine past and present into a single experience, and with the added resource of his artwork.

The pictures are Eisner's special contribution and what lifts the book into its own category. I've heard casual readers complain that Eisner's people are "cartoony," compared to his realistic city-scapes, and in his comic strips, the contrast does take getting used to (though it is worth the effort); this may explain why his Spirit comics have not been as commercially successful as lesser, more conventional strips. However, in *A Contract with God*, the exaggerated features of the characters work for the whole. The child in us does not remember the adults we met as they actually were; he remembers them as archetypes—as caricatures, almost. He remembers them as Eisner draws them. Similarly, we do not recall every detail of the houses and streets we inhabited as children, as anyone who has ever visited a childhood neighborhood after a long absence will testify: we recall *impressions*, the sort of mnemonic sketches Eisner draws. The Bronx of *A Contract with God* is much less precisely rendered than the Central City of *The Spirit*, and that is surely a conscious decision of a thinking artist intent on introducing us to his private, interior experience instead of reproducing the world as most of us see it. Eisner even puts the ink the book is printed in to his artistic uses: it is sepia brown, a close approximation to the monochrome psychologists say is the color of dreams—and memories.

I realize I'm making *A Contract with God* seem very complicated. It isn't. What Eisner has accomplished needs to be seen; once it is, everything is plain, and no explanation or elaboration is necessary.

R. C. HARVEY

Harvey is a comics critic, scholar, and cartoonist, and a pioneer in the field of comics studies with books such as *The Art of the Funnies* (1994) and *The Art of the Comic Book* (1996). In the 1970s, he regularly wrote for *RBCC* and *The Comics Journal*.

On *A Contract with God* and the Graphic Novel†

If the graphic novel is the future for the comic strip, then it doubtless ought to build on and develop the essence of the medium.

The technical hallmarks of comic strip art (or "sequential art," as Will Eisner calls it; probably a better name, actually)—the things about it that make it unique—are speech balloons and narrative breakdown.

Speech balloons breathe into comic strips their peculiar life. In all other graphic representations, characters are doomed to wordless posturing and pantomime. In comic strips they speak. And their speeches are

† From *Rocket's Blast Comicollector* 150 (December 1979): 57–60. Reprinted with permission of the author. Robert C. Harvey has authored more than a dozen books of comics history and cartoonist biography, and at his website, RCHarvey.com, he posts *Rants & Raves*, a twice-monthly magazine of comics news and reviews, cartooning history and lore. Notes are by the editor of this Norton Critical Edition.

made in the same mode as the rest of the strip: the graphic, visual, mode. We see and read the words of the characters just as we see the characters themselves and "read" their actions. Films are made in a hybrid mode—audio-visual. Comic strips are all visual, a seamless optic exercise.

Moreover, the inclusion of speech balloons within the pictures gives the words and pictures concurrence—the life-like illusion that the characters we see are speaking even as we see them, just as we simultaneously hear and see people in life.

If speech balloons give comic strips their peculiar life, then narrative breakdown gives that life duration, an existence beyond a moment, Narrative breakdown is to a comic strip what time is to life. In fact, "timing"—pace as well as duration—is the second of the unique ingredients of comic strip art. The sequential arrangement of panels cannot help but create time in some general way, but skillful manipulation of the sequencing can control time and use it to dramatic advantage. The sequencing of panels controls the amount and order of information divulged as well as the order and duration of events. Manipulating these aspects of a story creates pace, suspense, mood, and the like.

Ordinary mainstream literary prose does all of this, too; comic strips differ in that the pictures as well as the words manipulate time. For instance, action can be speeded up by sequences of pictures in which the scene shifts rapidly from panel to panel. Whatever the graphic novel is to be (or is), it seems to be that it must incorporate these two essential aspects of comic strip art if it is to be of the same species as comic strip art. The graphic novel may have other characteristics as well, but speech balloons and narrative breakdown seem to be vital ingredients. Without those traits, the graphic novel will be simply something else—another kind of graphic story, surely, but not of the same order as the comic strip.

Steranko's CHANDLER (1976),[1] for example, is called a graphic novel, but it doesn't meet the criterion I've mentioned. For all its brilliant visual effects, the pace of the story is controlled by the prose that runs in uniform columns under the pictures. The pictures create the story's mood, but they add no new information to the story: they simply illustrate the narrative. Although CHANDLER's theme is a mature one, in form and function the book is no different from the average illustrated children's book. It does not represent a new art form—or a new development in the art of the comic strip.

In Will Eisner's A CONTRACT WITH GOD we have something else again. To begin with, the collection of four stories delves into themes much more serious than CHANDLER. With their intimate glimpses into the private and sometimes seamy lives of New York tenement dwellers of the 1930s, the stories capture with bittersweet nostalgia the spirit of threadbare existence and the pitifully exalted albeit doomed aspirations that often flower briefly if vainly in such barren soil.

In the lead story that gives the book its title, Eisner tells a story with several layers of meaning. On one level, it may be a parable of the

1. Jim Steranko (b. 1938) is an American cartoonist, one of the most influential comic book artists of the 1960s and '70s. His experimental visual novel, *Chandler: Red Tide*, in a digest format, was not well embraced by the comics community because of its refusal to follow comic conventions such as word balloons.

Jewish experience—the history of a "chosen people" whose "contract with God" has not, through much of that history, produced very often the kind of material benefit that one would expect for a "select" group. But there are deeper religious ramifications to this simple tale. "Is not all religion a contract between man—and God?" asks one character. The implication of Eisner's story is that however sincerely men are compelled to draw up such contracts, the documents are wholly one-sided—signed by only the human parties to the agreement. As such, the contracts are scarcely binding to a seemingly indifferent and arbitrary God. But they remain, as Eisner shows, a powerful and therefore genuine force in human affairs.

Eisner's book modifies the form of the comic strip to fit the book format. Depending upon the narrative need, some pages are single panels in the unfolding story; others are composed of 4–6 panels. Narrative prose falls within the pictures, and the characters speak in the customary speech balloons. Pace is controlled by both pictures and words—as in the ordinary comic strip. Eisner preserves the essential nature of the art of the comic strip in his graphic novel, but he injects no new and different element. (Not that he should—unless the graphic novel is supposed to embrace and develop some new facet of the comic strip medium. And that's still a question.)

I'm still not sure what a graphic novel is. If it is an expanded comic book, we probably can't find a better example than Eisner's book. If it is to be something more than a new way of coupling words and pictures, that new way must preserve the essential nature of comic strip art.

But whatever answer is to emerge, we'll doubtless be in a better position to see it clearly when we come to the next milestone.

PENNY KAGANOFF

Before becoming a senior editor at Simon & Schuster, Kaganoff was an editor and frequent reviewer at *Publisher's Weekly*, a trade magazine targeting librarians, booksellers, and others involved in making buying decisions in publishing.

Review of *Life Force* (1988)†

Beginning in the 1970s, Eisner, a dominant figure in comic strips since the '30s, extended his meditation in language and pictures to such graphic novels as *A Contract with God*. Here, he interweaves the lives of Jewish and Italian immigrants and WASP pariahs in a Bronx tenement during the Depression. The emotional oscillations that Eisner details—from wretched despair to giddy exuberance—are fueled by his characters' struggles to escape their ritualized poverty and the self-deceptions that social desperation breeds. Eisner is best at portraying the stunted immigrant world in Depression-era New York, but his characters tend toward ethnic stereotypes and their responses to life are reduced to

† From *Publishers Weekly* 233.12 (1988): 61. Reprinted with permission of the publisher through Copyright Clearance Center.

sentimentality. The death, despair and venality his protagonists suffer become easy scaffolds on which to hang banal treatments of hope, dreams fulfilled, love and will to live. The drawings are subtle and variegated; as always Eisner is a master of the pictorial, but this problematic work highlights the difficulties inherent in utilizing comics as a medium for serious interpretations of life.

DAVID SCHREINER

Schreiner was a longtime comics editor, first in the world of underground comix in the 1970s and then at Kitchen Sink Press from 1983 to 1993. After leaving Kitchen Sink, Schreiner continued to work with Eisner as his personal editor until Schreiner's death in 2003.

Notes from the Perimeter†

When I proposed a look at *A Life Force* shortly after its final installment in *Will Eisner's Quarterly* 5, he was skeptical. I strongly suspect that he consented to talk about the novel only because it had already been published.

In the long telephone conversations, we discussed structure, plot, influences and characters. Eisner was purposely vague when we discussed the themes of *A Life Force;* he continues to feel that what the novel is trying to say is something for a reader to decide.

Which is as it should be.

In certain parts of this article, I've given elements of a positive review to the novel. Eisner felt uncomfortable about this, too, feeling it could be interpreted as self-serving because it appears in a magazine bearing his name.

Those of ungenerous spirit might feel that way, but I'm not going to worry about them. The *Quarterly* is an appropriate place to begin a serious discussion of his novel, because the magazine appeals to the reader who is serious about Eisner's work in particular and the potential of the comics medium in general.

If comic books, or the comics medium, or sequential art is ever to grow beyond "two units destroying each other," works that attempt to stretch the envelope of assumed conventions must be accepted, supported, analyzed, *read*. A handful of artists—Gilbert Hernandez, Art Spiegelman, Harvey Pekar, Larry Gonick, Will Eisner, a few others—are making this attempt. If the form is to live, chances must be taken by writers and artists, and by readers.

In Eisner's case, it is noble, challenging work, not without its problems and failures, but also with its rewards—for artist and reader.

A man plods down an alley. A carpenter, he is out of work in the midst of the depression of the 1930s. He has vagrant dreams of immortality achieved through his work, but he is aging, and for him, work seemingly no longer exists.

He clutches his chest and sinks to the ground.

† From "Notes from the Perimeter: Commentary about *A Life Force*," *Will Eisner's Quarterly* 6 (1985): 31–35, 37–38. Reprinted with permission of the author's estate. The illustrations have been omitted. Notes are by the editor of this Norton Critical Edition.

Down there, he comes eye to body with a cockroach, shaken out of a carpet from two stories up. Man tells bug about their shared struggle for survival, and about the long odds both face these tough days.

Only man, man says, is afflicted with the question of "why." Why life, why live? Only man ponders the existence of God, asking the old question: who created Whom, or Who created whom? He tells the roach that the meaning of life, if any, is only a guess.

After saving the roach from the hobnailed boots of a passerby, at the considerable risk of his own life, the man is called to supper by his wife. He struggles to his feet, climbs up the tenement steps to his apartment at 55 Dropsie Avenue, the Bronx, and in answer to his wife's question about his day, says, "Today? Today, I saved the life of a cockroach."

So begins *A Life Force*. Will Eisner's latest graphic novel, which completed its serialization in *Will Eisner's Quarterly* No. 5. The man in the alley is Jacob Shtarkah, the central character in the novel, and about the farthest creation from a conventional comics "hero" or "antihero" as you can imagine.

Jacob Shtarkah might best be described as dumpy. The sagging of age is progressing relentlessly over his body; he has recurring heart problems; he is not—and never has been—what you would call handsome.

In the novel, he is saddled with an inescapable feeling that life has passed him by. He complains about this to himself and others at length. Life has been hard for Jacob Shtarkah.

Yet the man holds his dreams, and they feed his dim hope for a better future. Jacob doesn't seem to be a person who would ever seriously consider suicide, unlike one of the other characters in the book. Jacob is a survivor.

"When Jacob talks to the cockroach in the alley, he is speaking my thoughts," Eisner said recently in a discussion of *A Life Force*. "I wanted to draw some parallels between man's and the roach's survival. My objective was to present this debate Jacob has with himself to the reader. All of the things expressed in the novel are for the reader to decide. It's in the nature of an intellectual exercise."

Eisner goes beyond simple explication of plot to address questions about the human condition. Instead of merely showing us the "how" of a story. Eisner goes on to ask us about the "why" of life. By doing this, he requires more participation than a reader is normally prepared to give a comic book.

He asks us to think, and not only about the eternal verities. He requires us to fill in certain gaps about relationships in the story. He gives some background, but he asks the reader to imagine the Great Depression and its effects. While some of his audience may be all too familiar with that time, it's a good bet that the majority are not. And he asks us to draw much of the psychology and motivations of his characters from the impressions he gives of them.

Eisner points the direction, but we pick our own way through.

* * *

The economic upheaval of the 1930s spurred social upheaval both in the United States and abroad. The depression sped the growth of the labor movement in the United States. It also facilitated fascism and communism and brought to the surface anti-Semitic feelings. The latter engulfed Europe, and especially Germany, but it also smeared the United States. Eisner deals with all of this in *A Life Force*.

In *Quarterly* 3's episode, a teenager named Willie eschews the call of worldwide unity under the Red banner by staying at home to eat his mother's soup. Earlier, Willie had helped plan a mass demonstration in which an organizer from Moscow (he resembles Stalin) directed that young women with babies position themselves in front of the pickets, and take the brunt of the action when professional agitators provoked the police.

In 1929, Moscow had decided that no compromises or patient take overs of capitalist societies were needed, as obviously, capitalism was in its death throes. The Comintern[1] set a deliberate policy of violent confrontation.

In the early 1930s, the workers' rights to organize unions and to strike without reprisal were finally recognized. The labor movement was indeed a force to be reckoned with as desperately poor skilled and unskilled laborers at last found their cause being met with sympathy by the public at large, and by the government.

Organized crime saw this burgeoning movement as a potential gold mine, as it surely was, and began making their own violent inroads into this area of social progress.

All of this set the stage for much hysteria and confusion.

The labor movement in this country was often called communistic, and while there were communist organizers and even the take over of some of the unions, they were not so strong as management figures and certain orators liked to claim. The communists became, in fact, a convenient excuse for industrialists to resist union organizing with violence. Even after the unions won the right to organize through government legislation, it was not unheard of for pitched battles to occur at struck plants. Usually these battles involved clubs, bottles and fists, but in one famous case at a Ford plant in Michigan, guns wielded by hired management "goons" came into play. These tactics served to gain the unions more sympathy.

Criminal dabblings in the unions also led to some take overs, a few allegedly still extant. Gangster-run unions typically were organized to milk as much money as possible from members, while extorting as much as possible through "protection" from business owners. Eliminating the thugs from the ranks of organized labor was a much tougher proposition than eliminating the communists. The process continues today.

In 1934, the time *A Life Force* deals with, none of these distinctions were generally known. The idealistic Willie sees an egalitarian union as part of a united worker front marching toward a better world. His father sees union members as the bunch of hoodlums who busted up his shop and crippled Uncle Max. It was quite possible for them to come into conflict while not knowing that they were arguing about two different matters.

Eisner's chapter called "The Revolutionary" is autobiographical, at least as far as the events facing Willie are concerned: to leave his home, possibly forever, and become a Marxist sign painter with Ben; or to remain in the bosom of the family, where there is love and a bit of security.

1. Short for Communist International; the Comintern was an international organization advocating communism in the years following the Russian Revolution.

Willie is not in the line of great political activists who were never concerned with daily living. Especially in times of change and instability, the reality of getting through the day must be faced. It was typical of the time, Eisner says, for people to be faced with the choices facing Willie.

* * *

On background: "I'd be very disappointed if readers took *A Life Force* to be a Jewish novel. I don't consider it that at all. There are Jewish characters and situations because that is my background. That is how I grew up. But the things I'm talking about here are universal experiences. They may grow out of a Jewish experience, but everyone is concerned with what I'm talking about here. Survival and questioning the meaning of living are not unique to the Jews."

* * *

On working readers: "I used shorthand in the book. A graphic novel uses fixed images within a given plot, but within that, I'm asking the reader to stop and think while he or she is going along with me. The reader in this particular book has to be somewhat more sophisticated than the youngster who's had a very limited life experience. The action between Jacob and his wife is really done in shorthand. The reader has to supply the immediate meanings between the relationships. I'm not allowing the reader any choice in the matter of how these characters look, but when Rifka and Jacob interact, I'm asking the reader to supply a certain amount of imagination."

* * *

A Life Force is a work that gives the impression of a life going on for the characters outside the panel walls. You get the feeling that these people keep going on about their business after Eisner averts his gaze.

* * *

What happens to Willie, the sign painter, after this period? We know in a general way what happened to Eisner. But what were the personal choices that led him to choose the career he did? * * *

A fact about the novel is that none of the major characters are total creatures of good and evil. Jacob is one example. He is dissatisfied with his life, and he has good reason to be.

Yet, it's hard to feel pity for him because he's complaining all the time about his dissatisfaction. While self-pity is almost never immediately recognizable in oneself, it's always instantly apparent in someone else. Self-pity and griping in others irritates us; for one thing, it breaks our concentration on our own self-pity and griping. Jacob's whining keeps the reader from plunging into despair over his—and let's make no mistake about this—extremely hard lot in life. Jacob has enough despair for reader and character alike.

But Jacob's attitudes reflect universal human traits. Self-absorption is a fact of life. We *are* always dissatisfied. We want *more*. Or maybe just *different*. At the end of the novel, Jacob is still dissatisfied, even though his material life has improved considerably. Such is life.

* * *

On bitterness: "Sometimes my work may convey a sense of bitterness on the outside, but really it's not. You can't come out of the scrimmage of life without some aches and bruises that you refer to once in awhile. Looking back, you ask 'why did that have to happen?' You see people whose lives have been twisted and torn apart, and you wonder why that had to happen. It's a start of a philosophy. As far as bitterness is concerned, I don't really know what that means. When I started *A Life Force,* I began with the question 'Are we no different from the cockroach?', but by the time I finished it, I answered my own question and I don't think I left a bitter taste."

* * *

On influences: "Both *A Life Force* and *A Contract With God* are influenced mostly by the theatre. I see them as a kind of live theatre. Many people identify my work with the motion picture. *The Spirit* is always equated to films, and there's no doubt some influence involved, because films were part of my early visual and literary nutrition.

"But I was always fascinated with theatre. The lighting in these works is theatrical, and that's not too far away from life experiences. As a city dweller, you live in a kind of stage set. Lighting comes from above. Your perspective vision is either from above or from below, or with converging lines of perspective going upward or downward. There isn't too much that you see on a long horizon.

"Artists see light and set their stages under the influence of where they grew up. Early environment is important. I don't think in terms of large panoramas, as an artist who grew up in a rural area might.

"Influences are funny things. In the comics business, that word generally means stealing or swiping. Every thing influences me. Watching WPA [Works Project Administration] theatre in lofts during the depression influenced me. New York and Florida influence me.

"You generally pick from things that are well done in other areas and try to introduce them into what you're doing. When I was in the Art Students League,[2] I'd go over to the ballet on 59th Street. It was a way I had of learning action and anatomy in motion. Pantomime. There's rhythm, movement, timing.

"In *A Life Force,* I was thinking of the structure of *War and Peace.*[3] That was done on a monumental, historical landscape, yet it dealt with individual lives, all interlocked. I didn't sit down with the firm intention of imitating Tolstoy. But if I had never read *War and Peace,* I might not have understood that it could be done."

* * *

There are two problems associated with graphic novels that concern Eisner. One has to do with the medium itself. The other has to do with the audience.

An advantage an artist has in graphic narrative is that the art can eliminate much of a setting's description. When Jacob walks down the alley at

2. Founded in 1875, this educational institution has served as a training ground for generations of artists, including prominent cartoonists such as Eisner, Otto Soglow, and Jules Feiffer.
3. Novel by the Russian author Leo Tolstoy (1828–1910) set against the backdrop of the Napoleonic Wars and the impact of the French invasion of Russia on five families.

the beginning of the book, Eisner spends no time at all with word descriptions of buildings soaring in the background, the lattice-work fire escapes coming down to the street, the debris on the ground. There is no narration about Jacob's shuffling, defeated walk, his look of a man punched in the stomach. It's in the art.

There is a flip side. "Visuals are precise," Eisner said. "If you draw a man with a fat nose, it leaves very little room for the reader to conjecture what the size of his nose is.

"In text, you're creating word analogies. Writers deal with allusions in the sense that they can, through dialogue and description, evoke images and feelings which the reader can embellish in his or her own mind.

"We have two mediums which are not necessarily meant to replace each other. Visuals can't entirely replace words; they can replace descriptions and actions, often in exciting ways.

"I've had a problem with stereotypes in this line of work. I got some complaints from readers that Rabbi Bensohn is a stereotype. They wanted to see a different type of person. I got some feedback from one of my students, who thought the Italians were portrayed through stereotypes.

"The fact is, this medium deals in stereotypes. It is a big obstacle, because you have to portray something visually, and the reader is cut off from deciding what these people look like. It is a continuing struggle to break through this inherent problem."

The other quandary for graphic novels or works in Eisner's mold is that while the reader doesn't have to provide a visual image for each character, she has to draw on experience to get the full impact of the novel.

"The reader doesn't have to contribute much if I'm showing two mutants tearing each other apart. There is really nothing to relate to there, except for a personal satisfaction in seeing two people or two units destroy each other.

"It's another matter in a novel attempting to deal with reality. The audience is there somewhere, it's just a matter of reaching them. I'm not able to reach them yet in the comic book stores."

* * *

Each time Eisner approaches the serious graphic storytelling form, he takes a few more steps in his personal quest to break new ground in sequential art. His first graphic novel. *A Contract With God,* owes much to his *Spirit* stories in that they are short, episodic pieces, each self-contained, each with its own plot, climax and conclusion.

A Life Force is more in the nature of a true novel in that the major characters appear in each segment, there are a series of little climaxes which spin the characters' lives forward but do not leave them in a position where they either live happily ever after, or die miserable, grimy deaths. The plot leads to a climax and then a conclusion of sorts, but there are other conclusions down the road for all these characters.

Life goes on.

"*A Contract With God* was basically written with a *Grand Hotel*[4] scheme in mind. The tenement was used as a vehicle in which the people were

4. A 1932 film starring a large cast of Hollywood celebrities. Various stories occur simultaneously within the world of the Grand Hotel.

living, a microcosm of life, an ant hill of some kind. The original title was *A Tenement in the Bronx,* and it was really built around the superintendent, who appeared in each episode. I wrote each chapter independently, and they were very, very clearly defined in my mind.

"*A Life Force* was much more unified. One of the problems I faced there was that the characters took on lives of their own—as they often do—and sometimes I was forced to change the story outline because the characters just wouldn't perform the way I originally intended."

* * *

On his graphic novels: "It must be understood that I'm trying, perhaps presumptuously, to achieve a literary level—not in a dictionary sense, but in a broader sense. I realize that I'm dealing with a medium that has some limitations. I'm constantly reaching to the perimeters of this medium, and I haven't yet found the total point of no return. I think every time I go to work on something. I find that I have pushed it a little farther, and there's always more yet to go."

GARY GROTH

Groth is the co-founder of Fantagraphic Books and editor-in-chief of *The Comics Journal.* As a critic, Groth has long devoted himself to proving that comics can be art—and to demanding that comics live up to that expectation.

A Second Opinion†

Will Eisner is, given his stature, one of the most problematic artistic figures in the history of comics. Universally acknowledged as a master of the form, belonging in anyone's pantheon of great comics artists alongside such figures as Carl Barks, Harvey Kurtzman, and R. Crumb,[1] he is also the most compromised and qualified member of the elite.

There are, it seems to me, two Will Eisners: the populist who defends mass-market junk and the elitist who champions comics as a form of literature; a shrewd businessman who prides himself on dealmaking and market savvy and an artist whose aspirations rise above the marketplace; an artist who uses his (and others') gifts to package utilitarian products-to-order and an artist who strives to explicate the human condition.

These aren't glib dichotomies, the kind of dualities that could be dug up by scrutinizing anyone's career long enough: I believe Eisner's twin alliance to commerce and art has had a consistently deleterious affect on his art. Prior to *The Spirit,* Eisner ran what was basically a sweat shop

† From *The Comics Journal* 119 (January 1988): 3–7. Reprinted with permission of the publisher. Notes are by the editor of this Norton Critical Edition.

1. Robert Crumb (b. 1943), American cartoonist and the most influential figure of the underground comix movement of the 1960s and '70s. *Carl Barks:* American cartoonist and painter (1901–2000), best known for his work as the primary artist for Donald Duck comic books from 1942 to 1966. Although he worked anonymously throughout most his career, he was identified and tracked down by fans in the early '60s. *Harvey Kurtzman:* American cartoonist (1924–1993) and editor of several influential satirical magazines, including *Mad* and *Help*!

with Jerry Iger that cranked out comics pages in volume for comics publishers, which was basically an exploitive adjunct to publishers who were well-known as exploiters of skill. *The Spirit* was created in 1940 at the request of some financiers who wanted to produce a comic strip newspaper supplement. Eisner has often said that *The Spirit* was an artistic compromise. The comics supplement had to appeal to a wide, largely middle-class readership, so the Spirit needed a mask and a costume of sorts so as to imitate the prevalent comic book icons of the time, and the supplement had to truck in "action, adventure, suspense." Eisner took pride in his work and wanted to do the best he could (or the best he could get away with, which I believe, later in his career, became one and the same), so for his inspiration he avoided serious literature of the time—which was celebrating a revolution of socially committed realism in the hands of such authors as Dreiser, Norris, Farrell,[2] and others—and went straight to Hollywood schmaltz. His femme fatales were straight out of Jean Harlow/Veronica Lake/Lauren Bacall.[3] The brush work imitated *film noir*.[4] The sentiment belonged to Warner Brothers. It was a shrewd strategy for the time; in fact, it was probably the only strategy an intelligent artist seeking a degree of autonomy could pursue, given the cultural and artistic circumstances. Still, there is evidence that such pragmatic eagerness to compromise with the dictates of the marketplace, if such it was (we will never know for sure) has affected his vision as an artist.

The Spirit stories were great fun, but at what point did great fun turn into a major literary experience? If the old *Spirit* stories are considered classics—and the pedantic overkill accompanying each story in Kitchen Sink's *Spirit* reprint series insists that they are—Eisner's new work from *A Contract With God* to his latest, *The Building*, are considered classics-in-the-making. In fact, no other American author—not Bellow, Roth, Vidal, Mailer, Capote, Styron,[5] or anyone else—can expect the unanimous prostrate critical reception that routinely greets each new Eisner book. If Eisner were to write his name 500 times on a chalkboard. Don Thompson would give him one of his schoolmarmish As, and

2. James T. Farrell (1904–1979), once-popular Irish-American author, best known for his Studs Lonigan trilogy. *Dreiser*: Theodore Dreiser (1871–1945), American novelist and journalist, a prominent figure in the naturalist movement in American literature. *Norris:* Frank Norris (1870–1902), American novelist and journalist, also a prominent figure in the naturalist movement.
3. *Jean Harlow*: American actress (1911–1937) and a leading Hollywood sex symbol in the 1930s. *Veronica Lake*: American actress (1922–1973), whose career was prominent in the 1940s, especially in film noir (see following note). On Lauren Bacall, see note 4 on p. 211.
4. A subgenre of crime film that came into popularity in the 1940s and '50s, characterized by low-key lighting and morally ambiguous characters who have wandered from the straight-and-narrow.
5. William Styron (1925–2006), American novelist and essayist, author of the controversial, Pulitzer Prize–winning historical novel *The Confessions of Nat Turner* (1967). In his final decades he wrote extensively about his struggles with depression. *Bellow*: Saul Bellow (1915–2005), Canadian-American writer, who along with authors such as Malamud and Roth (see note 3 on p. 237) helped bring prominent attention to Jewish American fiction. *Vidal*: Gore Vidal (1925–2012), American novelist, essayist, and critic, known for his willingness to engage in provocation and debate with some of the most prominent authors and public figures of his day. *Mailer*: Norman Mailer (1923–2007), American novelist, journalist, and essayist, who served as a key figure in the New Journalism school that would ultimately take shape as what is now known as creative nonfiction. *Capote*: Truman Capote (1924–1984), American novelist, screenwriter, playwright, and essayist, perhaps most remembered today for his nonfiction novel *In Cold Blood* (1966).

Dale Luciano[6] would proclaim it "a major new work by an established master of the form."

* * *

The elements of Eisner's *Spirit* that were acceptable in that context have become an obstacle to the serious aims in Eisner's more "mature" work. The sentimentality that "humanized" the *Spirit* stories was offset by the humor: in Eisner's new work there is no room for humor, only sentimentality. When all this Hollywood schmaltziness is placed in a serious, indeed stridently "literary" endeavor, it merely becomes obnoxious.

* * *

It's always a little dangerous and perhaps a little foolish to speculate as to why the life's work of an artist takes the trajectory it does, but few comics artists have offered us as long a career as Eisner's, and few artists' careers have shown as consistent a pattern to them as Eisner's. Ultimately, it's a chicken-or-egg question, but I should like to venture that Eisner was deeply scarred by the early comics industry's totalitarian money ethic that was hostile to meaningful artistic considerations or the intellectual and spiritual needs of its profession. Certainly Eisner tried to walk a tight rope, but one cannot do this for decades at a time and remain unaffected by it. If artists with talent succumb to the overwhelming climate of junk-making *today*, what must the pressures have been like in Eisner's time? Smothering, I'd say. Cartoonists of Eisner's generation (Milton Caniff is a good example) pride themselves on being entertainment merchants; they talk eagerly of pleasing their clients, pleasing their publisher, pleasing their editor, pleasing their audience. To this generation, art served the needs of commerce, and this attitude was institutionalized into an ethic.

This ethic is consistently followed throughout Eisner's career. After *The Spirit*, Eisner founded American Visuals, a commercial art house that went on to secure a contract with the U.S. Army to produce *P.S.* magazine, a monthly instructional periodical (propaganda organ) for Army personnel. Part of Eisner's contribution was to design strips that attempted, in Eisner's words, "to produce 'attitude conditioning'"—a phrase that surely couldn't have existed before this century. (Eisner modestly refers to his afilliation with *P.S.* as "a success story.") He continued to attempt to condition attitudes throughout the Viet Nam war; all such instruction had to cater to the (low) educational level and cultural prejudices of the Army management's perception of the average GI. Eisner had become an education merchant, but the same rules applied: pleasing a client.

The new client is Literature, so the schmaltz and sentimentality take on a solemnity, the characters become Symbols imbued with a higher meaning, and Theme takes the place of attitude conditioning. Eisner's client has always been someone or something outside of himself, whereas the truly independent artist knows that the only client worth following is oneself.

6. American comics critic, who wrote frequently for the *Comics Journal* in the 1980s and '90s. *Don Thompson*: American comics critic and historian (1935–1994), and a founding figure in the development of modern fandom.

EDDIE CAMPBELL

As a cartoonist, Campbell has collaborated on such important works as *From Hell* (with Alan Moore) and also devoted himself to a long-running autobiographical comic series. He is also a comics critic and historian.

Genius and How It Got that Way—Part III†

In modern times being "different" is for some reason more important than being "good." Being "derivative" is the most heinous crime an artist, writer, or musician can commit. "At least he tried to do something different" you may hear in defense of the most awful piece of shit. Trying to do it *well* doesn't count for anything anymore. To earn a place in the roll call of great art, one has to introduce a new idea that nobody else thought of—*only* one, because this is also the age of specialization. Art couldn't put its own boot on—Cézanne put it on, Picasso tied the laces, Matisse buffed up the polish on it, and Duchamp[1] took it off again, etc. etc. The neurosis of innovation hovers over the creative world. In the real flesh-and-blood world, however, Laurel and Hardy[2] were comic geniuses because their films were funny and because they're *still* funny over 50 years later. They were "different" only insofar as "good" is different from both "bad" and "indifferent."

In comic books Will Eisner has long been regarded as one of the geniuses of the form, and popular mythology assigns him a specialized area of innovation. It is said that he gave comics all the intricacies of cinematic timing. And when we read Eisner's work now and it seems a little old-fashioned, we might be inclined to think, well, his day of moving and changing and advancing is past. So it is most refreshing to find that even in his heyday his associates found him just the same. Jules Feiffer, who was on Eisner's production team for *The Spirit* in the late '40s: "The others in the office in the early days would talk about how old-fashioned he was and would put down the work as terribly dated." And *those* guys went on to real slick stuff in the '50s which is mostly forgotten. Eisner left comics in the '50s—I think he got caught up in the challenges of being successful at business for its own sake—and came back in the late '70s, totally unmoved and unchanged by the game as it is now. But the man created some of the most engaging reading of the '80s, all of it published by Kitchen Sink. The latest is *Invisible People*—three issues, each a short story in the classic American mold. The first, just to give you a sampling, is about a clothes presser called Pincus Pleatnik, a somewhat

† From *Reflex Magazine* 31 (1992): 60. Reprinted with permission of Eddie Campbell. Notes are by the editor of this Norton Critical Edition.

1. Marcel Duchamp (1887–1968), French artist and writer and a leading figure in the experimental Dada movement. Perhaps his most famous work is *Nude Descending a Staircase, No. 2* (1912), a key exhibit in the 1913 Armory Show, which brought modern art from Europe to the United States. *Cézanne*: Paul Cézanne (1839–1906), French Postimpressionist artist, who paved the way for later modernist movements, such as Cubism. *Picasso*: Pablo Picasso (1881–1973), Spanish artist, who cofounded the Cubist movement and continuously experimented with new styles and techniques throughout his career. *Matisse*: Henri Matisse (1869–1954), French artist, whose experiments with color and flattened forms helped break the hold of naturalistic 19th-century art for 20th-century painters.
2. British comedian Stan Laurel (1890–1965) and American Oliver Hardy (1892–1957) were a popular comedy duo. Together they appeared in more than 100 films.

Dickensian[3] approach that only Will Eisner would not be embarrassed to give us: "I set his story during the grey 1930s because it was a time when life seemed easier to define." But these are not the '30s of Steinbeck or Cain;[4] and indeed, Eisner knows he was there and we weren't, so we have to take his word for it. It's all metaphorical anyway. But good. Bloody good, old-fashioned, crafted stories in a medium where "storytelling" is everything and "telling stories" an art kept alive only by a few souls who have refused to be swayed by changing fashion in a world where people have forgotten how to talk to each other.

I actually met the great man once; three years back, we were on the same panel at one of those comics conventions. The theme was comics about real life, and afterwards I spoke to Eisner and promised to send a copy of my book when it came out a couple of months later. Well, I almost put the book in an envelope, then I thought, aw, the great Will Eisner won't want to feel obligated to read my stupid little book, so I never sent it. But three years on, occasionally when I'm a few glasses of wine to the good, I picture Will out there in Florida going down to his mailbox at the end of the garden every day to see if Eddie's book's arrived yet.

Invisible People—my favorite read this month and another month maybe several years later, etc.

RON EVRY

A Quilt in the Bronx†

Look, this book is the reason you read comics, OK? Now go out and buy it, read it, then come back and read the rest of this. I'll wait.

Back already? Good. Here we go, then: It is a sign of the vitality of the comic book art form that a man who helped define what a comic book was in the medium's earliest days is still pushing the boundaries of what it can be today. Will Eisner's *Dropsie Avenue: The Neighborhood* achieves a complexity of structure that deserves detailed examination and analysis. Even a cursory examination of it reveals that Eisner's book works on multiple levels, and repeated readings show that apparently simple themes and plot lines nest within each other deeply.

For example, some of the characters come and go quickly, giving the misleading impression that they are not very well rounded. This is misleading. Actually, the main character is Dropsie Avenue itself, and its story is told through its relationship with dozens of people over a period of 125 years. Very few characters in comic books have had this detailed a portrait painted, and Eisner's book explores both how Dropsie Avenue affects those individuals and how they in turn affect Dropsie Avenue,

3. Referencing the style and themes of the English novelist Charles Dickens (1812–1870), "Dickensian" suggests a focus on often grim conditions facing working-class characters in the modern city and the use of grotesque characters in the service of social critique.
4. Two American writers: John Steinbeck (1902–1962) wrote the Pulitzer Prize–winning novel *The Grapes of Wrath* (1939), which captured the plight of Depression-era America perhaps better than any work from the period. James M. Cain (1892–1977) wrote several important hard-boiled crime novels in the 1930s and '40s, including *The Postman Always Rings Twice* (1934).

† From *Hogan's Alley* 3 (1995): 137–38. Reprinted with permission of Ron Evry.

Eisner explained to *Hogan's Alley*, "I'm weaving a quilt. I'm constantly connecting threads."

A quilt indeed. There are approximately 50 significant characters of varying degrees of importance in the book. The interconnectivity of the stories create a sense of vibrancy, but there are some links among three or four of them that express the deepest themes.

The first major link develops from a pattern often repeated over the years, of one group decrying the arrival of another. Also, the eventual demise of the neighborhood is prefigured even as it is birthed: in flame. Dirk Van Dropsie's fear of the English moving into the area and chasing out the Dutch results in fiery death, foreshadowing Hendrik Dropsie's torching of his own home thirty years later. The O'Briens' arrival starts the cycle anew as the English slowly make way for the Irish.

In Eisner's carefully plotted sequences, it is not the socially ambitious O'Brien who creates a lasting mark on Dropsie Avenue, but rather his "lower-class" rival, Timothy O'Leary. The O'Briens' efforts to fit in with the upper crust come to naught, even as O'Leary's son, the neighborhood priest, becomes spiritual leader of the newly arriving Irish. Decades later, as an elevated railway station's proximity turns the street into tenements, even more Irish pour in. The last free standing private home, belonging to old Mrs. Shepard and her granddaughter, the crippled Rowena, provides the reader with the second major link in the overall story. Rowena marries her mute "Prince Charming" and moves out of her wonderful home with its "magic garden," perhaps the final remnant of Dropsie's Dutch farmland heritage. In what turns out to be a significant transitional device, Father O'Leary's wedding gift, a box of seeds and money, becomes his gift to the Dropsie Avenue of the 1990s.

Where Rowena's home stood becomes the site of the Moroni Building, a tenement that opens the neighborhood to the Italians. Izzy Cash Clothes, a neighborhood garment peddler, pushes his cart, saves his money, and in the worst days of the Depression buys the Moroni Building, opens up the neighborhood to Jews. Among the Jewish families settling on Dropsie Avenue are the Golds. Their son, Abie, applies street savvy to become a key figure in the life and resurrection of the street toward the book's end. Abie Gold's role in the story might be the glue that connects all the other links. Gold's importance likely comes from Eisner's identification with the character, as he too grew up in various New York tenements in a variety of ethnic neighborhoods.

The last major link among the book's themes is the character of Ruby Brown, the first black child raised on Dropsie Avenue. The connections from her story to the Van Dropsies' are traceable in a line of interconnected tales.

When Dropsie Avenue becomes like so many other Bronx neighborhoods of the last decade, burned up and "bombed out," it is through the interaction of Rowena, Abie and Ruby that new life comes to the street. Since each of the three has a unique vision of what Dropsie Avenue was, their confrontations with one another provide insight as to what makes a neighborhood a living place.

The now-ancient Rowena buys the burned-out neighborhood from the city, using the financial empire built up from the seeds and money Father O'Leary provided as a wedding gift. Her dream is to restore it to the tree-lined street of houses where she grew up. The adult Ruby Brown, the city official Rowena must deal with (Father O'Leary's successor, Father Gianelli, helped Ruby get the grant she needed for college—he too planted seeds, in a way), introduces the old woman to Abie Gold. Gold, now the executor of Izzy Cash Clothes's estate, is offered the opportunity to manage Rowena's dream housing project.

"You're too late with too much," Abie tells Rowena. "Where were you with your money when it began to decay?" he asks. Rowena's answer ties up all the themes in the book: "Who can mark the point at which neighborhoods start to die!" Eisner specifically used an exclamation point here rather than a question mark. Dropsie Avenue is a variety of neighborhoods, not always defined by ethnic or racial lines, but sometimes by economic class, and sometimes by the efforts of the people in it to make it a decent place. All through the century, the character of the neighborhood changes, sometimes slightly, as it transforms from a few abutting mansions, to a pleasantly tree-lined street of small, single-family homes, to—almost overnight—tenements.

Eisner had planned to make the character Danny Smith, who returns to Dropsie with his French bride after World War I, a much larger part of the tale and had actually drawn more pages, but he cut out many of them due to space considerations. "Space is your friend and your enemy," he said. "In telling such a big story, one needs to try to evoke meaningful material with good imagery."

Oddly enough, Eisner's proclivity for inundating his characters with rainstorms (Kurtzman called them "Eisenshpritzes") is subdued for such a huge book. There are three snowfalls but only two showers, both of them judiciously placed near the end: one at Polo Palermo's funeral, possibly signifying the washing away of the character's influence on the Avenue (for good or ill, Palermo's stock in trade was Influence itself), the other at Abie and Ruby's meeting long after the neighborhood is in ruins, perhaps also washing away Abie's expressed idea that memories are what makes a neighborhood. For in the end, as in the beginnings, a neighborhood's life is in its people. It is in the here and now, not in the images of the past.

"The '30s and '40s were big turning points," Eisner mentioned when asked if his own personal experience during those decades had anything to do with his story focusing a bit more on that time. "The street was really alive at that point, but an unperceptible deterioration began to take place," he said. If the Dropsie Avenue of the '30s and '40s seemed to be more alive to Will Eisner than any other time, perhaps it is because the people that lived there then were making the most out of what they had. They set up their shops, their businesses, and their clubs all on the street on which they lived. The Dropsie Avenue of stately mansions, the Dropsie Avenue of tree-lined homes and the Dropsie Avenue of crumbling firetraps and drug addicts had no place for those things. Without people maneuvering behind the scenes to make the place better for themselves and their families, the only behind-the-scenes activities were the finishers (people who buy and strip buildings) and the leeches trying to squeeze out everything they could.

The resurrection of Dropsie Avenue ends the book on an uncertain note, with hints of racial animosity among the new residents of the revitalized street and new deterioration setting in. Yet uncertainty is a fixture of modern urban existence. People who live their lives today without knowing their next-door neighbors face terrible uncertainty. Are neighborhoods without roots, common interests or activities truly neighborhoods? Are they doomed to a lifeless end like the bombed-out streets of the Bronx? If Eisner's book offers any hope on this subject, it is that a single person *can* make a major difference.

PAUL J. GRANT

Dropsie Avenue: Eisner Returns to the Neighborhood†

With *Dropsie Avenue*, his latest graphic novel, Will Eisner returns again to the fictitious Bronx neighborhood he first introduced in 1978's *A Contract with God*. However, where his previous works used the locale as a backdrop against which human stories were enacted, this time the human stories serve to delineate the story of the gradual corruption and destruction of the urban microcosm known as the South Bronx. This time, the street is the main character, as it weathers 120 years of change. Beginning in 1870, when the Dutch burghers are looking askance at these English newcomers who are lowering property values, *Dropsie Avenue* sees a variety of ethnic groups (Irish, Italians, Jews, Blacks, and Hispanics, in roughly that order) come and flee, and a variety of hopes thrive and fail. Not coincidentally, the book begins with fire, and fire becomes the final harsh judge of the neighborhood's viability.

Eisner, who grew up in the Bronx, knows this landscape first hand, but had to do more historical research than usual. "These are people I grew up with and knew," he explained, "but in this particular book, I had to draw on fixed historical patterns, rather than in the case of *To the Heart of the Storm* (1991), where I drew on my life and my own personal experiences to create a history. This was kind of a composite, built on what I saw and then extended onto a historical point of view. I had a very difficult canvas to work on here. I was dealing with an extensive historical work, and I had to thread it together and make it as authentic as possible. Believability was important."

Some will doubtless read *Dropsie Avenue* and accuse Eisner of resorting to ethnic stereotypes. This is a criticism he not only understands, but welcomes: "I have a very strong feeling about stereotypes. It is almost impossible to function in this medium without the use of stereotypes, which are a very important part of the language of the medium. Without the use of stereotypes, you cannot successfully achieve instant recognition of a character. So I have absolutely no apology."

Eisner has also been accused of sentimentalizing the past in earlier works. Although there are many sentimental parts in *Dropsie Avenue*, the novel has a hard, cynical edge. Eisner concedes that this work was largely fueled by his anger. "As I got into this thing, the more I realized there was a lot of inexcusable greed and moral corruption that goes into the

† From *The Comics Journal* 177 (May 1995): 30–31. Reprinted with permission of the author's estate. Note is by the editor of this Norton Critical Edition.

destruction of the neighborhood. The whole point of doing a book like this is to show the disintegration is not physical, but rather a result of human dynamics . . . an internal force."

Even the more sympathetic characters, like streetwise lawyer Abie Gold or the crippled romantic Rowena (a girl who's read *The Secret Garden*[1] one too many times) are touched by the overall corruption. Abie, who is essentially a do-gooder who honestly cares about the community, acts as fixer and advisor to Polo Palermo, the local ward heeler. "I was trying to create a balance there, to show that within the frame of this general disintegration the individuals visibly involved are not in themselves inherently corrupt," Eisner explains.

Covering over a century in under 200 pages requires a fair degree of condensation, yet through the novel's vignettes, the broader picture clearly emerges. One sacrifice that Eisner had to make, to some extent, was subtlety. "This medium requires broad strokes, and does not permit layers of infinite detail for fear of boring the reader. So I had to deal with these people in obvious actions, rather than refining it." He adds, self-deprecatingly, "Maybe someday when I become more sophisticated in this medium, I'll be able to refine down the actions and the interplay into something more akin to the detailed descriptions characteristic of a finely wrought novel."

Dropsie Avenue is powerful stuff, wrenched from real-life events, and a far cry from the typical comics fare. When asked who he sees as his target audience, Eisner laughs and replies, "Whenever I'm asked this, I always say my reader is a 40-year-old man who's just had his wallet stolen in a subway in New York." He continues, on a more serious note. "I'm addressing myself not so much to an age group but to a group of people who have similar experiences and can understand what I'm saying. Certainly, I cannot expect a callow youngster who has had maybe 12 to 15 years of life experiences, whose life has centered around MTV, to be interested in the disintegration of a neighborhood or be concerned about why it disintegrates. But there are things one can do in this medium to raise the level of the storytelling to reach the intellect of the reader. I'm consciously trying, in my work, to make contact in a context with the internal emotions of people."

Eisner's art remains expressive and resolutely low-tech. Over the last twenty years, he's changed and refined his style in the service of his stories. "The more complex and introspective my stories become, the more I find that the artwork need not be as bravura as it was when I was doing *The Spirit,* when the artwork dominated the scene as much as possible. Now I find that I tend to want to minimize my drawing, and try to convey the story as quickly and easily as I can. I spend more time determining a posture, revising until I can get the exact gesture that I want that will convey an inner meaning. Over the years, I've come to realize that one of the great impediments in comics is the tremendous burden on the artist to convey an internal emotion. In a medium that has devoted itself to externalism, this has become the real artistic challenge for me."

1. A 1911 children's novel by the English-American author Frances Hodgson Burnett (1849–1924).

* * *

Eisner continues gamely to work in a format—the graphic novel—within this industry that most publishers have largely abandoned, but he maintains hope for the format and the medium as well. "I'm betting on the fact that the audience for the comic medium is getting older, and their standards are going to get closer to what I'm doing, which is why I undertook this task in 1974 in the first place."

After more than 50 years in the industry, Will Eisner remains optimistic about its—and his own—future. "Fifty years ago, comics were essentially regarded as an entertainment form," he recalls. "Today, there's a growing acceptance of them as a literary form, which is something that was never even thought about then. The comic medium has become integrated in our reading culture, and can provide a message other than mindless mayhem. This is an area that still is virgin territory, not yet fully exploited."

Those that explore it, however, will undoubtedly find Eisner's footprints there before them. After half a century, *Dropsie Avenue* shows that he is still one of the medium's most powerful and innovative storytellers.

CRITICISM

ANDREW J. KUNKA

A Contract with God, *The First Kingdom*, and the 'Graphic Novel': The Will Eisner / Jack Katz Letters†

In 1974, Jack Katz sent Will Eisner Book 1 of Katz's epic fantasy series, *The First Kingdom*, and asked the venerable creator for some feedback on the comic. This began a correspondence that continued through the end of *The First Kingdom* in 1986. In this first letter, dated August 7, 1974, Katz describes his project as "a graphic novel" some four years before Eisner published his own first, self-identified "graphic novel," *A Contract with God*. For years following the publication of *A Contract with God* in 1978, Eisner frequently retold the story of how he came up with the descriptive term on his own, in a moment of inspiration while pitching the book to a publisher. The 1974 letter from Jack Katz not only reveals that Eisner was exposed to the term "graphic novel" years before he claimed to have come up with it, but it also shows Eisner and Katz engaged in a discussion of the future of comics and their shared desire to move the medium forward into more sophisticated literary territory as Eisner was developing his plans for his own groundbreaking work.

That conversation continued as Katz and Eisner exchanged letters regularly through the twelve-year run of *The First Kingdom*, with Katz sending Eisner each of the series' twenty-four issues. The correspondence looks, at first, to be mostly one-sided: Katz initiates each exchange, and Eisner regularly provides constructive feedback and praise on Katz's work. Eisner seems to get little out of the exchanges other than the good feeling of helping and encouraging a fellow creator. However, when these letters are placed in the context of other conversations and influences Eisner experienced at this time, our understanding of their importance for him increases. Eisner's biographers (Bob Andelman and Michael Schumacher), friends (especially Denis Kitchen), and others have documented the influence that underground comix had in inspiring Eisner to produce *A Contract with God*, but the letters between Katz and Eisner also show another crucial step in that process. In terms of genre, style, and content, *The First Kingdom* and *A Contract with God* bear little or no resemblance to one another, but both represent efforts by their respective creators to follow in the steps of the undergrounds and expand the literary potential of comics while also expressing intensely personal artistic visions. The letters between Eisner and Katz, along with other comments Eisner made in the late 1960s and early 1970s, trace another, important strand of influence on *A Contract with God*, through the genre work that Katz was doing with epic science fiction and fantasy in *The First Kingdom*. When addressing this period, histories of the comics industry often ignore or only briefly mention the work of Katz and others, like Gil Kane, who were innovating new ways of telling stories and expanding the

† From *Inks: The Journal of the Comics Studies Society* 1.1 (Columbus, OH: Ohio State UP, Spring 2017): 27–39. Reprinted with permission from Ohio State UP. Unless otherwise indicated, notes are by the author. Many of the author's notes have been omitted, and some of his references have been edited.

potential of the comics medium in the years leading up to Eisner's creation of *A Contract with God*. However, Jack Katz's groundbreaking work in the early 1970s served as a critical influence on Eisner's *A Contract with God* and on the development of the graphic novel as a whole.

The story of how Will Eisner first used the term "graphic novel" is a familiar part of his biography: when trying to pitch *A Contract with God*—then called *The Tenement*—to Bantam Books president Oscar Dystal, Eisner wanted to come up with a term that would distinguish his new work from the stigma of "comic books": "I looked at it and realized that if I said, 'A comic book,' he would hang up."[1] On the fly, Eisner came up with the term "graphic novel" to describe the book, and Dystal expressed interest. However, when Eisner showed Dystal the work, the publisher responded, "You know, this is still a comic. . . . We don't publish this kind of stuff."[2] As Eisner later commented, "I thought I had invented the term, . . . but I discovered later that some guy thought about it a few years before I used the term. He had never used it successfully and had never intended it the way I did, which was to develop what I believe was viable literature in this medium."[3]

That "guy" was early fanzine writer and retailer Richard Kyle, who used the term beginning in 1964 in the pages of the fanzine *K-A CAPA alpha* and, later, as a reviewer for Bill Spicer's magazines—*Fantasy Illustrated* and *Graphic Story Magazine*—and his own *Graphic Story World*. Whether Kyle "used it unsuccessfully" or "intended it the way [Eisner] did" is debatable. In the November 1964 issue of *K-A CAPA alpha*, Kyle wrote a short essay on the future of comic books in the "Richard Kyle's Wonderworld" column. After dismissing previous terms like Charles Biro's "illustories" or EC Comics' "picto-fiction," Kyle lands on the term "graphic": "And so, in future issues of *Wonderworld*, when you find me using the terms 'graphic story' and 'graphic novel' to describe the artistically serious 'comic book strip,' you'll know what I mean. I may even use it on some that aren't so serious."[4] This definition seems similar to Eisner's own use of the term.

It is now fairly common knowledge that Eisner invented neither the term itself nor the form that we call a "graphic novel," but it is fair to say that he popularized the term when he later used it to promote *A Contract with God* upon publication from Baronet Books in 1978. * * * For better or worse, the term has stuck as the descriptor and category for any book-length work or square-bound volume in the comics medium, as well as a marketing term for bookstores to separate most such works from the "Humor" and "Science Fiction" sections where they were previously located. Therefore, the concern here is not with the origins of the term or how it first seeped into the cultural consciousness, all of which has been well documented. Instead, I will be focusing on the ways in which the letters between Katz and Eisner reveal how Eisner first became exposed to the term years earlier than previously cited. These letters, then, can be

1. Quoted in Michael Schumacher, *Will Eisner: A Dreamer's Life in Comics* (New York: Bloomsbury, 2010), 200.
2. Schumacher, *Will Eisner*, 201.
3. Schumacher, *Will Eisner*, 201. Bob Andelman tells a similar version of the story in his biography, *Will Eisner: A Spirited Life* (Milwaukie, OR: M Press, 2005), 290–91.
4. Richard Kyle, "Richard Kyle's Wonderworld," *CAPA-alpha* 2 (November 1964): 3.

seen as part of an alternative narrative to the story that Eisner told about his first conceptualization of the term "graphic novel." In addition, that exposure was an important and overlooked component of the inspiration that drove Eisner to create *A Contract with God* and later works, which makes this information gleaned from these letters more significant than a debate over the origins of what was ultimately first and foremost a marketing term.

In his introductory letter, Katz writes, "Here is the first book of a series of 24 books which it will take to complete the epic. . . . What I am starting is a graphic novel in which every incident is illustrated." Katz then goes on to explain the plot and themes of the entire epic at length. On August 26, 1974, Eisner responds in his typical polite and encouraging fashion: "My compliments to you on an imaginative piece of work. There is strength, drama and great picture value. I'm particularly impressed with the enormity of your undertaking. It is efforts like this that move the standards of our art form upward." So, in this first exchange, Katz uses the term "graphic novel" to describe *The First Kingdom*, and Eisner acknowledges the project's scope and potential significance.

* * *

Eisner is keenly attentive to Katz's progress, which means that Eisner reflected back on earlier letters and likely recalled Katz's use of "graphic novel" when it came time to pitch *A Contract with God*. Eisner's gracious feedback (common in his letters to other creators as well) clearly has an emotional, professional, and motivational impact on Katz. A more challenging question, however, is this: What, if anything, was the impact of Katz on Eisner's work? Or, did Eisner get anything out of this exchange that he wasn't getting out of other influences he was exposed to at this time?

On the surface, one can find little in common between Eisner's *A Contract with God* and Katz's *The First Kingdom*, other than the fact that they are both ambitious projects that broke with many of the conventions of the comics medium and comics publishing. However, the timing of these letters coincides with the period in which Eisner was planning and composing his first graphic novel. Some of Eisner's other influences during this time have been well documented, such as his exposure to underground comix through Denis Kitchen and the success of his *Spirit* reprints through Warren Publishing. Eisner first met Kitchen while attending the 1971 New York Comic Art Convention, organized by Phil Seuling. According to Michael Schumacher, Eisner "hadn't seen any underground comix prior to [this convention], but he'd heard more than enough about them to spark his curiosity."[5] What made Eisner curious, Schumacher explains, was the potential underground comix revealed for expanding both the market and the content of comics to a new audience. The underground publishing model appealed to Eisner because the comix remained on store shelves longer than newsstand comics, and they underwent multiple printings. The underground publishers also offered royalties and allowed creators to retain their own copyrights. Eisner would test out this new publishing model in 1973 with two issues of *Spirit* reprints published by Kitchen Sink Press.

5. Schumacher, *Will Eisner*, 165.

The following year, Eisner shifted publication of *Spirit* reprints to Warren, who offered not only the same copyright retention, but also higher royalties and wider newsstand distribution in a magazine format. Warren's *The Spirit Magazine* ran from April 1974 to October 1976 (to be picked up later by Kitchen Sink after Warren cancelled the title). Schumacher explains the importance of the Warren reprints: "With Warren, Eisner was now back in the entertainment comics business, working steadily in a field he had abandoned long ago, learning more about the purchasing habits of comics fans, and preparing himself . . . for his entry into the ultimate in comics for adults—the graphic novel."[6] The experience with Warren and Kitchen, then, answered both artistic and commercial questions Eisner had as he transitioned into new work: What was his reputation with contemporary readers? Did his work have an audience? What publishing models were now available for more sophisticated work?

Therefore, in 1974, when the letters between Eisner and Katz began, Eisner was in a time of transition. He had also just started teaching at the School of Visual Arts, where he saw a new generation of comic artists at work. He had attended his first comic convention in 1971, and in that same year, he stopped working on *PS: The Preventative Maintenance Monthly* magazine for the US Army. During this time, he expressed to Kitchen and others a desire to push the comics medium into an area of greater literary and artistic respect. So, when Eisner wrote in their first exchange that Katz's project "move[s] the standards of our art form upwards," Katz was clearly contributing to Eisner's developing thoughts on the medium at that time.

Like Eisner, Katz found inspiration in the undergrounds to launch his own ambitious and deeply personal comics project. *The First Kingdom* is an elaborate science fiction/fantasy narrative that serves as a vehicle for Katz's metaphysical and philosophical explorations. From the outset, Katz planned for twenty-four chapters (mirroring the twenty-four books of *The Iliad* and *The Odyssey*),[7] to be published at the pace of two chapters per year for twelve years. The series was originally published by Comics & Comix and, later, by Bud Plant. In a 2010 interview with Jim Amash, Katz explains, "I gave [Comics & Comix] the first, I think, 25 pages of *The First Kingdom,* and they jumped at it because undergrounds were really going hot and heavy at that time. It was the one place I could get the stuff done without any editorial interference. And they were just happy to have the books, and I was happy to do something that was totally my vision. I had worried about finding a place that would allow me to do it my way."[8] Therefore, while market concerns were in play for Katz, he prioritized the opportunity to express his own personal vision. That vision carried him through the twelve-year publishing schedule, despite the personal and economic sacrifices necessary to complete it.

6. Schumacher, *Will Eisner,* 186.
7. Traditionally attributed to the ancient Greek poet Homer, about whom nothing definitive is known, the two works date to around the 8th century BCE. *The Iliad* tells the story of the heroes of Trojan War and *The Odyssey* tells the story of the long, difficult journey home for one of those heroes, Odysseus, King of Ithaca [*Editor*].
8. Jim Amash, "'I'm Trying to Prod People to Think': Interview with Golden & Silver Age Artist Jack Katz—Part II," *Alter Ego* 92 (March 2010): 54.

* * *

Eisner's thoughts about the future of comics and their literary potential date back well before *A Contract with God* and the correspondence with Katz, and even before his 1971 meeting with Denis Kitchen. In 1968, John Benson interviewed Eisner for the sixth issue of *witzend,* a magazine originally published by artist Wallace Wood in 1966 to showcase comic artists' work outside of the control of mainstream publishers and to allow those artists to retain ownership of their work. * * * In the interview, Eisner reveals that he had read Bill Spicer's *Graphic Story Magazine* 9. That series featured comic stories, interviews, essays, and reviews of contemporary comics. Issue 9 includes two unconventional comic stories: a new chapter of George Metzger's ongoing serial "Master Tyme and Mobius Tripp" and Vincent Davis's politically charged allegory "The Last Weapon," based on a story by Robert Sheckley. When Benson asks Eisner specifically about "Master Tyme," Eisner responds, "Fascinating stuff; great stuff. There's tremendous talent around, tremendous. It's too bad these kids are going to have a hell of a time finding a mass audience."[9] Because Eisner knew of *witzend* and had read *Graphic Story Magazine* in the late 1960s, he had been exposed to underground comix (or, at least, "proto-underground") before his meeting with Kitchen, though he may not have seen them as such at the time. With these unconventional comics, however, Eisner expresses concern about their commercial viability, wondering if these creators are "going to move 300,000 copies of the comic book." He was, therefore, at least thinking about these alternatives to conventional comics publishing as early as 1968.

Bill Spicer's *Graphic Story Magazine*, along with its precursor *Fantasy Illustrated* and Richard Kyle's later fanzine *Graphic Story World*, was one of the earliest venues in which the concept of the "graphic novel" was discussed by both fans and professionals. The term "graphic novel" does not appear in issue 9, so Eisner's awareness of the term cannot be traced back to that point. However, Richard Kyle does use the term in the previous issue (Fall 1967), during a discussion of Russ Manning's "The Aliens" series that ran in *Magnus, Robot Fighter*: "When the story is completed, it may form a graphic novel of unusual and impressive quality." The column also contains a review of Harvey's *Spirit* reprint comic, which increases the possibility that Eisner saw that issue. The same holds true for Kyle's "Graphic Story Review" column in *Fantasy Illustrated* 6 (Summer/Fall 1966).[1] (With issue 8, *Fantasy Illustrated* became *Graphic Story Magazine.*) In this column, Kyle reviews the first issue of Harvey's *Spirit* reprints and the Gold Key *Tarzan of the Apes* comic, among others. Kyle writes, "If the tales of The Spirit represent an almost complete development of the techniques of the graphic short story, the Gold Key adaptations of Edgar Rice Burroughs's Tarzan novels represent the first steps in the creation of the graphic novel."[2] So, in these two columns, Kyle reviews

9. John Benson, "Having Something to Say," *witzend* 6 (Spring 1969). Reprinted in *Will Eisner: Conversations*, 22. Metzger later contributed to *Gothic Blimp Works, Brain Fantasy,* and other underground comix in the late 1960s and early 1970s. For more on Metzger's role in underground comix, see Rosenkranz, *Rebel Visions: The Underground Comix Revolution—1963–1975* (Seattle: Fantagraphics, 2008).
1. Richard Kyle, "Richard Kyle's Graphic Story Review," *Graphic Story Magazine* 8 (Fall 1967): 31.
2. Richard Kyle, "Graphic Story Review," *Fantasy Illustrated* 6 (Summer/Fall 1966): 4.

Spirit reprints and discusses the "graphic novel" as a concept that signals comics' future development. If Eisner were a regular reader of *Graphic Story Magazine* or *Fantasy Illustrated*, or he came across Kyle's *Spirit* reviews, then a direct connection between Kyle's origination of the term and Eisner's exposure to it could be made. Given Eisner's concern about his reputation among comics fans at the time, he possibly would have seen these reviews. At the very least, the Benson interview shows that Eisner was already invested in discussion of the future of comics as "graphic stories" as early as 1968—a discussion that frames the earliest uses of the term "graphic novel."

Eisner was also aware of other projects that had attempted to offer readers more sophisticated, "adult" comics that followed in the spirit of the undergrounds, but with varying degrees of success. For example, Eisner was familiar with *Star*Reach,* the science fiction anthology series that Mike Friedrich had begun publishing in 1974. Friedrich attempted what he called "ground-level" comics, to distinguish the work in *Star* Reach* from both the undergrounds and the "above ground" mainstream comics that publishers like DC and Marvel produced. On February 28, 1978, months before *A Contract with God* was published, Eisner wrote a letter to Friedrich, expressing interest in *Star*Reach*: "I truly believe we are still at the beginnings of the mature use of comics as visual literature or narrative art, and I hope to keep on being part of it—hopefully in the vanguard."

What may have made Katz's influence different from that of the undergrounds and works like *Star*Reach* was that Katz and Eisner were from the same generation: roughly ten years separate the two creators, and both had experience in the industry in the 1940s and 1950s. Eisner began his comic career in 1936, at the age of 19, and he went on to found one of the first comic production studios with Jerry Iger. Katz's career began in 1943, at the age of 16, working for various studios and publishers before landing a regular job with King Features Syndicate in 1946. This small age gap and overlapping careers stand in contrast with Denis Kitchen and the other underground comix creators Eisner met around this time, who were often 25–30 years younger. It is one thing to see a younger generation pushing the medium in a new direction; it is another to see a contemporary jumping in to the fray at the age of 47, as Katz was when *The First Kingdom* started. Katz's project, then, may have pushed Eisner another step closer to creating his own innovative project.

As indicated in the Benson interview, Eisner had also read the work of another contemporary: Gil Kane's *His Name Is Savage*, the magazine-sized spy thriller that Kane released in 1968.*** The forty-page comic story features Savage, a special agent for The Committee who fights for the future of the United States against the evil General Simon Mace. Like Jim Warren, Kane wanted to circumvent the Comics Code's content restrictions by publishing in a magazine-sized format. The magazine, however, was not a success, with 200,000 copies printed and only 20,000 distributed. Kane claimed that the publishers behind the Comics Code sabotaged the magazine at the distributor level in order to discourage competition. Whatever the case, the magazine failed, and Kane did not produce a second issue. Eisner specifically laments the failure of *Savage:*

"Sorry Gil's magazine failed. . . . I believe he's got the right idea."[3] This discussion leads Eisner and Benson to talk about Eisner's ideas for the current comics marketplace and the potential for someone to create something new and innovative (Eisner even uses the phrase "a novel in comic form," which is getting him pretty close to "graphic novel"). The failure of Kane's *Savage* may have discouraged Eisner's entry into the market at the time, serving as a cautionary tale and contributing to his more measured progress over the next ten years.

In this context, *The First Kingdom* presented for Eisner yet another project similar in its ambitions to the underground comix and works like Kane's *Savage*, where creators were doing new things with comics—exploring new markets and content—and all of these works clearly had the cumulative effect of inspiring Eisner. Eisner's moves toward *A Contract with God*, however, were tentative: he tested the market out first with the *Spirit* reprints, which was a safe move in terms of maintaining his legacy with that creation and seeing if his name still had resonance with comics readers. Katz, on the other hand, dove right in to the relatively untested direct-sales and mail-order markets, with primarily the undergrounds as precedent, and he eschewed paid work to realize his vision. Kane and Katz can be seen as polar influences on Eisner: Kane's magazine was a direct and calculated attempt (and failure) to reach a mass adult audience with comics, while Katz didn't seem to share such ambitions, focusing primarily on his own vision and story, and on what the project meant for the medium as a whole. Ultimately, *Savage* and *The First Kingdom* are genre works, while Eisner's ambition seemed to be directing him to projects he felt would have had more literary or artistic value. And their status as works in genres that were already familiar and popular in mainstream comics has caused them to be overlooked in considerations of the graphic novel's historical development, which tends to center on more "literary" projects like *A Contract with God* and Art Spiegelman's *Maus*. Eisner's literary ambitions, therefore, make *A Contract with God* a more palatable origin point for the development of the graphic novel.

As Eisner was thinking about the future of comics in the 1970s, one crucial component of that development concerned what to call the new type of comic book that would push the medium forward. Eisner was aware that "comic book" had a stigma attached to it that may have been holding the medium back. He was also concerned that this new work would need to be both commercially and critically successful, and so the terms under which it would be marketed were especially important. As Schumacher acknowledges, Eisner tried out and rejected other options: Eisner found "graphic novel" to be "a 'limited term,' although his preferred 'graphic literature' or 'graphic story' came across sounding a little too academic for bookstore owners and readers alike, just as the term *sequential art* would rub some readers the wrong way."[4] He would continue using "sequential art" as his definition of the medium and as part of the title of his 1985 instructional text, *Comics and Sequential Art*. That

3. Benson, "Having Something to Say," 21.
4. Schumacher, *Will Eisner*, 201.

term, like the others he considered, seemed too pretentious for what Eisner wanted to accomplish, while "graphic novel" struck a balance between artistic or literary merits and commercial concerns. Therefore, Eisner's choice of "graphic novel" to describe *A Contract with God* was not simply a random choice made on the spur of the moment, but a more measured and calculated choice to navigate his seemingly diametrically opposed ambitions.

Katz continued corresponding with Eisner through the end of *The First Kingdom* in 1986. Late in 1984, Katz wrote to Eisner requesting a foreword for issue 23, the penultimate volume of *The First Kingdom*. Katz refers to "silhouette power problems" and "anatomy" critiques that have come up in earlier letters, so Eisner continued to offer advice on Katz's art ten years after their first exchange. Katz writes, "Will, a foreword from you will mean a great deal to me. In a sense, it will validate the effort I've put in." Katz goes on to ruminate about the vision that drives him to complete this work: "We are all working toward our own personal ideal. One we call upon from our personal inner vision. I'm still trying to reach the excellence which I see and am striving for. And there is no greater authority than excellence. Will, you and a handful of artists will leave a legacy in our field. All I've ever wanted to do was to earn my way into that select group."[5] Heading into the home stretch on what will be a twelve-year-long project, Katz considers how personal vision and legacy have served as the primary motives for his work. The commercial success or failure of the work never came into play for Katz as much as it did for Eisner.

In his foreword to *First Kingdom* 23 (1986), Eisner recalls seeing the series from the beginning and recognizes the risk Katz took: "I was, I confess, more impressed then with the fact that a well regarded professional had the courage to leave the security of the establishment comic book marketplace and strike out for a financially uncertain independence."[6] This compliment also identifies Katz as Eisner's contemporary. The foreword continues, "To me, this was very important because he was, by example, helping to establish a beachead [*sic*] for the 'free-agent' comic book artist and writer who happily populates the field today. Certainly he carved a position for the graphic novel concept and helped establish a category for work produced with literary intent." Most of Eisner's compliments here are reserved for the form and ambition of Katz's project, leaving aside the quality of the content. However, Eisner gives Katz some credit here, though not going so far as to say that Katz used the term "graphic novel" before him. At the very least, Eisner places Katz on a historical continuum leading toward the development of "the graphic novel concept," which would also include *A Contract with God*. Eisner also acknowledges Katz's rejection of the art/commerce dilemma that had so troubled Eisner.

Comics history is filled with stories that achieve the level of legend and often remain unchallenged. One of the jobs of comics scholarship and research is to correct, expand, and modify the historical and biographical

5. Jack Katz to Will Eisner, December 28, 1984. Will Eisner Archives, Billy Ireland Cartoon Library & Museum.
6. Will Eisner, Foreword, *The First Kingdom* 23 (1986): n.p.

record. The letters between Eisner and Katz might at first seem to offer only a footnote in Eisner's career, but they in fact help us see more clearly the pathway leading up to his creation of *A Contract with God*. It is entirely possible that Eisner could have forgotten Katz's use of the term "graphic novel," and the phrase just floated through his transom at the moment when he needed it. However, the letters between Katz and Eisner offer an alternative narrative—that Katz provided a significant influence on Eisner both through the ambition of his own epic project and through his use of "graphic novel" to describe it, and that influence contributed to Eisner's creation of *A Contract with God*. These letters also fall in line with other discussions that Eisner engaged in going back to the late 1960s, which came about through his exposure to underground comix and other experiments. Finally, what emerges is a useful contrast between two creators of the same generation, both recognizing new potential in the medium to which they have devoted their careers, but with each one willing to take different degrees of risk to participate in that growth.

PAUL WILLIAMS

Did *A Contract with God* Popularize the "Graphic Novel"?[†]

Writer and editor Archie Goodwin displayed his knowledge of comics history in the essay "Stalking the Great Graphic Dream" (1980), published in Marvel's *Epic Illustrated*. He began with [Richard] Kyle's construction of the "graphic story" as "something more serious of intent and greater in scope than [. . .] *comics*." According to Goodwin, by 1967, the contributors to *FI* [*Fantasy Illustrated*] and *GSM* [*Graphic Story Magazine*] generally agreed "that the next bright light on the comics horizon had to be the graphic *novel*."[1] Goodwin evaluated a cohort of long comics narratives that might be considered examples of "graphic novels," but he judged that few of them met Kyle's criteria. The essay listed over a dozen viable contenders, most of which fell into the genres of SF, fantasy, espionage thriller, or hard-boiled detective fiction. There was one notable absentee: despite declaring that 1978 saw a bumper crop of graphic novels, Goodwin did not mention Will Eisner's *A Contract with God*. He did refer to Eisner, hailing him as "the architect of graphic narrative" and noting that the creator was "working on a novel-length serial [entitled] *Life on Another Planet*."[2] A short-story cycle set in 1930s New York, it would seem that Eisner's *Contract* was not enough of a novel to be worth mentioning in Goodwin's essay. The absence of *Contract* from Goodwin's list of 1970s graphic novels will surprise any reader who knows their

† From *Dreaming the Graphic Novel: The Novelization of Comics* (New Brunswick, NJ: Rutgers University Press, 2020), pp. 111–17, 222–23. Copyright © 2020 by Paul Williams. Reprinted by permission of Rutgers University Press. Notes are by the author. Some of the author's notes have been omitted, and some of his references have been edited. Bracketed page references are to this Norton Critical Edition.

1. Archie Goodwin, "Stalking the Great Graphic Dream," *Epic Illustrated* 4 (Winter 1980): 36 (italics in original).
2. Goodwin, "Stalking," 40.

comics historiography, where the standard position is that this volume "first put the term [*graphic novel*] into wide circulation."[3] If we analyze the book's initial reception, it seems wrong to privilege *Contract* as popularizing *graphic novel* during the 1978–1980 period; indeed, it seems wrong to single out any one text for this purpose.

*** *Contract* was published in 1978, the year that occurrences of *graphic novel* exploded in frequency. But what happens if we drill deeper into the data for 1978? *Graphic novels* came up a lot, but did *Contract*? The short answer is no. Of the sixty-eight occurrences of *graphic novel* (or *graphic fantasy novel* or *graphic novelization* or *graphic novelist*) in 1978 I have seen, only four referred to *Contract*. By way of contrast, fifteen referred to Delany and Chaykin's *Empire*, six to McGregor and Gulacy's *Sabre*, and twenty-six to Katz's *The First Kingdom*. *Contract* was officially published on November 15, 1978 (the date printed inside the paperback edition is October 1978), so let's spread our net a little wider. If we examine instances of *graphic novel* recorded between the start of October 1978 and the end of 1980, does *Contract* assume a new prominence?

Yes: *Contract* is mentioned in 20 out of 109 paratexts, though that includes unpublished personal correspondence to and from Eisner. As a point of comparison, I found eighteen references to *The First Kingdom* as a *graphic novel*, seven to *Sabre*, thirteen to *Empire*, nine to Moench and Nino's *More Than Human*, and seven to Lee and Kirby's *Silver Surfer*. So across every paratext, *Contract* was alluded to more often than any other graphic novel—but this is skewed by the fact that I consulted Eisner's papers but visited few holdings dedicated to other specific *creators*. If we examine published paratexts from October 1978 to December 1980, we have sixty-six publications that contain references to *graphic novels*. Excluding multiple citations to the same graphic novel in any single issue of a comic/fanzine/catalog, *Contract* is invoked as a *graphic novel* fourteen times, compared to thirteen for *The First Kingdom*, twelve for *Empire*, nine for *More Than Human*, and seven for *Sabre*. *Contract* beats *The First Kingdom* by a nose?

Some texts identifying the latest "graphic novels" mentioned *Contract* but declined to elect Eisner's book as an example of them. Advertisements for Monkey's Retreat Retail-Mail Order, which appeared several times in *TBG* [*The Buyer's Guide for Comic Fandom*] in October and November 1978, were trading *Silver Surfer* and *More Than Human* as "graphic novels" but did not categorize *Contract* as such. *** In December 1979, the fan Al Turniansky urged his peers to get hold of a copy of *Contract*, "a magnificent example of the things that can be done with Illustories," choosing not to call it a *graphic novel*. Certainly, this could have been a promotion of Turniansky's preferred nomenclature of "Illustories" rather than a rejection of the idea that Eisner's book deserved the label *graphic novel*; after mentioning *Contract*, Turniansky related an anecdote about "Graphic Novels."[4]

Readers often rhapsodized over Eisner's achievement but showed little readiness to call *Contract* a graphic novel. Comics writer Dennis O'Neil's

3. Christopher Pizzino, *Arresting Development: Comics at the Boundaries of Literature* (Austin: University of Texas Press, 2016), 49.
4. Al Turniansky and Chris Mortika, "IAM's, I Said," *CAPA-alpha* 182 (December 1979): [74].

review called it "a near-masterpiece" without naming it as a novel, though he did write that Eisner was using the resources of the "novelist" [237]. Fan Ron Harris thought it was "near perfect" but "an anthology of graphic short stories."[5] SF writer Harlan Ellison and comics writer Doug Moench cited it as a high point of innovation but not as any kind of novel.[6] Mike Valerio told his fellow CAPA-alphans to "check it out" but thought *Contract* was not equal to Eisner's "definitive work" on *The Spirit* and added, "Despite the cover-claim that this collection is a graphic novel, the four stories are not interlocked in any way other than that they share a common backdrop" [233]. Jon Harvey's review of *Contract* in *Fantasy Media* was favorable and reprinted the paperback's cover but did not refer to these "very adult tales" as any kind of novel.[7] An interview with Eisner published in the fall 1979 issue of *Funnyworld* mentioned *Contract*'s recent publication but went no further.[8] Letters from editors, journalists, and publishers articulated the emotional pull of Eisner's book and urged him to produce more of them, but up to the end of 1980, only a few correspondents called it a *graphic novel*. Writing to order more copies of the book, Richard Kyle was effusive about *Contract*'s qualities, and he called it "the finest 'straight' work yet done in the graphic story format," but even Kyle—the person who invented the term—did not call *Contract* a *graphic novel* [231].

In a letter to Norman Goldfind, presumably written around August 1978 (and republished that year in *The Spirit* magazine [1977–1983]), Eisner thanked his publisher "for your faith in this effort" and described the book "as an experiment to see whether themes other than cops and robbers can be successfully dealt with in this artform." The letter did not refer to *novels* or *graphic novels*, so perhaps at this point, Eisner was undecided on the best possible label. He told Goldfind that "for want of a better description," he called this "quartet of stories [. . .] 'eyewitness fiction.' That is to say that they are compounded of events + people I have known at first hand" [203]. Earlier in 1978, Denis Kitchen was still coming to terms with the novelistic nature of *Contract*, writing to Eisner in February 1978 to propose adding pages from "your new 'Bronx' comic/novel" to *The Spirit* periodical.[9] Personal correspondence indicates that from October 1978 onward, Eisner readily called the book a *graphic novel*, but promotional paratexts had not settled on this preferred moniker. An anonymous article previewing *Contract* in *The Spirit* 19 (October 1978) called it a *comix novel* and a *graphic novel*, and it was as a *comic novel* that it was listed in the April 1979 *Krupp Dealers' Catalog*.[1 * * *]

The book did not receive unanimous praise, and Bill Sherman was scathing of its storytelling ("bloated," "laughable," "illogical," "pretentious," "mawkish"). Sherman used scare quotes to question its taxonomic status, writing that *Contract* "is Eisner's graphic 'novel,' a series of four

5. Harris, "Argh," *CAPA-alpha* 174 (April 1979): [2.32].
6. Doug Moench, interview, *TCJ* 48 (Summer 1979): 61; Harlan Ellison, interview with Gary Groth, *The Comics Journal* 53 (Winter 1980), 99.
7. Jon Harvey, review of *A Contract with God* by Will Eisner, *Fantasy Media*, Will Eisner Papers, box 24, folder II, 22.
8. Will Eisner, "Moved by the Spirit," interview with Tom Andrae, *Funnyworld* 21 (Fall 1979): 20–27.
9. Denis Kitchen, letter to Will Eisner, February 15, 1978, Will Eisner Papers, box 28, folder 1.
1. "*A Contract with God and Other Tenement Stories* by Will Eisner," *Spirit* 19 (October 1978): 2–3; "New Comix," *Krupp Dealers' Catalog* 32 (April 1979): 8.

stories set in the depression era Bronx" [235]. Other members of *CAPA-alpha* were struck by Sherman's hostility, though it is hard to tell whether Chester Cox's terse two sentences ("Second bad review of Eisner's Contract. Hmmm?") were raising an eyebrow at Sherman's isolated sentiment or concurring that the book was not the triumph claimed elsewhere. Sherman's vitriol earned support to his cause, with other newsletters agreeing that *Contract* was "vastly overrated" and merely "competent" compared to Eisner's work on *The Spirit*. One remark even impugned Eisner's motives: "I'm willing to let Eisner [. . .] hack out stuff for narcissism and money; after all that [he's] given to me, I figure I owe [him] at least that much."[2] Perhaps most surprising, some people just weren't that bothered; as fan Cara Sherman put it, "I didn't care for the sepia printing [. . .] and I decided not to get it this time around, though normally I'm an Eisner fiend."[3] Referring to it as "a book of four stories written and drawn by Will Eisner in a free form comic strip," James Van Hise gave the book a seven out of ten in the *Rocket's Blast Comicollector.* He tended to be a generous reviewer (in the same issue, he awarded Wally Wood's *The Wizard King* ten out of ten) but was unimpressed by *Contract*, deriding the stories' poor plotting and stating that "it lacks a true direction" as an integral project. Furthermore, "too many of the people are painted in the easy bold stroke of the cliché." Reception was sufficiently hostile for the fan Dale Luciano to publicly defend the book, protesting in *TCJ* [*The Comics Journal*] that "I wouldn't dream of calling this wonderful, moving, and deeply personal effort a 'failure,' yet I've seen it virtually dismissed by various unsympathetic, pop-oriented reviewers as 'too personalized' and 'Not up to Eisner's work on *The Spirit*.'" He cited Van Hise's bland review as one of the worst offenders.[4]

To be clear, *Contract* was *not* widely hated. Eisner was nominated in the Outstanding Comic Book (Story) category at the 1979 National Cartoonists Society awards, and he accepted the nomination assuming that this was precipitated by his "graphic novel" *A Contract with God*. In December 1979, the fan-critic Robert C. Harvey wrote that if the "graphic novel" is defined as "an expanded comic book," then "we probably can't find a better example than Eisner's book" (though he added that if "it is to be something more than a new way of coupling words and pictures, that new way must preserve the essential nature of the comic strip art"—then Kane's *Blackmark* was the stronger candidate) [240]. An exchange of letters between Eisner and writer Michael Fleisher suggests that by 1984, *Contract* had become a rare gem, difficult to track down but of great value, and the book was mentioned during a meeting at DC "as the zenith of what the more ambitious formats have produced."[5] By the mid-1980s, *Contract* had been translated into Spanish, French, Italian, Danish, Finnish, German, and Yiddish, and the book's decent-but-unspectacular domestic sales (fewer than ten thousand copies) were much less consequential now that total sales around the world were "close to 50,000 copies." In

2. Chester Cox, "Kaos," *CAPA-alpha* 176 (June 1979): [1.21]; Bob Soron, "Grooble!," *CAPA-alpha* 180 (October 1979): [2.53]; Mark Worden, "Uk! Wuk!!," *CAPA-alpha* 180 (October 1979): [1.118].
3. Cara Sherman, "Thanatophile," *CAPA-alpha* 180 (October 1979): 1.
4. Dale Luciano, letter, *TCJ* 61 (Winter 1981): 41.
5. Michael Fleisher, letter to Will Eisner, January 26, 1984, Will Eisner Papers, box 25, folder 12.

1985, Eisner told an interviewer that since using *graphic novel* on the cover of *Contract*, "the word 'graphic novel' has been used pretty widely, and I'm very pleased in that, because I feel that somehow or other, the concept has found acceptance." He did not "claim to have invented graphic novels," pointing to Lynd Ward's books as a precedent, but neither did he comment on the role played by Kyle, Spicer, or others.[6] Eisner's unparalleled esteem was signaled in 1990, when the first Eisner Awards, recognizing excellence in the field of comics, were presented at the San Diego Comic-Con. In 1995, he was given the Milton Caniff Lifetime Achievement Award, and when he celebrated his eightieth birthday in 1997, his comics were available in more than a dozen languages. Biographer Michael Schumacher explains that Eisner was an "icon" of U.S. comics around the world, epitomized by a version of The Spirit that appeared on the Berlin Wall.[7] Where *Contract*'s reputation was specifically concerned, in 1998, an International Graphic Novel Conference was organized at the University of Massachusetts to mark twenty years since its first publication. *Time* magazine celebrated "The Graphic Novel Silver Anniversary" in November 2003 in acknowledgment of *Contract*'s originary status, and in 2005, W. W. Norton & Company, a New York–based publishing house well known for scholarly editions of canonical literature, published the hardcover *The Contract with God Trilogy: Life on Dropsie Avenue*. This reprinted Eisner's 1978 graphic novel together with two others set on the same Bronx street; in 2017, Norton issued a remastered edition of *Contract* commemorating the centenary of Eisner's birth. Few other graphic novels have been reprinted with so much care and attention to textual fidelity, especially one first published before the late 1980s graphic novel boom.

Contract's originality, quality, and influence are not under question, nor its status as a milestone in the history of the graphic novel, but that status was much less obvious before the end of 1980: its immediate reception was generally warm and occasionally euphoric but not unanimous, and some readers were dismissive, unimpressed, or viciously critical. Eisner's own impatience with *Contract*'s novelness bubbled near the surface when he talked about his follow-up project: "[*Life on Another Planet*] was really an attempt on my part to prove that one could do, and I put this in italics, *a proper novel*, with all the structures that a novel has, the thread of a theme, the main thrust of an idea, the continuity of characters throughout, the development of a single plot into a drama. That book was my attempt to prove that a serious subject, and a seriously fabricated novel could be attempted in this medium."[8] The readers of *The Spirit* magazine expressed the same thoughts to Eisner in their letters—that *LOAP*, "more than 'A Contract with God,' can be truly called a graphic novel."[9]

6. Eisner, interview with Dale Luciano, *TCJ* 100 (July 1985): 86.
7. Constructed in 1961 by the Communist-controlled government of East Germany, the Wall effectively cut East Berlin off from West Berlin until being torn down in 1989 [*Editor*].
8. Eisner, interview with Dale Luciano, 86 (italics in original). See also Will Eisner, "A Talk with Will Eisner," interview with Ted White, Mitch Berger, and Mike Barson, in Inge, *Will Eisner: A Dreamer's Life in Comics* (New York: Bloomsbury, 2010), 85; and Will Eisner, interview with Jim Higgins, *Reflex Magazine* 1.10 (1989): 33.
9. Randy Reynaldo, letter to Will Eisner, June 18, 1979, Will Eisner Papers, box 26, folder 5.

* * * We would do well to locate *Contract* in the broader novelization of comics * * *, reading it as signally important but never the sole popularizer of graphic novels as a concept or a phrase. * * * [T]his does not diminish Eisner's importance to comics history. Several creators recollect that upon publication, *Contract* inspired them to think more ambitiously about the possibilities of comics by proving that a trade press would publish a graphic novel whose content was not that usually found in a 1970s comic.[1] But this should be understood alongside the fact that, in terms of comics-world discourse more generally, the book's exceptionalism was loudly pronounced only in the 1980s and after, by which point other seminal graphic novels (such as Los Bros Hernandez's *Love and Rockets*, vol. 1, 1981–1996) were also being singled out.

JEREMY DAUBER

Comic Books, Tragic Stories: Will Eisner's American Jewish History†

In recent years, we have witnessed a significant increase in writing by scholars and literary and cultural critics on the genre of the comic book, corresponding to an increased legitimacy given to the comic book industry and its writers and artists more generally. * * *

* * *

Much of the recent critical excitement * * * has come not from the classic newsstand comic books but rather from the comic book's full-form version, known as the graphic novel, which is generally published on glossier paper and between harder covers and perhaps best known for its greater degree of literary sophistication and (arguably) aesthetic ambition. Certainly, this field has blossomed in recent years not only in objective terms but also in the eyes of the cultural gatekeepers: When graphic novelists such as Daniel Clowes are prominently featured on the pages of the *New Yorker* and Chris Ware has a weekly feature in the *New York Times Magazine*, then it is clear that what once may have been an underground trend has now emerged firmly into the mainstream.

Many of the graphic novels that have received the most attention (though not those of Ware and Clowes) focus on issues of history, nationality, and ethnicity, often refracted through a personal lens; this is certainly true of Marjane Satrapi's *Persepolis*, which describes the author's experiences growing up in Iran during the Islamic revolution; Joe Sacco's "graphic journalism" covering his time in Gorazde (*Safe Haven Gorazde*) and the West Bank (*Palestine*); and, most notable for people in the field of Jewish studies in general and American Jewish writing in particular, the

1. Levitz, interview with the author; Bob Andelman, *Will Eisner: A Spirited Life* (Milwaukie, Oreg.: M Press, 2005), 294; Schumacher, *Will Eisner*, back cover.

† From *AJS Review* 30.2 (Cambridge, Eng.: Cambridge University Press, 2006): 277–79, 285, 287–94, 297–99, 301–04. Reprinted with permission of University of Pennsylvania Press. Unless indicated otherwise, notes are by the author. Most of the author's notes have been omitted, and some of his references have been edited. Bracketed page references are to this Norton Critical Edition.

work of Art Spiegelman. Spiegelman's two-volume graphic novel biography of his father's experiences during the Holocaust, *Maus* (subtitled "My Father Bleeds History"), combines the riveting testimony of a survivor with a second-generation writer's powerful examination of issues of history, memory, and the responsibility and ability of art to capture that historical memory.

But Spiegelman, for all his merits, was neither the first graphic artist to address Jewish history as seen through personal history nor, despite his honored place in the pantheon of graphic novelists, the most central. It is less well known that one of the central figures of the comics industry in the United States during its formative "golden age"—and the man generally considered the creator of the "graphic novel" more generally—was also, in the last decades of his life, working increasingly on Jewish themes.

The year 2005 saw the passing of Will Eisner, and the posthumous release of his final work—*The Plot: The Secret Story of the Protocols of the Elders of Zion*—provides a useful opportunity to examine his literary output over the better part of six decades. * * * Eisner was not only one of the field's practical innovators but also one of its leading theoreticians; his works on what he referred to as "sequential narrative and graphic art" allow us also to interpret his poetics and to see how Eisner's American Jewish history and biography have been essential in shaping not merely a canonical oeuvre but also the contours of a new and rapidly expanding medium.

* * *

Eisner's Jewish Work: Autobiographies

As mentioned previously, Eisner is known in the field of comics for two fairly distinct achievements: his creation of the Spirit, a groundbreaking adventure hero (but an adventure hero nonetheless), and his invention of the graphic novel, in which he felt freer to explore the literary and autobiographical potential that he had always claimed lay within the "sequential art" form. Eisner said that he found expressing his personal opinions in *A Contract with God* "very, very hard to do, because all my early years I was hiding behind a guy with a mask. I always did speak candidly about my opinions on life, but never about *me*."[1]

* * *

Thirty-five years later, Eisner's developing perspective on not only the nature of the medium but also the kinds of stories that the medium could tell is evident. In his discussions about the medium, he refers to the graphic novel as "a form capable of dealing with much more sophisticated themes than are being dealt with now" and "a *means*, not an *end*."[2] Eisner's innovation in *A Contract with God* was to recreate the medium of the graphic novel as both a genre suited to autobiographical expression and, perhaps because of the added degree of mimetic possibility stemming from the combination of typographical and visual representation, to ethnographic exploration. Eisner writes in his preface to *A Contract with God,*

1. Will Eisner, *Will Eisner's Shop Talk* (Milwaukie, OR: Dark Horse Comics, 2001), 259.
2. Eisner, *Shop Talk*, 73, 170; see also 118, 236.

> In this book, I have attempted to create a narrative that deals with intimate themes. In the four stories, housed in a tenement, I undertook to draw on memory culled from my own experiences and that of my contemporaries. I tried to tell how it was in a corner of America that is still to be revisited.

Eisner's explanation contains the somewhat contradictory implications of any autobiographer or life writer, particularly one with an explicit polemic purpose: on the one hand, his desire to present the graphic novel as a fitting medium for the presentation of the personal requires the creation of intimacy; on the other, as in the case of *The Spirit,* the desire for popular appeal (here not only on behalf of his own work but on behalf of the form itself), which yields to an argument concerning the product's ethnographic value—not merely as an end in itself but as an attempt to truthfully portray an ethnic group as an essential part of understanding the diverse American experience. This is hardly an uncommon strategy among early American Jewish writers, reminding us to contextualize Eisner's graphic novel work as deeply continuous with that of his generational peers, produced in the late 1930s, not the late 1970s.

Though other scholars have addressed the tensions between personal revelation, polemic, and ethnography in American Jewish autobiography and Jewish life writing more generally, the addition of the graphic element, and particularly Eisner's own highly theorized approach to his medium, demands an analysis that incorporates both the visual and textual aspects of the work. * * *

* * *

Eisner uses *A Contract with God* to tell stories of the immigrant and first-generation American Jewish urban experience, particularly in the tenements of the Bronx. Eisner writes more abstractly about cities and their relationship to his art in his collections *City People Notebook* and *Will Eisner's New York: The Big City.* In those works, he notes that "life deep in a big city affects the basic sensibilities and influences the character of one's conduct in a way that affirms environment's triumph over all of us," particularly along the perceptual and cognitive axes of time, smell, and space, which he terms "the most influential and pervasive environmental phenomena."[3] Though much can be said about the first two categories, this essay will focus primarily on his treatment of space.

In these notebooks and sketchbooks, Eisner's dissolution of the traditional panel structure is frequently apparent; large open spaces are often used to accentuate feelings of alienation and unease rather than a sense of possibility. But the overwhelming picture of Eisner's city is that of density and crowding, which allows the graphic novelist's eye both to catch telling and thus literary details, as well as to generate the kinds of encounters that lead to worthwhile stories. In the more narratively developed *A Contract with God*, it becomes clear that there is some thematic connection for the constriction of space faced by the denizens of Eisner's tenements and the constrictions placed on Eisner's art by the conventions of the newspaper comic strip and the comic book—that in telling the

3. Will Eisner, *City People Notebook* (New York: DC Comics, 1989, 2000), 3–4.

stories of these individuals, he is able to provide them with the freedom in their representation that they could not get in their lives.

Eisner writes in his preface,

> It is important to understand the times and the place in which these stories were set. Fundamentally, they were not unlike the way the world of today is for those who live in crowded proximity and in depersonalized housing. The importance of dealing with the ebb and flow of city existence and the overriding effort to escape it never seems to change for the inhabitants.

Indeed, the stories that make up *A Contract with God* are tales of how attempts at liberation are merely prescriptions for another kind of bondage. In the title story, Frimme Hersh has escaped eastern Europe, which is presented in the story as simply a source of constant and near-annihilatory antisemitic attacks, because of his virtue and his ability to make a contract with God, which he writes on a stone: the confinement of virtue for happiness. This happiness is made manifest in the form of an adopted daughter, Rechele, a foundling whom he raises as his own. When Rechele dies of a sudden illness, Frimme Hersh declares himself free of the contract and transforms himself from a pious Hasid into a stereotypical slumlord, complete with shaven beard and Gentile mistress. Eventually, he seeks a kind of return; perhaps spurred by his mistress's offer to convert to Judaism, he goes to the synagogue where he used to work and asks the rabbis there to draw up a new contract with God. After some time, they agree, saying, "is not all religion a contract between man and God . . . he is asking us to provide him with a guiding document so that he might live in harmony with God . . . can we truly deny him this?" They do so, and as he studies the contract later that night, happy to return to his former life, he dies suddenly of a heart attack. Eisner writes,

> At the exact moment of Hersh's last earthly breath . . . a mighty bolt of lightning struck the city . . . Not a drop of rain fell . . . only an angry wind swirled about the tenements. On Dropsie Avenue the old tenements seemed to tremble in the storm. It reminded the tenements of that day, years ago, when Frimme Hersh argued with God and terminated their contract. [58–59]

In an epilogue, another new arrival finds the stone on which Frimme Hersh wrote his original contract and, knowing nothing of the transpiring intervening events, signs it as well. Thus, someone else's own contractual obligations with God begin.

Naturally, Eisner references larger theological issues, as well as previous literary treatments of those issues: Frimme Hersh's insistence that the rabbis create a contract with God recalls the hasidic tales surrounding Rabbi Levi Yitzchak of Berdichev, for example.[4] But one of Eisner's main arguments seems to be that no one is ever really free—or, for that matter, ever really happy. God seems to provide despair, at least existentially speaking, when one violates the contract and agony when one maintains it.

4. See, for example, the tale titled "The Deal" in Martin Buber, *Tales of the Hasidim* (New York: Schocken Books, 1991), 1:209–10. [*Yitzchak of Berdichev:* Hasidic rabbi and Jewish leader, (1740–1809), considered by some to be the founder of Hasidism in Poland—*Editor.*]

Liberation is at best a matter of perspective. In telling this story, then, Eisner is also creating a metaphor of American Jewish existence and the questions of violating tradition as well as maintaining it, both speaking to his own autobiographical experiences and creating an ethnic-national narrative.

But Eisner is an artist as well, one who believes strongly in art's ability to establish and support thematic positions articulated by the writer (particularly when the writer and artist are the same). As a result, it is surely intentional that *A Contract with God*'s visual presentation constantly evokes a sense of claustrophobia. Characters are constantly viewed through doorframes, window sills, and a curtain of rain that threatens, Noah-like, to engulf everything. Though the melodramatic aspects of the presentation of the story certainly lend credence to a reading of the presentation as Eisner's willingness to show off his love of storm and stress—to say nothing of tipping his hat to the pathetic fallacy[5]—it may be possible to suggest that the visuals here once more serve to demonstrate the way in which confinement is a major theme in Eisner's work, one that allows him to *define*: to define Jews as a particular kind of people, to define his memories in a kind of specific context.

This, then, is one kind of tragic Jewish story that Eisner collocates with American Jewish history: tenement life as a place of dreams often denied, promises broken, and pain, suffering, and poverty triumphant. It is a mood that pervades many of Eisner's autobiographical or quasi-autobiographical works; though a full discussion must await further study, suffice it to say that works about his neighborhood are often imbued with this sense of negativity or despair. For example, *The Neighborhood: Dropsie Avenue* (1995), a history of one Bronx neighborhood's rise, decline, and potential rise once more, told through the interwoven stories of its denizens, is a story told almost entirely through lurid tones and depictions. From the very beginning, the avenue's story is built on a horrific accidental death in *grand guignol* style: A child is accidentally burnt to death, a fate that will echo in the final dynamiting of the avenue's last tenement with a legless Vietnam veteran turned drug dealer inside it. The avenue's history, in Eisner's retelling, is filled with horrors, from corruption to gang violence to prostitution to drugs to inter-ethnic strife to the Prohibition equivalent of a drive-by shooting.

This is not to say that Eisner, a witness to life's disappointments and his traditional neighborhood's decline, is unrelentingly nihilist or negative. Like many who lived through the Great Depression, Eisner is struck by the tenacity of the American community—and particularly the immigrant American Jewish community—to continue on in the face of manifold obstacles and massive suffering. In his account of the Great Depression years in the Bronx, *A Life Force* (first published in sections in the 1980s and 1990s), Eisner constantly compares the tenement dwellers, who "remained holding fast to their beachhead simply because they had only just arrived from other, more hostile places [and] carried with them the tabernacle of a life force they hardly understood" to the cockroaches that infest their tenements. In chapters such as "Izzy the Cockroach and the Meaning of Life," the graphic novel's main protagonist,

5. The attribution in literature of human emotions to natural, nonhuman objects [*Editor*].

Jacob Shtarkah (Yiddish for "strong man"), wonders in the course of his hard, unrecompensed life and his unhappy marriage whether there is anything to life in the Great Depression beyond sheer animal survival. In Shtarkah's soliloquies on seeing a cockroach clinging to life, Eisner further develops his philosophical approach to the relation between man and God:

> Well, there are only two possibilities! Either, man created God . . . or, God created man! If . . . man created God . . . then, the reason for life is only in the mind of man!! If, on the other hand, God created man, then the reason for living is still only a guess! . . . After all is said and done, who really knows the will of God? . . . So, in either case, both man and cockroach are in serious trouble. Because staying alive seems to be the only thing on which everybody agrees! [114–15]

By the end of *A Life Force,* though, things have changed just enough to suggest that the possibility of dreaming of a better life—even if one's particular dreams have been crushed—constitutes proof of the actual existence of different, improved circumstances. * * *

* * * For Eisner, it is the dreaming of romance, not the romance itself, that matters: It is not for nothing that Eisner gives one of his most straightforwardly autobiographical and most optimistic graphic novels—a thinly disguised account of his own upward move from the tenements to the successful comic book business—the title *The Dreamer.* Eisner's own life story is, for him, proof of the potentially happy ending of the American Jewish story.

* * *

Well before 2003, Eisner articulated his perspective on stereotype and caricature in his lectures and corresponding books on the subject; he refers to the stereotype as "a fact of life" and "an accursed necessity." Based on a vaguely evolutionary argument that "modern humans still retain instincts developed as primordials" and thus have a long-standing understanding of the meanings of a given set of facial configurations and gestures, as well as a sense of symbols that are "universally valid," Eisner asserts that because comic book drawings "depend on the reader's stored memory of experience to visualize an idea or process quickly," images must be simplified into easily repeatable symbols—"ergo, stereotypes."[6] Eisner's argument is a bit subtler than this sketch suggests: He does point out, for example, that "when the plot is arranged to support it," the stereotypes of, say, doctor visuals "can be abandoned in favor of a type suitable to the story environment."[7] In general, however, his defense of caricature and stereotype is a robust one.

However, Eisner's utilitarian approach, which attempts to maximize effective communication by appealing to universally recognizable images, can be seen to generate its own problems. Take, for example, the portrayals of Jews in Eisner's early graphic novels. As early as *A Contract with*

6. Will Eisner, *Graphic Storytelling and Visual Narrative* (Tamarac, FL: Poorhouse Press, 1996), 17–20; and Will Eisner, *Comics and Sequential Art* (Tamarac, FL: Poorhouse Press, 1985), 13–15. According to Eisner, in determining and identifying these symbols, gestures, and body language, the artist draws on "personal observations and an inventory of gestures, common and comprehensible to the reader" (*Comics and Sequential Art,* 101).
7. Eisner, *Graphic Storytelling and Visual Narrative,* 18.

God, Eisner relies on stereotyped images of Jews throughout the piece. Though Eisner proudly speaks of "actuality," the hyperrealism he employs subtly deforms image to reflect both communicative and thematic concerns. It seems clear that, even with the difference of shaven beard and hair loss, Frimme Hersh before he breaks the contract only vaguely resembles the "Frim" Hersh of afterward in terms of posture, weight, and specifically facial features. In making this change, one can see how complexly and problematically Eisner has drawn on the typical antisemitic image of the Jewish capitalist, with his thick lips and jowls, to make his point.

In *The Neighborhood: Dropsie Avenue,* many different ethnic groups move in (and out) of the neighborhood. The Jews who do are primarily represented in the graphic novel by two characters: Izzy Cashclothes and Abie Gold. In both cases, Eisner traffics in Jewish stereotype, both visually and characterologically: Izzy is drawn as a short, crude, hairy man (and thanks to the perspective that comics provide, he is drawn as approximately three feet tall). Starting as a peddler, he works his way up to being a tenement slumlord. Abie Gold, by contrast, is presented as the fighting Jewish liberal. He represents all of the various ethnicities as a ward councilman, and—significantly for Eisner's vision—brings together the various elements of the neighborhood through his own life: He marries an Italian girl from the neighborhood, allowing, in several scenes, for cooperation between the priest and the rabbi. Portrayed with the high forehead and the glasses of an intellectual, Gold uses his law practice not for the accumulation of wealth but to support the poor and dispossessed. It may be that Eisner's portrayal of Jews in *The Neighborhood* allows him to work out his mixed feelings about Jewish ethnicity by concretizing them in various forms. But what is clear is that in doing so, he engages with—and perhaps problematically, perpetuates—the tragic history of Jewish representation in graphic media more generally.

Such considerations inevitably affect and arguably catalyze Eisner's research into caricature and antisemitic prejudice, which reach their height in his preparation for *Fagin the Jew*:

> Upon examining the illustrations of the original editions of Oliver Twist,[8] I found an unquestionable example of visual defamation in classic literature. The memory of their awful use by the Nazis in World War II, one hundred years later, added evidence to the persistence of evil stereotyping. Combating it became an obsessive pursuit, and I realized that I had no choice but to undertake a truer portrait of Fagin by telling his life story in the only way I could.

* * *

We begin to see Eisner's growing sense that visual media are a strong source of not only propaganda but counterpropaganda as well, and it is therefore somewhat unsurprising that Eisner's next work after *Fagin the Jew* is dedicated to polemically combating one of the most infamous

8. Fagin is the antagonist in the novel *Oliver Twist* by Charles Dickens (see note 3 on p. 251). Dickens's Fagin draws on antisemitic stereotypes of Jews as greedy and manipulative [*Editor*].

pieces of propaganda in the history of antisemitic prejudice, *The Plot: The Secret Story of the Protocols of the Elders of Zion* (2005).[9]

In his introduction to *The Plot,* Eisner once more explains the catalyst for his latest creation in terms of personal history, national history, and the history of the graphic novel. Asserting that *The Plot* "marks an effort to deploy this powerful medium to address a matter of immense personal concern," he writes about his own experiences with American antisemitism and his parents' European "shtetl attitude . . . who advised that we should 'be quiet and not offend the goyim,'"[1] which led to his investigation of antisemitism's sources and, eventually, an examination of the Protocols of the Elders of Zion.[2] However, in *The Plot,* Eisner is finally able to bring together his twin goals of championing graphic novels and Jewish causes. He argues that the "hundreds of books and competent scholarly studies" that have exposed the fraudulent nature of the Protocols have failed because of their esoteric language or their ability to preach only to those convinced of their position, and he suggests that his own medium may succeed where other media have failed:

> I have spent my career in the application of sequential art as a form of narrative language. With the widespread acceptance of the graphic narrative as a vehicle of popular literature, there is now an opportunity to deal head on with this propaganda in a more accessible language. It is my hope that, perhaps, this work will drive yet another nail into the coffin of this terrifying vampire-like fraud.[3]

* * *

The Plot marks a new movement in Eisner's work into the mainstream; published by a mainstream press, W. W. Norton, and boasting an introduction by an unquestionably major figure in the literary world, Umberto Eco,[4] it paved the way for the new release of hardbound versions of all his graphic novels. Whether this pulpit will allow Eisner's perspective on prejudice and on his past to be accepted more widely, is, of course, impossible to know. But it may be enough to encourage more thinking about a major American Jewish writer and a less considered means of American Jewish writing.

9. *Protocols of the Elders of Zion* is an antisemitic text first published in Russia in 1903, purporting to be "documentary" evidence of a Jewish conspiracy to take over the world. It is widely believed to be singularly influential in the resurgence of antisemitism in the 20th century [*Editor*].
1. Non-Jews [*Editor*].
2. Eisner, *The Plot: The Secret Story of the Protocols of the Elders of Zion* (New York: W. W. Norton, 2006), 1.
3. Ibid., 3.
4. Italian scholar, philosopher, political essayist, and novelist (1932–2016). In addition to novels such as *The Name of the Rose* (1980), Eco contributed to a wide range of fields, including the study of fascism, popular culture studies, and medieval studies [*Editor*].

GREG M. SMITH

Will Eisner, Vaudevillian of the Cityscape†

To appreciate Will Eisner's comics, the reader must juggle two seemingly contradictory tendencies in his work. On the one hand, Eisner demonstrates a masterful command of the formal expressiveness of comics. His mature works frequently foreground comics as *comics*, making the reader aware of frame borders, panels, and gutters as devices, not as simple conveyors of the depicted world. Eisner is, therefore, a modernist extraordinaire, a twentieth-century artist deeply concerned with the nature of the medium. On the other hand, Eisner appears to be a retrograde figure bogged down in melodramatic content from the nineteenth century. His stories can be maudlin, with sentimental stock characters gesticulating wildly in emotional paroxysms. The old-fashioned content of his stories seems to be at odds with the modernist impulses governing his formal play. This chapter argues that a key backdrop for understanding the contradictions of Will Eisner's comics is American vaudeville. This popular theatrical form not only provides characters and dramatic structures for his stories, but it also ties Eisner to the modern urban landscape. Melodrama is a response to the changing face of the city, and Eisner's obsession with making the city speak in his comics leads him to his formal experiments. Vaudeville and melodrama are important underpinnings that structure Eisner's work, creating the tensions between modernity and the past that exist throughout his comics.

* * *

Eisner asserted that throughout his career he argued for a more sophisticated vision of comics that took advantage of their full potential. He recalled one particular occasion when he was extolling the beauties of comics to his fellow practitioners: "[Newspaper cartoonist] Rube Goldberg told me that what I was saying was bullshit. He said, 'Shit, boy, you're a vaudevillian. Don't forget this is vaudeville'" (Brownstein 2005: 63). I contend that, although Eisner aspired to "serious" work, he never did forget the lesson he learned from Goldberg and from his early experiences with American popular theater. The expressive forms and narrative structures of vaudeville show their imprint throughout Eisner's career.

American popular theater of the late nineteenth and early twentieth century depends on an understanding of gesture that is quite different from the norms of "realism" and "naturalism" that eventually laid claim to American stage and film acting. Instead of comparing melodramatic theatrical acting to the styles that later displaced it, it is more helpful to situate these turn-of-the-century performance styles in the theories that governed their practice. The work of François Delsarte[1] sought to provide

† From *Comics and the City: Urban Space in Print, Picture and Sequence*, ed. Jörn Ahrens and Arno Meteling (London: Continuum, 2010), pp. 183–97. Reprinted with permission of Bloomsbury Press. Notes are by the editor of this Norton Critical Edition. Some of the author's parenthetical references have been omitted. Bracketed page references are to this Norton Critical Edition.

1. French singer and orator (1811–1871), best known for developing the Delsarte System, which sought to coach artists in conveying emotion by connecting with their inner feelings and translating them through the body.

a conventionalized language for actors and dancers to convey emotion to an audience. He advocated bold gestures to give acting power, as opposed to subtler movements that were less clear. Delsarte studied patterns of gesture in everyday life, and he honed a system of archetypal postures based on these investigations. Horror, for example, could be effectively displayed by putting one hand to the head and the other palm outstretched and upright to ward off the horrific being. When actors wished to depict moments of high emotion, it was necessary for them to put their bodies into a characteristic posture in order for emotion to transfer directly to the audience. Unlike later Stanislavsky-based theories that made conventional forms the antithesis of good acting, conventional gestures are crucial for Delsarte. Spoken language is conventional too, but it does not access the deeper structures of the emotions in the way that the expressive human body can. A codified system of characteristic gestures combines the clarity of language with the emotional power of the human figure.

Genevieve Stebbins's 1886 book *The Delsarte System of Expression* was a hit, influencing stage practice worldwide but particularly in America. The drawn illustrations of this book resemble a comic, with figures demonstrating various conventional postures. These figures bear particular resemblance to the postures found in Eisner's comics. When Eisner wants to give a lesson on "expressive anatomy" in his *Comics and Sequential Art*, he produces an illustration that seems almost straight out of Delsarte. He sketches a "micro-dictionary of gestures": a series of silhouettes in exaggerated postures to demonstrate particular emotions: anger, fear, joy, surprise, and so on. His fictional comics repeatedly demonstrate this tendency to pose his characters in Delsartian expressive positions. In the Spirit story entitled "Wild Rice," the villainess tries to manipulate her captors with a display of theatrical acting. Her head back against the wall, tears flowing, she balls up her fists to rail against the world, saying, "Yes . . . Fun while it lasted . . . *While it lasted* . . . That's how it's been all my life . . . Is there no way to escape?" He continues this emphasis on broad gesture in his later graphic novels. When Frimme Hersh's daughter dies in *A Contract with God*, the Hasidic man throws his head back and raises both arms, his knees buckled, crying out to God, "NO! Not to me . . . You can't do this . . . We have a contract!!" [28]. When Jacob Shtarka tells his wife, Rifka, that he wants a divorce in *A Life Force*, she runs through a series of dramatic postures, one after the other, depicting her excessive grief: She puts both hands to her head and opens her mouth wide; she lays one hand on her breast, the other clutching her head; then she collapses onto a chair maintaining her hand positions.

Like many comic artists, Eisner recognized that he could depict his characters in any of a range of poses. In order for his visual storytelling to be clear, he needed to capture a particularly strong posture for his characters. When looking for a model of how to position figures in the most dramatically powerful way, he would reasonably turn to the American popular theater, influenced by the widely disseminated theories of Delsarte.

Theater provided structural principles for Eisner's page layouts as well. Eisner often treats the single page (or a pair of comics pages) as the comics equivalent of the stage scene, maintaining a unity of time and space across the page, then moving to another continuous time-space on the following page. Eisner frequently takes advantage of the "natural" break between pages to transition to another place and time, as if a curtain descends on the scene at page's end only to rise again at the top of the next page. Eisner explicitly acknowledged his theatrical roots in a published conversation with Frank Miller:

> . . . each page is . . . like theater, it's a scene. A [comic] book is a series of scenes, like what I first was exposed to when I saw vaudeville as a kid: there were scenes that were called blackouts. Blackouts were little vignette scenes where the joke was told visually, and at the end of the joke all the lights went out.
>
> (Brownstein 2005: 83)

In this anecdote, Eisner emphasizes the comic scene structure of vaudeville, but his own work leans toward the dramatic, and so it borrows also from the dramatic structures of vaudeville.

Eisner's page "scenes" tend to end at a moment of dramatic suspension of the action, a moment known in American popular theater as a "tableau." A tableau, according to Ben Brewster and Lea Jacobs, was a pictorial effect onstage in which characters "froze" into a static posture. This often occurred at the ends of scenes because once dramatic action has halted, it is difficult (though not unheard of) to put the characters back into motion in a somewhat believable fashion. The tableau, therefore, is a highly theatrical, non-naturalistic effect that suspends action in order for the audience to linger over, contemplating both the aesthetics of the frozen *mise-en-scène* and the dramatic tension between the characters.

The tableau often occurs at a narrative "situation." In the parlance of the time, a dramatic situation was a moment in which the "linear progress of the narrative is arrested or blocked" (Brewster and Jacobs 1997: 24). Situations are points at which opposing forces meet. The characters freeze because they reach a physical impasse: If one character moves, then the entire direction of the narrative changes. Brewster and Jacobs say: "Situations thus exist on the cusp of actions; they give rise to actions and are in turn altered by them . . . [They are] an unstable constellation of forces precariously held in check but nonetheless liable to break out into action" (Brewster and Jacobs 1997: 23). Tableaux, therefore, give pictorial embodiment to the narrative situation. A situation is more than just a stilled action; it is a highly energized pause where characters are on the verge of doing something narratively significant.

The scenes in Eisner's stories often end in a situation/tableau where the characters take an exaggerated posture at the height of the scene's action. When Willie's shop-owner father discovers that his son is making pro-union signs for a mass demonstration in *A Life Force*, he tells Willie and his friend to "get out of my house!" pointing one hand dramatically in the air, eyes closed, while the two youngsters look at each other in bewilderment. Sometimes such moments are quiet stoppages of action. When Father O'Leary tells Neil in *Dropsie Avenue* that both his parents have died, the priest asks "Is there anything I can do? After all, we are neighbors, Neil!!" The final panel shows Neil slumped over his piano, his shoulders sagging as the father leaves, and Neil says, "Nothing!" At the ends of pages/scenes, Eisner loves to freeze the action with his characters at their most expressive position, depicting a moment where something must change before the story can move forward. In so doing, he duplicates the frozen tableaux and narrative situations developed in American popular theater.

In making the link to tableaux and situations, I want to say something more than the obvious observation that comics are composed of still images. Of course every image on a comics page is frozen, but the panels at the ends of Eisner's scenes tend to present a particular kind of stilled action. These scenes show us a moment of action halted at an instant where the opposing character forces have stalemated each other. This differs from previous panels in the scene that tend to show intermediate stages with actions in progress, one action leading to the next, and not the tense constriction of potential energy that characterizes the situation.

Theatrical situations become principles that operate in a variety of narrative forms, but they most importantly serve as a structuring principle for melodrama. Melodrama places less emphasis on a strong linear character-driven line of action than more realistic drama does. Instead, as Brewster and Jacobs argue, melodrama maximizes the number of sensational situations, stringing them together with minimal narrative connective tissue. Characters in a melodrama lurch from dramatic reversal to reversal in ways that can be psychologically implausible, and this causes melodrama to be maligned by those who do not understand its distinctive structures. The skill for a melodramatist is to lead an audience from one emotionally affecting situation to another.

Melodrama, then, models the experience of moving through the modern world, being battered from all sides by intense sensations that have little connection to each other. To the immigrants emerging into the strange new world of the modern city, the urban environment presented them with a series of shocks. Modernity severs the ties between the individual and their former cultural context, forcing them away from the insulation of rural life to deal with a dizzying array of unfamiliar people and situations. The modern city dweller develops the ability to evaluate strangers based on their public presentation of self, and melodrama is obsessed with this unveiling of the underlying moral order. Melodrama is concerned with revealing who is truly moral, in spite of their public face. The esteemed landlord can be exposed as a tyrant; the proper husband might be a brutal wife-beater behind closed doors; or publishers can renege on their dealings with struggling comics artists. By participating in a melodramatic narrative, audiences can hone their skills at the urban survival skill of evaluating strangers through close observation of their actions and emotions.

Modernity, then, places the individual in a disorienting world of speed and mobility. The promise of modernity is that it will bring the world under the rational control of planners, that people will be more protected from the vagaries of nature as they participate in the steady rhythms of scheduled industrial labor and modern leisure. However, the fear that modernity produces is that individuals are more susceptible to fortune's reversals. In this seemingly more rational world, disaster is outside the individual's control in the form of industrial accidents, factory layoffs during economic downturns, or violence at the hands of criminals. This provides the social justification for the lack of classical causality in the melodrama. If external events can intervene to cause chaos in an individual's life in the real world, then certainly melodrama can move from one sensational, relatively unmotivated emotional crisis to another. The spectacle of overwrought suffering is the central pleasure provided by melodrama, just as walking down the urban street can present a series of displays of strangers caught in moments of high emotion. Melodrama, to this way of thinking, is both a reaction to modernity and an attempt to gain a certain measure of control over its excesses. Melodrama, far from being a retrograde practice, can be seen as being deeply embroiled in the contemporary experience.

Vaudeville adapted the melodramatic form (which developed over centuries) into a modular form, as is befitting the compartmentalized world of the modern city. Vaudeville presented a conveyor belt of disparate emotional sensations, each one only minimally related to the preceding one. A juggling act might follow an operatic tenor singing an aria, followed by a comedian, a short dramatic scene, and a coterie of dancers. Vaudeville's structure took maximal advantage of a centralized distribution network of performers, thus allowing theater managers to treat individual acts as interchangeable parts, following the lead of the assembly line. Many different arrangements could result because there was no necessary dramatic logic that forced the components into a particular order.

The city encloses people into modules as well, providing standardized domiciles (in the form of apartment buildings) and routinized work schedules in factories. The city places people in a range of compartments of different sizes and forms, and Eisner's comics explore the multiple forms of urban compartmentalization and containment. His stories present melodramatic narratives of people trapped by their circumstances, railing against the cruel injustice of these narrative impasses. Eisner's enclosed figures embody Delsartian postures, making their emotional plight clearly legible to their audience.

Transposing these melodramatic narratives from their stage heritage to the medium of comics creates a distinctive opportunity that could not exist in the theater. In depicting these stories of enclosure, Eisner begins to be interested in the formal possibilities posed by the urban landscape. His work becomes increasingly concerned with tracing the multiple forms of the cityscape and noting how each one can frame these entrapped characters. Eisner's comics form a catalog of how architecture can become a frame and how these frames can become prisons.

* * *

Eisner's pages often begin and end with exits through doors, further accentuating the connection between his pages and the structure of theatrical scenes. Just as in film, there is no need for a comic's character to exit the scene. In theater, an actor who is onstage has to get off the stage. In film this can be accomplished with a cut; in comics with a simple transition to another time and place. Eisner's tendency to begin or end scenes in doorways both points to his fascination with the formal possibilities that doors present and the strong theatrical heritage that influences his comics' staging.

Windows similarly play a strong role in Eisner's formal architectural play. The cover to *Dropsie Avenue* is a brick-building front with each of the sets of characters in the neighborhood seen through various windows. The layout of the cover draws attention to the similarity between these windows and the layout of panels in a comic page. In one of Eisner's famous splash pages that often began his Spirit stories, the Spirit stares through the bars of the window of the police station as rain falls outside, and the bars duplicate the rectangular layout of the standard comics page. The elegant flashbacks in *To the Heart of the Storm* often begin as World War II serviceman Willie looks out of the train as he returns home, and what he sees through the frame of the window triggers his memories. Similarly in one of the short pieces in *New York: The Big City* appropriately entitled "Theater," a man looks out a subway window at a passing scene of two lovers framed by their bedroom window, a frame within a frame. The obvious connection between windows and doors is that they usually (but not always) echo the rectangular shape of the standard comic's frame. They offer a fairly naturalized opportunity to emphasize the relationship between the diegetic space and the usually unacknowledged border that frames the action. Eisner's formalist tendencies rarely extend so far that he calls attention to the expressive capacity of the panel border without some motivation. His modernist practice, therefore, is limited, seeking grounding in the story world instead of flaunting formal play with the frame for its own purposes.

An outgrowth of Eisner's interest in architecture is his emphasis on the shapes made by light. Once he began to play with doors and windows, there is a natural progression to the squares of light produced by these architectural features. After all, in comics both the doors and their attached shadows are simply rectangles, just as comics' frames often are. It is just as easy to draw an outline of cast light as it is to draw an outline of a window letting the light in.

In addition, comics can heighten dramatic "lighting" because drawing makes "lighting effects" possible that could not be achieved in real life. Real theatrical lighting requires very powerful lighting instruments in order to create a distinct edge, and no lighting instrument can define an outline as clear and sharp as an inked line. The lighting in Eisner's compositions is often described as following film noir practice, but this is not quite accurate. Eisner's lighting effects can be *more* noir than film noir, accomplishing effects that no actual film lighting could.

These lighting effects eventually take on a kind of tangible form. As the connections between cast shadows and drawn frames become more foregrounded, it becomes possible for these lighting effects to serve as a kind of stage on which the action occurs. In the * * * Sand Saref story, the light spilling through the open doorway illuminates a square in the black frame, providing a landing for the suitor's fall in the otherwise abstract space. In later works, the square of light begins to drift away from its moorings to become pure space. The short work "Sermonette" begins with a street preacher shouting in an alley between buildings. As the sermon continues, the buildings disappear, leaving the street preacher declaiming on an abstract rectangle of space. In these moments, the grounding in naturalism is tenuous at best. Here we see light and shadow as almost pure outline, using them to frame and enclose the action just as strongly as doors and windows do. Here we see light being used in ways that greatly exceed the theatrical practice that gave rise to these effects. Adapting melodramatic stories of entrapment to comics created opportunities for Eisner to experiment in distinctive ways with comics'

The naturalized frame: Windows frame the flashback images within the panel

From: *To the Heart of the Storm* (New York: Norton, 2008), 35.

depiction of spatial enclosures. Adapting lighting effects from theater to comics made them more theatrical in ways that exceed the source.

The naturalized play that Eisner is most known for is his handling of rain and water. This tendency is so pronounced in Eisner's work that Harvey Kurtzman gave it a name: "Eisenshpritz." Rain creates spectacular vistas in the Spirit's Central city, such as the splash page in "Life Below," in which rain drips across a stone structure that spells out the Spirit's name. Rain functions like light in Eisner's comics, as a naturalized feature of the environment that greatly exceeds its grounding in reality. It hugs and flows around the urban landscape, accentuating its contours just as light does. Rain acts like shading, creating dramatic spatial effects. As Eisner works later in his life, he begins using less of the spectacular Eisenshpritz that distinguished his early career, instead using the same kinds of lines as shading. The lines that might have been rain in the Spirit become patches of shading in his later graphic novels.

* * *

At the same time Eisner's artistic style begins to extend more and more outside the confines of the frame boundaries. This tendency has always been present in Eisner's work, although he does this only to a limited extent in his run on the Spirit. When Eisner reemerges in mainstream comics with his graphic novel *A Contract with God*, he seems energized by the innovative work of comics artists in the 60s and 70s. Once practitioners such as Neal Adams and Jim Steranko began extending their art outside the classical container of the panel, this seems to embolden Eisner in his later graphic novels to make good on his nascent tendency to play with the panel border. Thus freed, Eisner's later works can fully explore the tropes of containment and liberation in his stories. His characters can be imprisoned within their narrative confines and within the borders traced by Eisner's lines, but they can also find freedom, expressed both in story terms and by having characters sail outside the classical panel. In his later works, Eisner's form and content are free to interact in lyrical counterpoint to present his vision of the city.

* * *

Eisner's city is rarely experienced as a whole, except when viewed from enough distance to see the (abstracted) skyline. The city as seen from the street is a series of specific locales. Throughout this chapter I have listed various archetypal urban locations that Eisner uses: stoops, doorways, drain grates, windows, alleys, and so on. Eisner's city is a city of fragments because that is how his characters perceive the urban landscape. His characters feel modernity not as an overall totalizing force but as a series of details and occurrences that have personal bearing on their lives.

The city architecture impinges on the people who inhabit it, uncomfortably shoving them up against each other like characters on a comics page. Will Eisner sees the city as a prison, but mostly he sees that prison as being created by other people. In *The Name of the Game*, marriage is a trap that constrains multiple generations of the Arnheim family. In *Family Matter*, mute patriarch Ben is confined to a wheelchair by a stroke, leaving him to be tortured by his family, who air their grievances in front of him. "Mortal Combat" tells a story of a couple whose chance at romantic happiness is destroyed by an overbearing parent. There is no escaping other people in the city, and so relationships make Eisner's characters into jailors.

The emphasis in Eisner then is not on the city itself but on the personal lived experience of the city. The city can retreat to the background, providing a backdrop for his characters. It can be reduced to lived fragments or to abstract outlines. The city is rarely far away, however. The urban environment cannot be separated from these characters' lives because they bear its indelible marks, just as melodrama is inconceivable without the shaping provided by modernity.

Works Cited

Brewster, Ben and Lea Jacobs. *Theatre to Cinema: Stage Pictorialism and the Early Feature Film*. Oxford: Oxford University Press, 1997.

Brooks, Peter. *The Melodramatic Imagination: Balzac, Henry James, Melodrama, and the Mode of Excess*. New Haven, CT: Yale University Press, 1995.

Brownstein, Charles. *Eisner/Miller*. Milwaukie, OR: Dark Horse Comics, 2005.

Eisner, Will. *Comics and Sequential Art*. New York: Norton, 2008.

Eisner, Will. *Graphic Storytelling and Visual Narrative*. New York: Norton, 2008.

Gledhill, Christine. "Historicizing Melodrama." In: *Home Is Where the Heart Is: Studies in Melodrama and the Woman's Film*. London: BFI Publishing, 1987. 14–39.

Singer, Ben. *Melodrama and Modernity: Early Sensational Cinema and Its Contexts*. New York: Columbia University Press, 2001.

Stebbins, Genevieve. *The Delsarte System of Expression*. New York: Edgar Warner, 1886.

DEREK PARKER ROYAL

There Goes the Neighborhood: Cycling Ethnoracial Tensions in Will Eisner's *Dropsie Avenue*†

In his *Contract with God* trilogy Will Eisner, one of the earliest and most vocal advocates of the graphic novel, sets out to narrate the life of Dropsie Avenue, a neighborhood in the Bronx housing residents of diverse ethnic backgrounds. His first two books in the trilogy—*A Contract with God* (1978) and *A Life Force* (1988)—focus primarily on the lives of Jewish families caught in the struggles of Depression-era America, reminiscent of both Isaac Bashevis Singer's shtetl portraits and the kind of Jewish social realism found in the work of Anzia Yezierska and Michael Gold.[1] However, the third book in the trilogy, *Dropsie Avenue: The Neighborhood* (1995), is strikingly different from its predecessors in that it is not restricted to an individual family or a cast of three or four characters. What is more, and also unlike the previous works in the trilogy, *Dropsie Avenue* does not primarily concern itself with Jewish issues, culture, or families. Instead, Eisner's story is projected onto a much broader canvas, American ethnoracial relations as a whole and the process of urban assimilation. The narrative sweep of the graphic novel encompasses Dropsie Avenue residents from the 1870s to the late twentieth century, revealing its multi-ethnic evolution and the turmoil generated by such diverse encounters. What is significant about the last in Eisner's trilogy is the ways in which the author uses comics to represent the ongoing dynamics of the modern ethnic neighborhood. Through both word and picture, Eisner offers a critical—if not downright cynical—reading of the traditional "melting pot" myth, resistant to any romantic notions of multicultural nationhood that any "cartoony" representations might initially suggest. On the contrary, the very form of his efforts—the fluid sweep of his graphics, his non-traditional uses of framing, and his employment of contrastive tones—reveals a rather stark, even neo-naturalistic, analysis of relations between American ethnic communities. As Laurence Roth says of the three Dropsie Avenue narratives, "the special contracts promised between America and its citizens . . . are redrawn by Eisner as distinctly unglamorous and unfulfilled agreements."[2] What is more, Eisner's bittersweet rendition of the Dropsie Avenue neighborhood (much like the one in which the author grew up) is further complicated by what he apparently sees as the cyclical nature of ethnoracial tensions—a fitting metaphor, given the fact that the book itself is part of a larger graphic narrative cycle.

† From *Shofar* 29.2 (Winter 2011): 120–36, 140–44. Reprinted with permission of Purdue University Press. Unless indicated otherwise, notes are by the author. The author's page references and most of his footnotes have been omitted, and some of his references have been edited. Some illustrations have been omitted. Bracketed page references are to this Norton Critical Edition.

1. American writer and Communist activist (1894–1967), whose work focused on the experiences of the proletariat and on growing up poor and Jewish in the Lower East Side of New York City. *Isaac Bashevis Singer*: see note 3 on p. 237. *Anzia Yezierska*: Polish-born American writer (1880–1970), who emigrated with her family in early adolescence, and whose work often focused on the lives of immigrants living in the Lower East Side of New York City [*Editor*].
2. Laurence Roth, "Drawing Contracts: Will Eisner's Legacy," *The Jewish Quarterly Review*, Vol. 97, No. 3 (2007): 466.

In drawing together the various actions that occur and recur, cycle-like, throughout the text, Eisner employs several highly revealing and visually sophisticated graphic signifiers that dramatically underscore the violence and alienation that can result within multi-ethnic communities. They include a metaphoric emphasis on windows, references to fire, and the presence of "For Sale" or "For Rent" signs, and it is the use of these visual themes that will be the focus of the current essay. These cyclically recurring images function as a form of illustrated shorthand, coded disclosures of the seemingly never-ending, and apparently futile, attempts of diverse populations to work out their differences and live in mutual respect. They serve as visual leitmotifs that not only underscore the pessimistic tone of the graphic novel, but also interlink the sprawling action of the narrative—assorted sequences that, taken together, can certainly be read as a metaphor for the breakdown in American ethnoracial relations. In other words, the many references to windows, fire, and signs serve the paradoxical function of binding together into a cohesive whole a series of varied and disjointed episodes that are intended to emphasize social fragmentation.

The plot of *Dropsie Avenue* is fairly simple. It begins in 1870, in the living room of the Van Dropsies, a Dutch family from New York's earliest wave of immigrant settlers, where they are discussing the relatively recent arrival of the English into their neighborhood, a region that we now know as the Bronx. Dirk Van Dropsie complains that the English are gaining the economic upper hand on the Dutch residents, and on one drunken night sets fire to a neighbor's crops as an act of protest. In the process Dirk accidentally kills his niece by immolation, he is then shot by his brother-in-law, the Dropsie family goes into seclusion until their house is eventually destroyed by fire, and then soon after a "For Sale" sign is placed on the property. Several years later, the newly rich O'Brien family purchases the lot, wanting desperately to move up in social circles and enhance their lifestyle in the now predominantly English neighborhood, and then just as the Van Dropsies had earlier scrutinized the English, the O'Briens are scrutinized by the English neighbors across the street. These early scenes in this graphic novel set the stage for many of the images and themes that will recur throughout. "Established" residents will become unsettled by the arrival of newer immigrants, complain about the "colorful" changes—color as signifier of difference resonates throughout this work—eventually sell their homes and move away from Dropsie Avenue. The newer immigrants will then become the "established" neighbors, eventually bemoaning the fact that an even newer and more "colorful" group of arrivals have started to move in. This continues throughout the graphic novel, with the English being replaced by the Irish, who are replaced by the Italians, followed by the Germans, Jews, and Hispanics (primarily Puerto Ricans), and then finally by the African Americans.

The central figure in this drama is the Dropsie neighborhood itself, a setting that becomes a character, metaphorically living and breathing with a life force all its own. In fact, several times throughout the graphic novel individuals comment on how neighborhoods have a life cycle much like people. As one of the book's dominant figures, Abie Gold, speculates, "Maybe a neighborhood has a life cycle . . . like people!" And if the neighborhood is the central character in this novel, it is one that is as chaotic and fragmented as the relationships among its inhabitants. What binds these various episodes together are a series of interlocking themes and images—such as those of fire, signs, and windows—that connect, or cycle, its long string of individual stories. In this way, *Dropsie Avenue* is much like Eisner's 1978 graphic novel, *A Contract with God,* a text that relies on the short-story cycle form as way of bringing together its seemingly disparate narratives. However, *Dropsie Avenue* is more, and in the fullest sense, novelistic than the earlier work, with its more tightly woven scenes and its structuring imagery. In fact, it is a graphic novel whose visuals dramatically outweigh its verbiage in narrative significance.

Inside Looking Out, Outside Looking In

Perhaps the most common theme in *Dropsie Avenue* can be summed up by the fatalistic adage, "There goes the neighborhood." Individuals from one ethnic community are constantly throwing up their hands at the arrival of individuals from another ethnic group, and this throwing up of the hands can be read at different times as resignation, resistance, and relocation. The resignation comes in the form of moderate voices within an established community, accepting the presence of a new group of residents and aware of the potential for growth and progress among different people. In Eisner's text, this pragmatic approach to ethnic diversity is often clothed in religious garb—for instance, there are occasions when Father O'Leary, Father Gianelli, Rabbi Goodstein, and the African American reverend Dr. Washington acknowledge the reality of the changing neighborhood and adjust their outlooks accordingly—but it also comes in more secular forms. Abie Gold and Polo Palmero, a lawyer and a political boss, are two of the most developed characters in the novel and understand the social necessity, as well as the personal profits, that come of good community relations.

While examples of resignation and even understanding can be found throughout *Dropsie Avenue,* scenes of resistance and relocation are far more plentiful. One way in which Eisner represents ethnoracial discord is through the use of windows as a visual theme. The artist uses windows and glass imagery not only to illustrate (literally) the various barriers separating one ethnic group from another, but also as a commentary on the process of obtaining "insider" status. In this way, we can read *Dropsie Avenue* as a visual discourse on whiteness, or the means through which certain individuals and groups identify themselves as "white," thereby positioning themselves within a perceived middle class—or at least distinctly separate from what they see as common laborers or recent immigrants—and assuming the various entitlements and privileges such a status provides. Window imagery functions as a way of representing both insider and outsider status, and the graphic novel is filled with examples of "privileged" characters inside their domains looking out at others, or perspectives of individuals outside looking in on those in positions of authority. As such, Eisner provides us not only with examples of ethnoracial identity formation, how individuals contextualize themselves within certain ethnic and racial groupings, but also with the process of what Karen Brodkin calls "ethnoracial assignment," which is "about popularly held classifications and their deployment by those with national

Figure 1. Reprinted from *Dropsie Avenue* by Will Eisner. 14. Copyright © 1995 by Will Eisner, Copyright © 2006 by the Estate of Will Eisner. Used with permission of the publisher, W. W. Norton & Company, Inc.

power to make them matter economically, politically, and socially to the individuals classified."[3]

The opening episodes of *Dropsie Avenue* are an effective demonstration of this. In the first scene, Hendrik Van Dropsie, the Dutch landowner whose father bought the property from the Van Bronks, is looking out of his window and talking with his family about the growing presence of the English. Hendrik's brother-in-law, Dirk, complains that the English are buying up everything and, standing by the window, claims that soon the new residents will "make things bad" for the Van Dropsies [167] and damns them for not belonging [168]. A similar context is drawn after the Van Dropsie house is burned to the ground. When Sean O'Brien, a *nouveau riche* Irish owner of a construction company, builds a mansion in the neighborhood, the Skidmore family (part of the now dominant English presence on Dropsie Avenue) stands by their window and bemoans the O'Briens' presence (Fig. 1). Looking out at their unwanted neighbors, they complain that Mrs. O'Brien walks down the street "as if she owns the neighborhood," and laugh at them because "they don't even know they don't belong." This use of window imagery occurs repeatedly throughout the graphic novel, linking together the separate episodes and demonstrating patterns of exclusiveness among the various ethnic residents of Dropsie Avenue.

Windows are also used to establish authority and privilege from an inverse perspective. There are a number of scenes where Eisner forces the reader, through visual framing and perspective, to look in on those with economic power, individuals who have "made it" in the neighborhood and who now have some political voice. One of the most frequently recurring characters in the graphic novel is the Ashkenazi ragman, Izzy Cash, so called because of his singsong cries as he pushes his cart down

3. Karen Brodkin, *How the Jews Became White Folks, and What That Says about Race in America* (New Brunswick, NJ: Rutgers University Press, 1998), p. 3.

Figure 2. Reprinted from *Dropsie Avenue* by Will Eisner. 131. Copyright © 1995 by Will Eisner, Copyright © 2006 by the Estate of Will Eisner. Used with permission of the publisher, W. W. Norton & Company, Inc.

the street: "I cash clothes" [179]. He becomes the central economic power on Dropsie Avenue, and even his name suggests as much. He is one of the only figures in the novel who is observed through windows from an outside perspective. When he buys his first building from the borough bank, we are introduced to this transaction as if we were standing outside the bank window looking in [187]. When he is present at a hearing because he is accused of being a slumlord, we observe the action from the outside and through the door's windows. And before Izzy begins selling off his property, having a "bad feeling about Dropsie Avenue" and realizing that it is going downhill, we see him discussing this matter with his assistant as if we were looking through the window of his office door (Fig. 2). The latter example is particularly telling, in that as we observe Izzy Cash through the door window—as if we were outside of the room—he is looking outside of his office window at the crumbling neighborhood below. In other words, the distance between the haves and the have nots is compounded. In these scenes with Izzy, the outsider is the focalizer. It is as if the reader

Figure 3. Reprinted from *Dropsie Avenue* by Will Eisner. 158, 161. Copyright © 1995 by Will Eisner, Copyright © 2006 by the Estate of Will Eisner. Used with permission of the publisher, W. W. Norton & Company, Inc.

is serving as a narrative proxy for the disempowered other as he or she looks in on, and is separated from, those with economic clout.

* * *

As these many examples clearly demonstrate, Eisner's use of windows emphasizes the economic and social divisions resulting from ethnoracial turmoil, and it reveals the almost cyclical process through which immigrant communities establish themselves in order to be considered "white" . . . or the violence that can result from being excluded from such social privilege. The window imagery also helps to give form to his sprawling narrative, with the repeated use of windows binding together the book's many episodes. In fact, one can even read the recurring image as a metafictional device. It is as if Eisner is drawing our attention to his project by showing us that windows are visually similar to the various panels that make up the comic page. This becomes apparent toward the end of the graphic novel, when we see the last remaining tenement building minutes before it is demolished. And at the Dropsie Avenue Reunion, the pictures on "The Old Neighborhood as We Remember It" display board recall the multi-paned building just three pages earlier (Fig. 3). The reunion photographs can even be seen as "windows" into the past. Yet, as these final visual references suggest—the boarded up windows and the pictures of a dead past—Dropsie Avenue no longer embodies the dreams of its earliest residents. Even the final attempts to revive the neighborhood, bankrolled by the Rowena Plant Corporation, fall prey to the suspicions of and prejudices against the ethnic other.

Firestorms of Ethnoracial Animosity

Another way in which Eisner reveals fear and bigotry in *Dropsie Avenue*, and also gives form to his narrative, is though fire imagery. Throughout the text, fire is directly linked to the anger and discontent among the neighborhood residents, and they come in a variety of forms, from budding embers of personal resentment to full-scale emotional explosions from the community at large. In fact, the graphic novel more or less begins with such imagery. In the opening scene, Dirk's anger at the growing English presence is expressed through conflagration [168]. He attempts to destroy the English crops, thereby removing any economic threat that the new arrivals may pose. Screaming "Burn them out!" Dirk literalizes the inner fires of his hatred, and in doing so he ignites a flame that consumes not only the English crops, but also his niece, Helda Van Dropsie. In these opening pages of his graphic novel, Eisner is pointing out, rather overtly, the underlying nature of the Dropsie neighborhood, illustrating through its very namesake the fire-laden forces of destruction that will propel the rest of the narrative.

While the opening scenes with the Van Dropsie family may be a rather heavy-handed way to symbolize hatred, other scenes in the book reveal a more nuanced use of fire imagery. One such episode occurs in a brief exchange between Coleen O'Brien and her brother Neil (Fig. 4). It is around 1900, approximately thirty years after the opening crop fire, and the O'Brien family currently owns the old Van Dropsie property, now centrally located within a largely English population. In this scene Coleen tells her brother about her affair with Charles Livermore, from a well-to-do Anglo ancestry, which ended because the Livermore family would not let their son marry, in Coleen's words, "a low class Irish girl." What is significant about this series of panels is the way in which Eisner uses Coleen's cigarette smoke as a means to revealing ethnic resentment. As she pours out her story to Neil, her words are literally framed by the smoke that she exhales. Unlike the opening scenes with Van Dropsie, the hate portrayed in this episode visually begins as a small flame at the top of the page and then is slowly revealed through the burning down of Coleen's cigarette, the smoke of which encompasses the insult and rumor leveled against the young Irish woman.

Eisner uses a similar technique several pages later, when a group of neighborhood residents, now primarily Irish, congregate to discuss the recent immigrant arrivals (Fig. 5). It is the early days of World War I, and the "Dropsie Avenue Property Owner's Association" has gathered to discuss a possible solution to the growing German population. "Them Krauts is movin' in," one resident exclaims, and the men decide to hold a patriotic block party as a way of "cleaning up the neighborhood." Their frustrations, as well as their unfounded fears, are initially revealed through their tobacco smoke, and this framing device immediately follows the image of a "For Sale" sign, a panel that serves as a segue between Neil O'Brien's story and the owner's association's clash with their German neighbors. * * *

* * * Elsewhere, Eisner uses much more dramatic means to express ethnic discontent (Fig. 6). In illustrating the U.S. entering the Second World War, he juxtaposes images of Dropsie Avenue (the street shot at the top part of the page) with scenes of destruction from the war, a conflict that was largely waged over issues of ethnoracial differences. With both the newspaper headlines screaming war and the mushroom cloud on the

Figure 4. Reprinted from *Dropsie Avenue* by Will Eisner. 20. Copyright © 1995 by Will Eisner, Copyright © 2006 by the Estate of Will Eisner. Used with permission of the publisher, W. W. Norton & Company, Inc.

Figure 5. Reprinted from *Dropsie Avenue* by Will Eisner, 30. Copyright © 1995 by Will Eisner, Copyright © 2006 by the Estate of Will Eisner. Used with permission of the publisher, W. W. Norton & Company, Inc.

left hand of the panel, Eisner links the ethnic resentments on Dropsie Avenue with images of war-ravaged Europe. What is more, the bright streetlight at the bottom right of the page not only pulls the eye downward from the pre-war scenes of Dropsie Avenue, thereby facilitating a condensed temporal segue, but it also centers the subsequent action in midst of ruin. This is the only time in the graphic novel that Eisner takes his story, albeit briefly, outside of the Dropsie Avenue setting. And it is significant that it is Berlin, of all places—now a burned out shell of a city—that becomes the symbolic embodiment of destruction and is directly linked to the Dropsie neighborhood. These images of fiery destruction gain even more import when compared to scenes near the end of the novel, when the last standing building along Dropsie Avenue is destroyed (Fig. 7). In an effort to stem crime and further economic decay, the city planners decide to demolish what is left of the "bombed out" neighborhood so as to start anew, a situation that parallels the decimation of the Nazi capital. The parallel is thematic as well as visual. The explosive cloud from the demolition is a graphic echo of the atomic cloud found in Figure 6—down to its mushroom shape—and the aerial shot of the leveled buildings on Dropsie Avenue are likewise a direct link to the bombed out buildings of Berlin.

* * *

Figure 6. Reprinted from *Dropsie Avenue* by Will Eisner. 83. Copyright © 1995 by Will Eisner, Copyright © 2006 by the Estate of Will Eisner. Used with permission of the publisher, W. W. Norton & Company, Inc.

Sign, Sign, Everywhere a Sign

Given the violence and the desperation that seems to permeate the text, it should come as no surprise that an outside force, some *deus ex machina*, may be needed to bring any promising change to Eisner's neighborhood. This "saving" force comes in the form of Rowena Shepard—and her suggestive surname—a once youthful and innocent gardener who lived in the shadows of the tenements occupying the neighborhood's last remaining private home. In the 1970s, after demolition teams have completely leveled the area, she returns to work with Abie Gold and Rubie Brown, an idealistic African American City Planning Director who had grown up on

Figure 7. Reprinted from *Dropsie Avenue* by Will Eisner. 159. Copyright © 1995 by Will Eisner, Copyright © 2006 by the Estate of Will Eisner. Used with permission of the publisher, W. W. Norton & Company, Inc.

Dropsie Avenue, in rebuilding the neighborhood. Rowena is now an aged millionaire, having successfully transformed her love of gardening into a thriving floral company, and she wants to use her money to recreate the neighborhood. * * * Abie reads Rowena's letter—whose text is framed in dreamy and reminiscent word bubbles—about her memories of Dropsie [196]. Throughout the text, Rowena is associated with magical transformation—in earlier scenes in the novel she sits in her wheelchair among her many roses, calling herself the princess of a "magic garden," a place where she meets a young mute boy whom she calls her "prince from an

Figure 8. Reprinted from *Dropsie Avenue* by Will Eisner. 113. Copyright © 1995 by Will Eisner, Copyright © 2006 by the Estate of Will Eisner. Used with permission of the publisher, W. W. Norton & Company, Inc.

enchanted kingdom"—and "magic" is what she attempts to bring back to Dropsie Avenue. It is here where Eisner's text flirts most closely with sentimentality, potentially providing unrealistically easy answers to the complex problems underlying his fictional landscape. Indeed, Eisner has been known at times to stray into the world of schmaltz, turning otherwise serious and provocative premises into maudlin storylines. This can be seen in such texts as *Fagin the Jew* (2003), his graphic narrative revision of Dickens's *Oliver Twist*,[4] or even *The Dreamer* (1986) and *Minor Miracles* (2000), stories that rely heavily on the melodramatic.

However, although *Dropsie Avenue* may at times threaten to become sentimental, the text ultimately resists such trite responses to ethnic turmoil. Eisner does this with another visual motif that runs throughout the text: the "For Sale" or "For Rent" sign. Whenever there is dramatic change in the neighborhood, the threat of racial hatred, or a new ethnic minority moving into a building or onto a block, "For Sale" or "For Rent" signs are never far behind (Fig. 8). This use of signs functions as an almost fatalistic counterweight to the optimism that springs from the neighborhood's more hopeful residents. * * * And as with the window and

4. See note 8 on p. 278 [*Editor*].

fire imagery, the repetitious use of "For Sale" or "For Rent" signs brings together the diverse episodes that make up the narrative.

Eisner uses this image most effectively in the final pages of the graphic novel. One day, after the Rowena Corporation has used its millions to "magically" create Dropsie Gardens, a residential community of affordable single-family homes, two neighbors, one black and one white, are out doing yard work and comment on their recently-arrived neighbors. We never see these new residents, but according to the homeowners they are families who have arrived "on leaky boats" and who decorate their houses in "weird colors" and "dinky ornaments" [198–99]. Again, "color" has infiltrated Dropsie Avenue, the neighbors are resentful, and the "For Sale" signs begin to go up. It is a "there goes the neighborhood" attitude all over again, and residents are once more suspicious and unsettled by ethnic diversity. As if to drive this point home, in the most recent edition of *Dropsie Avenue*—published in 2005 as a single-volume trilogy, and including *A Contract with God* and *A Life Force*—Eisner added two new illustrations. These are the final graphic commentaries of the graphic novel, and they show the Dropsie Gardens community slipping into disorder. In the first of these illustrations, the new houses on Dropsie Avenue are shown in disarray. Accompanying this image are the words of an extradiegetic narrator explaining,

> As it often happens to neighborhoods[,] Dropsie Avenue's ethnic mix began to change. The simple inexpensive home attracted a new group of people. Poorer and immigrant, they came with different cultural tastes and a less responsible attutude [sic] toward ownership and community. Soon they added brightly colored improvised structures to accommodate their large families. As earlier residents moved out, its character changed . . . visible evidence of implacable growth.

This detached, almost clinical, voice-over is then immediately followed by the book's final image. In it, we see the rain-drenched neighborhood sprinkled with "For Sale" signs, moving vans standing ready to assist in the relocation. It appears that the "fairytale" quality of the planned community is undermined once again by the cycles of violence and distrust, and not even Rowena's magic can change this fact.

Will Eisner's message in *Dropsie Avenue* isn't uplifting. Unlike the endings of some of his other graphic novels, this one is dark, blunt, and uncompromising. One could even call it neo-naturalistic, a fatalistic reading of ethnoracial relations in American. It is significant to note that this is the final text of the *Contract with God* trilogy, a series of narratives that explore interactions among disparate individuals and systems of faith. But whereas the earlier stories in the trilogy may have held out for the possibility of personal redemption, either through faith or even through art, there seems to be little chance of that happening within the larger community. *Dropsie Avenue* shows us a localized neighborhood trapped in the grip of ethnic intolerance, and even if its message is bleak, it is one that we should nonetheless heed, especially given our country's continued acts of racial intolerance, our ongoing rhetorical posturings concerning patriotism, and the current debates on immigration.

Will Eisner: A Chronology

1917	March 6	William Erwin Eisner born in New York City.
1933		Begins publishing work as a student at DeWitt Clinton High School in New York.
1934		Eisner's first paid job as an employee in the advertising department at the *New York American* newspaper.
1935		Studies briefly at the Art Students League in New York with George Bridgman and Robert Brachman.
1936		Works briefly as art director for the short-lived *Eve* magazine. Begins to publish in the short-lived anthology comic book *Wow, What a Magazine!* Following the failure of the comic after four issues, Eisner negotiates with Jerry Iger to form Eisner and Iger Studio to produce comics for other publishers.
1938		First appearance of Sheena, Queen of the Jungle, in *Wags* in Britain then in *Jumbo Comics* (Fiction House) in the U.S.—the first important comic book character created by Eisner.
1939		Contracts with "Busy" Arnold, head of Quality Comics, to begin developing a newspaper supplement comic book.
1940		*The Spirit* debuts as a comic book insert.
1941		*Spirit* daily strip debuts. The strip runs until March 1944.
1942		Reports for duty in the U.S. Army, first to Fort Dix in New Jersey before being quickly transferred to the Aberdeen Proving Ground in Maryland.
1945		At the end of World War II, Eisner returns to New York and resumes control of *The Spirit* comic book.
1948		Establishes American Visuals Corporation as a postwar home for his ongoing work with the U.S. Defense Department and to develop new markets for educational comics.
1950	June 15	Marries Ann Weingarten.
1951		*P*S, The Preventative Maintenance Monthly* begins publication by the U.S. Army. Eisner will serve as artistic director until 1972.
1952	October 5	Last *Spirit* newspaper supplement published.
1965		Begins a three-year tenure as president of the Bell McClure Syndicate and of the North American Newspaper Alliance, newspaper syndicates that distributed columns, articles, and comic strips to newspapers

nationwide. Jules Feiffer, Eisner's former assistant and now an established cartoonist, publishes *The Great Comic Book Heroes*, which helps inspire renewed interest in *The Spirit* and in Eisner's founding role in comic book history.

1966 Harvey Comics publishes the first of many reprints of *The Spirit*.

1970 Eisner's daughter, Alice, dies of leukemia.

1971 Eisner attends the Comic Art Convention in New York, where he is introduced to underground comix and meets Denis Kitchen.

1973 Denis Kitchen's Kitchen Sink Press publishes two issues of the *Spirit* magazine.

1974 Begins teaching sequential art at the School of Visual Arts in New York.

Establishes Poorhouse Press, which will publish several of his novelty titles, such as *Will Eisner's Incredible Facts, Amazing Statistics*, and *Monumental Trivia*.

Eisner takes the *Spirit* magazine to Warren Publishing.

1975 Eisner awarded the Franco-Belgian Grand Prix de la ville d'Angoulême for lifetime achievement.

1976 After sixteen issues with Warren Publishing, the *Spirit* magazine returns to Kitchen Sink Press. Eisner will maintain a partnership with Kitchen for the remainder of his career.

1978 *A Contract with God* is published by Baronet Books.

1983 First serialized in the *Spirit* magazine, *Life on Another Planet*, a science fiction graphic novel, is published by Kitchen Sink.

1985 *Comics and Sequential Art*, a pioneering text on the art and practice of graphic narrative, is published by Poorhouse.

1986 *The Dreamer*, a semiautobiographical graphic novel about the early years of the comic book industry in the 1930s, is published by Kitchen Sink.

Will Eisner's New York: The Big City, published by Kitchen Sink, collects urban sketches that Eisner created for Kitchen Sink's *Spirit* magazine.

1987 *The Building*, a collection of stories about four individuals whose lives are connected to the same building in New York, is published by Kitchen Sink.

1988 First serialized in *Will Eisner's Quarterly*, *Life Force* is published by Kitchen Sink.

The Eisner Awards are established. They continue today as the "Oscars of comics," celebrating the best work of the year.

1991 *To the Heart of the Storm*, a graphic memoir addressing immigrant life and antisemitism in America before and during World War II, is published by Kitchen Sink. The book wins the Eisner Award for 1992 for Best Graphic Album.

1992 *Invisible People* is serialized in three issues by Kitchen Sink before being collected in a single volume the following year.

1995 *Dropsie Avenue: The Neighborhood* is published by Kitchen Sink.

1995 The National Cartoonists Society awards Eisner the Milton Caniff Lifetime Achievement Award.

1996 *Graphic Storytelling and Visual Narrative*, a companion volume to *Comics and Sequential Art*, is published by Poorhouse.

1998 *Family Matter*, a graphic novel about a family reunion around an aging patriarch and the secrets that emerge, is published by Kitchen Sink.

2000 *Last Day in Vietnam*, a collection of stories of soldiers in Vietnam, Korea, and WWII, is published by Dark Horse Press.

Minor Miracles, a final collection of tales set in the Dropsie Avenue neighborhood, is published by DC Comics. *The Last Knight* is published by NBM as the first of a series of literary adaptations.

2001 *Moby Dick*, a comic adaptation of Herman Melville's monumental 1851 novel, is published by NBM.

The Name of the Game, an intergenerational family drama, is published by DC Comics.

2003 *Fagin the Jew*, a reimagining of the life of the "villain" from Charles Dickens's *Oliver Twist*, is published by Random House.

2005 January 3 Will Eisner dies in Laurendale, Florida.

The Plot: The Secret Story of the Protocols of the Elders of Zion, a nonfiction graphic account of the anti-semitic conspiracy theory, is published posthumously by W. W. Norton.

Selected Bibliography

• indicates works included or excerpted in this Norton Critical Edition.

Biographies and Backgrounds

Andelman, Bob. *Will Eisner: A Spirited Life*. Milwaukie, OR: M Press, 2005.

Couch, N. C. Christopher, and Stephen Weiner. *The Will Eisner Companion: The Pioneering Spirit of the Father of the Graphic Novel*. New York: DC Comics, 2004.

Eisner, Will. *Life, in Pictures: Autobiographical Stories*. New York: Norton, 2007.

Eisner, Will, and Frank Miller. *Eisner/Miller: A One-on-one Interview*. Milwaukie, OR: Dark Horse Books, 2005.

Gravett, Paul, and Denis Kitchen, eds. *Will Eisner: The Centennial Celebration*. Milwaukie, OR: Dark Horse Comics, 2017.

Groth, Gary, et al. The Will Eisner Memorial Issue. *The Comics Journal* 267 (April/May 2005).

Inge, M. Thomas, ed. *Will Eisner: Conversations*. Jackson: University Press of Mississippi, 2011.

Levitz, Paul. *Will Eisner: Champion of the Graphic Novel*. New York: Abrams Comic Arts, 2015.

Schumacher, Michael. *Will Eisner: A Dreamer's Life in Comics*. New York: Bloomsbury, 2010.

Criticism

Beronä, David A. "Breaking Taboos: Sexuality in the Work of Will Eisner and the Early Wordless Novels." *International Journal of Comic Art* 1:1 (Spring/Summer 1999): 90–103.

• Dauber, Jeremy. "Comic Books, Tragic Stories: Will Eisner's American Jewish History." *AJS Review* 30:2 (November 2006): 277–304.

Kaplan, Leonard V. "Will Eisner: Master of Graphic Wisdom." *Comics and Sacred Texts*, ed. Assaf Gamzou and Ken Koltun-Fromm. Jackson: University Press of Mississippi, 2018, 269–80.

Klingenstein, Susanne. "The Long Roots of Will Eisner's Quarrel with God." *Studies in American Jewish Literature* 26 (2007): 81–88.

• Kunka, Andrew. "*A Contract with God, The First Kingdom*, and the 'Graphic Novel': The Will Eisner / Jack Katz Letters." *Inks: The Journal of the Comics Studies Society* 1:1 (2017): 27–39.

Royal, Derek Parker. "Sequential Sketches of Ethnic Identity: Will Eisner's 'A Contract with God' as Graphic Cycle." *College Literature* 38:3 (Summer 2011): 150–67.

• ———. "There Goes the Neighborhood: Cycling Ethnoracial Tensions in Will Eisner's *Dropsie Avenue*." *Shofar* 29:2 (Winter 2011): 120–45.

• Smith, Greg M. "Will Eisner, Vaudevillian of the Cityscape." *Comics and the City: Urban Space in Print, Picture and Sequence*, ed. Jörn Ahrens and Arno Meteling. New York: Continuum, 2010, 183–98.

Tuusvuori, Jarkko. "Philosophy in the Bargain: *A Contract with God* (1978) by Will Eisner." *Graphic Novels as Philosophy*, ed. Jeff McLaughlin. Jackson: University Press of Mississippi, 2017, 17–40.

• Williams, Paul. *Dreaming the Graphic Novel: The Novelization of Comics*. New Brunswick: Rutgers University Press, 2020.